Views from Fort Battleford

Constructed Visions of an Anglo-Canadian West

Walter Hildebrandt

Canadian Plains Research Center
University of Regina
1994

Copyright @ Canadian Plains Research Center

Canadian Plains Research Center
University of Regina
Regina, Saskatchewan S4S 0A2
Canada

Canadian Cataloguing in Publication Data

Hildebrandt, Walter

Views from Fort Battleford

(Canadian plains studies ; 31)

Includes bibliographical references.
ISBN 0-88977-086-7

1. Northwest, Canadian - History - 1870-1905.
2. Battleford (Sask.) - History. 3. Indians of North
America - Prairie Provinces - Government relations.
4. Métis - Prairie Provinces - Government relations
5. North West Mounted Police (Canada) - History.
I. University of Regina. Canadian Plains Research
Center. II. Title. III. Series.

FC3217.H54 1994   971.05   C94-920253-3
F1060.9.H5 1994

Cover Design: Agnes Bray/Brian Mlazgar
Cover artwork by Appiisoomahka (William Singer). Appiisoomahka is a member of the Blood tribe and a Traditionalist. He presently attends Red Crow College. The painting represents Miserable Man and Poundmaker talking to Infantry Brigadier Lieutenant-Colonel Bowen van Straubenzie. The map included at the back of this book is reproduced courtesy of the Canada Map Office, Department of Energy, Mines and Resources.

Printed and bound in Canada by
Hignell Printing Limited, Winnipeg, Manitoba

Printed on acid-free paper

For Frits

CONTENTS

PREFACE

This book argues that the Anglo-Canadian presence in the Canadian West was established with little concern for those who were there before and with little sensitivity to the culture of the First Nations and Métis peoples who occupied the land for many hundreds of years before the first settlers arrived in the West. Using the area around Fort Battleford as a focus, the book outlines the way of life that existed on the prairies before the Canadian presence was established. It goes on to examine the various institutions that placed the Anglo-Canadian elite in a position of power by the 1880s. The book investigates the role of the North West Mounted Police and the North-West Field Force in establishing Canadian hegemony and analyzes government policies that were employed to control those who were seen as a threat in the wake of the 1885 Resistance. It concludes with a description of the various interpretations of Fort Battleford that have evolved over time.

When I began with the Parks Service in the late 1970s the history of Fort Battleford was being presented as a story of law and order, of valour and the establishment of civilization in the West. I was uncomfortable with this emphasis and worked to persuade administrators of the program that the Mounties did not enter a vacuum and that the civilization they thought they were bringing was as controversial then as it is now.

The material on which this book is based was compiled when I worked as an historian for the Canadian Parks Service in the 1980s. The book has been written from articles and manuscripts produced over the years to meet the program needs of interpreting the history of Fort Battleford to the public.

I would like to thank the many colleagues I have worked with over the years: historians, archaeologists, interpreters, engineers, architects, planners and guides. Also thanks to the Superintendents, some of whom remain unconvinced that the context for interpreting the history of Fort Battleford needed to be broadened. The always helpful and attentive assistance of archivists made my research so much easier, particularly while working at the National Archives of Canada, the Provincial Archives of Manitoba, the Provincial Archives of Alberta, the Glenbow Alberta Archives, the Saskatchewan Archives Board, and the Shortt Library. I am grateful to the Tootoosis family at the Poundmaker Reserve, especially the late John Tootoosis and Gordon, for their hospitality and generosity in sharing the history of their people with me. Once again I am indebted to Sarah Carter for more than can be listed here, and also to our daughter, Mary, who is always an inspiration to me. Also, special thanks to Bob Coutts for help with the photographs and to George Melnyk and Brian Mlazgar for editing, Rick Lalonde for the maps, and William Singer for the cover illustration. Thanks also to Frits Pannekoek who hired me fresh out of graduate school. Frits encouraged historians working for governments to experiment, to try different approaches, to apply the methodologies of cultural and social history for the writing of public history. He encouraged us to take risks and to not simply use our sites to prop up established nation-building narratives; I dedicate this book to him.

At the Chicago Columbian Exposition in 1893, the four hundredth anniversary provided the occasion for a straight forward celebration of all progress made since Columbus launched the conquest of the Western Hemisphere. But the five hundredth anniversary will come at an awkward point in our changing perceptions of history. The cult of "progress" has lost believers. The idea of a North America without industrial machinery, pollutants, pesticides, or nuclear waste does not immediately call to mind the words "primitive," "backward," or "savage." But more important, the 1992 commemoration planners must take into account that natives did not vanish; the descendants of the pre-Columbian Americans are very much alive — as are, in many cases, their memories and resentments of the conquest. In an age of attempted civility towards minorities, it seems poor taste, at best, to celebrate an invasion, a demographic catastrophe, and a conquest.

Patricia Limerick
The Legacy of Conquest

ONE

Conquest of the Prairie West

It is only a step from market to colony. The exploited have only to cheat, or to protest, and conquest immediately follows.

Fernand Braudel

Before the Mounties arrived on the western prairies, evidence of European culture could be found in the log houses and huts of pioneers and fur traders that sparsely dotted the landscape. The role of these early traders and settlers did not allow them to create exotic structures nor was there a need for any unduly grand display of power. The difference between early fur trade material culture and Native culture was not great. Accordingly, expressions of power by the police when they arrived were more overtly military or paramilitary, though the hegemonic function of culture was certainly present in the red coats and military discourse of the "March West." Thus, the red coats, lances and military equipment of the North West Mounted Police (NWMP) announced power: the power to act in the name of the law, to call in reinforcements and to embark on punitive expeditions. The solitary Mountie, mythologized by Anglo-Canadian culture, served as a floating signifier for those who knew how power operated. The mystery and romanticized military image of the NWMP served the function of force, but force is not the most efficient way to run a society, nor is it the cheapest. Sooner or later, new societies will seek a more efficient and cheaper means of maintaining power. Battleford provided a classic example of this process in the nineteenth-century Canadian West.

The study of social control has changed radically in recent years. Until the 1960s, the history of police forces was generally written in a narrative form that emphasized the gradual evolution of a humane system of punishment, policing and imprisonment. This process was initiated by a group of Enlightenment thinkers led by theorists like Beccarian and Bentham, along with religious men and women of conscience like the Evangelicals and Quakers who "set out to convince the political leadership of their societies that public punishments of the body like hanging, branding, whipping and even in some European countries, torture, were arbitrary, cruel and illegitimate, and that a new range of penalties, chiefly imprisonment or hard labour, could be at once humane, reformative and punitive."[1] It is suggested that these changes, initiated by enlightened reformers, led to a system of social control that was more humane than in the era previous to it; history progressing from "cruelty to enlightenment."

More recent revisionist histories were influenced by the work of Michel Foucault, and they dramatically altered the study of social control:

> the libertarian, populist politics of the 1960s revised historians' attitudes toward the size and intrusiveness of the modern state; the history of the prison, the school, the hospital, the asylum seemed more easily understood as a history of Leviathan than a history of reform.[2]

The focus of attention changed. This new perspective looked with scepticism at the projects of the eighteenth and nineteenth centuries, especially as they aimed to change the personalities of criminals. Institutions established and run by the state were thus viewed not as the means to "reform" and "educate" people, but rather as institutions responsible for limiting their freedom. The "Panoptic eye" became an homology for the new and modern ethic of social control in prisons where a guard situated high above in a tower could maintain surveillance over everyone in the prison. The design of the new prisons reflected an ideology which emphasized the need for society to control and reform its subjects in order for them to participate in the economic system.

In Canada, the political and social culture was imported from Europe. It shared the same ideology that produced an industrialized Europe, including the Christian values that accompanied capitalist culture. Introduced along with these cultural values were concepts of liberty and private property. The NWMP were the harbingers of a dramatically new social order in the Canadian West. They represented those who held power, a power that operated in many complex ways. "Putative power is dispersed through the social system: it is literally everywhere in the sense that the disciplinary ideology, the *savoir* which directs and legitimizes power, permeates all social groups (with the exception of the marginal and deviant), ordering the self-repression of the repressors themselves."[3]

The new system was effective. The Aboriginal peoples who had to cope with the police were confronted by only the first line of power — the police who were charged with keeping public order. Behind the police were many other forms of power, such as the military who were used so successfully in 1885. The systems of social control developed by Europeans were no longer just physical and institutional, but represented cultural and psychological tactics serving the same powerful ideology.[4] The NWMP thus were an arm of the law which was to restrain and guide Native people (as well as the incoming white settlers) into conformity with the dominant culture and society the Mounties represented and were to disseminate.

New Approaches to Aboriginal History

The concept of acculturation is used to examine the cultural confrontation between Natives and newcomers — two radically different cultures.[5] In the classic situation, the white trader-explorer-missionary, who is usually from a European country or empire, meets Aboriginal people. Acculturation explores how both sides change and adapt as a result of communication and through exchanges of material culture and information. This method helps us to understand, for example, how Native society changed due to the European goods it absorbed and how the colonizers adapted as a result of the survival techniques they learned from Aboriginal peoples.

Acculturation as a methodology was developed alongside the establishment of a new interdisciplinary approach to studying Native people: ethnohistory. This new discipline combined methods and approaches both from history and from anthropology in order to better understand Native society and culture. Traditionally, the discipline of history denied the validity of oral evidence and favoured written documents. Ethnographers, though sympathetic and expert in the use of oral evidence, were unfortunately not disposed to study the manner in which societies changed over time and were thus content to take a snapshot-in-time approach to studying Native societies. Though much important knowledge was brought to light through this approach, it led to the impression that Native societies were stagnant or locked in time. History and ethnology became specialized and mutually exclusive solitudes.

History as a discipline emphasized the diachronic (examining change over time), while ethnology focussed on the synchronic (that which remains the same over time). The cross-fertilization that occurred when these two disciplines were brought together raised new kinds of evidence for consideration and allowed different perspectives to emerge for understanding First Nations. The two approaches tempered each other. While Western European history sought to chronicle the progress and dynamism of peoples and cultures that were European in origin, ethnology sought to study the static and less overtly dynamic cultures of the Aboriginal world. The discipline of history tended to use an empirical and fragmentary approach to explain and gain knowledge about the past within a Newtonian-Cartesian paradigm, while ethnology attempted to study societies as a whole, seeking to understand how the parts related to each other. Historians basically focussed on understanding their own societies by looking from the past toward the present; ethnologists looked from the present and made use of contemporary structures as they looked back to the past.

The findings of the combined discipline of ethnohistory led to new perspectives for understanding Native societies and dynamics of change within them. To combat the idea that Native plains peoples simply roamed the prairies indiscriminantly, locked in a hopeless feast-or-famine conundrum, the "seasonal cycle" method of explaining their movements was developed. This corrected the impression that they wandered in an undirected and largely purposeless manner. It drew attention to the significance of Aboriginal movement and the way in which these people relied on their understanding and knowledge of the environment: its flora, fauna and weather. The seasonal-cycle approach helped to counter the prevailing notion of European culture: that there was progress or a sense of progress to history. The seasonal-cycle framework showed instead that those cultures not driven by ideas of progress could still live full and creative lives as they moved in response to seasonal change. Native people were content to live in their environment, taking from it only what they needed. To them, there was economic security in being able to survive without having to carry or accumulate cumbersome material goods.

European standards and discourses were very damaging and unsympathetic in their descriptions of the cultural institutions of Native society. They equated living in harmony with nature as "savage" while considering the exploitation of nature as "civilized." In actuality, Natives who moved with the seasonal cycles were far from "savage" or static:

> Native economies in America were not poorer, more precarious, or more miserable than their contemporary European counterparts. Indeed, recent studies of hunting and gathering societies suggest that natives of the western interior may have lived a life of relative comfort and plenty... The hunter-gatherer did not labour endlessly in quest of food. Indeed, it is apparent that when societies give up a hunt-based economy in favour of agriculture, they actually increase the per capita work-load... The hunting and gathering societies of the western interior achieved economic, political, and religious arrangements as satisfactory and as conducive to human happiness, for most members of the community, as those of any other society.[6]

The Cree on the Prairies

In the late nineteenth century, there were two reasons for choosing Fort Battleford as the site of a North West Mounted Police post. First, Battleford had been chosen as the new territorial capital. The members of the Territorial Council would therefore need a police force to protect them and enforce the laws they would pass. The police were thus a necessary adjunct to the administration of the North-West Territories. Second, and perhaps most important, was the presence of a large number of Aboriginal people in the area. The Thickwood and Eagle Hills areas to the north and east respectively had traditionally been wintering places for Cree and Assiniboine, but by the late nineteenth century, the buffalo no longer migrated north of the South Saskatchewan River and could no longer be relied upon as a primary source of food and clothing. As a result, the plains tribes began to settle on reserve land promised to them in Treaty 6. They chose the land around Fort Battleford, as they were familiar with the territory and small game could still be found.

Settlement onto reserves was a major watershed for the Cree. Ahead of them lay compliance to the laws of another culture and adjustment to subsistence agriculture that was controlled by government regulations. Behind them lay a long tradition of adaptation to the forest and plains environments, the fur trade, missionaries, diseases formerly unknown, alcohol and the disappearance of the buffalo. Rapid change in a few short years contrasted with previous times when change occurred more slowly, allowing for gradual adjustment.

After more than two centuries of contact with European culture, the Aboriginal way of life still stood in stark contrast to Euro-American culture. The plains tribes, especially the Cree, had adapted to the economic changes they had first faced with the arrival of the horse, then the gun, then the traders. At its core, Native culture absorbed change on its own terms and retained beliefs and practices that enabled it to thrive on the plains. The Christian, Western European world perceived the environment as hostile and advocated a systematic harvest of the land, while the Aboriginal people lived with this environment, not against it, and adapted to it as each season allowed or demanded.

The Cree, originally located in woodland areas to the east and north of the Great Lakes, were band societies in which the ultimate unit of organization was the family. They were not tribal units under a common leader. In small groups, they moved over their territory in search of game or to collect other food. Each family unit had an appointed leader. A number of bands could come together at various seasons, but this was rare and occurred only for short periods of time.

The scarcity of fish and game made very large gatherings of band people impossible. The inability to meet in large numbers meant that they rarely went to war with neighbouring peoples. In the woods, scattered in small groups, they were a difficult target for an enemy attack. By contrast, tribal societies were composed of much larger units that stayed together for longer periods of time. On the prairies, it was difficult to hide from neighbouring tribes, making tribal cohesiveness a necessity for self-defence and creating more opportunities for military conflict than in the heavily forested woodlands. Food was also more abundant on the plains. Up to the late 1870s, large herds of buffalo still migrated into Canadian territory, providing many plains tribes with a steady food supply and facilitating the organization of larger groups.

The nature of life on the plains demanded greater organization and social control. The annual buffalo hunt, for example, required many horsemen who needed to be tightly coordinated. Such pursuits made it necessary to have a firmer political organization. In the spring, when all the Indians gathered together before the buffalo hunt, a council of men elected a chief. The use of the horse contributed to the development of a more organized political structure, as it led to a mobile society in contrast with the isolated, foot-locomoted woodland bands. Thus the plains tribes could be readily mobilized for both political and military purposes.

Aboriginal Cosmology

As with the Europeans, Cree religious life was centred around the concept of one supreme being who had created the world. This was not a being who could be approached directly as with the Christian god, but could only be reached through intermediary spirits that resided in nature. Although their god was not believed to reside in any specific place or to be personalized in any way, it was nevertheless thought to have power over all things.

Cree religion expressed an affirmation of nature. The intermediary spirits could be found in birds and animals (such as the crow or bear), and other natural phenomena. Thunder, wind and sun were thought to contain the most powerful spirits. The powers of these spirits could be used by mortals if, in a vision, an image of the object appeared to the person. When this occurred, it was believed the powers of the spirit could be harnessed by the vision-seeker. The individual would then take on the name of the source of the power and be protected by the supernatural strength attributed to it. A spirit bundle might be made and carried by the person for protection or guidance. This religion affirmed the strength and power that the Natives felt resided in the world around them. They made this reverence of nature an integral part of their religious attitudes. Much of the Aboriginal art, whether tent drawings, clothing decoration, rock paintings, or on drums and other instruments, reflected a deep respect for the spiritual power of the natural world. Their sun motifs and animal paintings were the most obvious example of their worldview, which held nature, rather than humans, as sacred.

Though there were many ceremonies (both religious and otherwise), that showed this symbolic kinship with nature, the most commonly known and most central to Cree life was the Sun or Thirst Dance. By asking for spiritual strength from nature, this dance served not only as a symbolic rite of rebirth but was an opportunity for members of the tribe to earn the rite of passage into adulthood and for all those present to feel and ask for protection and power from the spirits of the natural world around them, especially the Thunderbird. One member of the band initiated the dance in order to fulfill a vow. The ceremony began when the pledgers, through rituals of song and dance, asked for the power to stage a dance, usually from the sun or thunder spirits. The pledger would engage assistants from his band to conduct the dance: they sang the songs with him and helped build the Sun Dance lodge. Traditionally, the Sun Dance lasted four days, during which time the participants fasted and abstained from sexual activity. It was believed that during these four days the spirit powers took pity on the dancers and would send rain to quench their thirst.

As the singers sang and the drums were beat, the men prepared themselves for the successful completion of their dance. Once completed, the spirits would bless those who had participated; this, in turn, bode well for the entire tribe. Prayers were said throughout the ceremony: "The burden of all prayers was that a ceremony very dear to the powers was about to be given, that the powers help the participants complete the Sun Dance, so that mankind might be blessed."[7] It was a communion with nature, a request for mercy by those who lived in the continual presence of the awesome elements that confronted them on the plains. In this humility, there was a peace offering to the natural world in which the Cree would be attempting to harvest what they needed for their own survival. The participants hoped to be worthy of what they would kill during the buffalo hunt. They wanted to appease the natural world they held in respect, but from which they also took. In this sense, the Sun Dance was a symbolic gesture towards the life-giving sun and the thunder with its accompanying rains.

The Fur Trade

The Aboriginals' role in the fur trade, their consequential move onto the plains, and the resulting diplomatic systems that emerged have only recently been explored by scholars. It is perhaps a telling comment on the bias of early western Canadian historians that so little has been written about the role played by the Natives in the history of the fur trade. The primary debate of more recent studies has focussed on the adaptability of the Natives to this system of trade. One side has argued that the role of the Natives changed very little and their basic institutions did not change dramatically as they traded with Europeans. It is contended that the Indians had traded among themselves long before they traded with Europeans. The other side of the argument claims that the Indians adjusted rapidly to the presence of traders and competed actively to obtain as many European goods as they could. They acted as "economic men," adapting to the marketplace as conditions allowed. The former view is put forward by A. Rotstein and E.E. Rich, while the latter is delineated by Arthur Ray and John Milloy.

According to Rotstein's argument, there was less change in Aboriginal society during the fur trade than some would believe. He states that it was the European trader who was forced to adapt to the Indians' trade practices and learn the protocol of their trade patterns.[8] He believes the fur trade was already imbedded in the Indian way of life prior to direct contact with Europeans, and that it was their alliances and intertribal relations that determined their actions, not their contact and trade with Europeans. Rotstein further argues that the motivating factor among the Natives was tribal and collective rather than individual. Thus, the alliance system among the Natives would be based more on collective determination of their economic activities than on individuals entering the marketplace motivated by their own desires for accumulation of material goods. Rotstein backs up his arguments by referring to accounts of missionaries, traders and explorers describing alliance systems among plains tribes. These sources are used to support the claim that elaborate diplomacy was already in place to control the territorial imperative of Natives in the North-West before the arrival of European traders. Elaborate trade ceremonies and methods of obtaining essential goods were also present before the entrenchment of fur-trade society. Indians thus adapted naturally to their role as middlemen in the fur trade, since this role fit patterns already known to them.

Rich agrees with Rotstein's basic argument, but the tone of his perspective is, by implication, more negative toward the Indians.[9] Rich states that the Natives were not "economic" men like most Europeans, in that they possessed no sense of property and were not motivated by a desire to accumulate wealth. He claims the Natives were firmly entrenched in their old ways and could not change to adapt to the fur trade in the same way as Europeans. Rich suggests the Native fell into the role of middleman, then exploited it to gain full advantage over the Hudson's Bay Company (HBC) and other Native groups. He finds it somewhat puzzling, and considers it an indication of inferiority, that the Aboriginal did not adopt European concepts of property and acquisitiveness.

On the other side of this debate, Ray maintains the Natives were continually and actively adjusting to the economic conditions confronting them.[10] The fur trade was a partnership between European and Aboriginal traders, both needing each other in some way. This partnership had a wide range of consequences for both sides, as each group had to make significant adaptations during the fur-trade period. Ray disagrees with Rotstein and Rich's view that the ceremonial practices introduced by Aboriginals were an affirmation of political position; instead, he argues that ceremonial activities were simply one aspect of trading. To support this, he states that the Cree traders were free to shop around for the best bargains for their furs, and in fact frequently did. They were not simply trading to maintain and mark out territory. He points out that before the arrival of the HBC, the Cree traded along the east-west axis established by North West Company traders from Montreal, and that even when the HBC moved to the bay area the Natives chose not to trade there. Ray states that the Cree trading with the HBC during these years held an advantage and bargained from a position of power with the company. Furthermore, he shows that it was not always (or even usually) the case that Aboriginal leaders were involved in trading; rather, various individuals from each tribe conducted the trade. This point diminishes the importance that Rotstein and Rich attach to the ceremony of the trade and shows that Aboriginals would often participate in trade individually, with the intent of making the best deal they could for the European goods they sought. Ray also demonstrates how the Cree traders often played the companies against each other to obtain their commodities. This situation helped the HBC decide that it would have to move inland if it was going to obtain quality furs and remain competitive with free traders and the North West Company.

Ray's propositions show that the Cree reacted to the marketplace, not to customs or rules that their own society or culture brought to bear on them. Exchange rates set by the competition were determined by the market, not by gift rituals. For example, when the English raised their prices the Natives went to the French to obtain needed goods. Often they were willing to pay higher prices when they wanted particular products, such as the superior English knives or tobacco. By the end of the seventeenth century, the ceremonial trade practices that transpired at the outset of bartering were less frequent and the pure market trade introduced by the English had become dominant. In accommodating some points made by Rotstein, Ray agrees that the Cree did not always trade to increase wealth. He notes that, as trading relations developed, individual Natives did gain status among their own people by gathering and accumulating European goods.

The significance of this debate between Ray and Rotstein lies in the analysis of Aboriginal motivations. These motivations enabled them to preserve a good part of the basic structure of their internal institutions, including their religious beliefs and kinship systems. These internal institutions were preserved, even though they made significant adaptations to the new economic environment necessitated by their pursuit of economic goals.

Post-Contact Cree Movement on the Plains

According to historian John Milloy, three distinct phases can be identified between the first direct contact with Europeans and the end of the fur-trade era around 1870. The first period began in 1670 with the alliance between the Cree and Blackfoot situated to the west. The second phase was the period in which the Cree developed a stronger alliance with the Mandan to the south, who also supplied them with horses. Milloy labels this phase as the Horse Wars era lasting from 1810-50, a time when the Cree were increasingly in need of horses and were seeking alliances to the west. The third phase is labelled the Buffalo War period of 1850-70, when the Cree were competing with other plains Natives for the diminishing buffalo herds which had become their source of food. By the end of this last phase, the fur trade was in decline and the Cree no longer played a crucial role in its function.

In the initial period of contact, the Cree lived along the shores of Hudson Bay, north of the Ojibwa. They became the first and primary consumers of European goods in the seventeenth century and began to carry the trade of these goods to other Natives to the south and west. Their strategic position gave them control of all the major waterways that flowed into the bay. They blocked the access to Hudson Bay to all but the Assiniboine, who became allies as the Cree moved south from the bay. During these early years of the fur trade, the Cree began a two-pronged push westward: one to the northwest and another along a more southerly route. By 1760, 100 years after their first contact with Europeans on Hudson Bay, they had pushed back the Beaver tribe to the north and had reached as far west as Lesser Slave Lake. This northern Cree society grew towards a greater dependence on European goods. After an initial period of relative prosperity, these traders were extended far beyond their traditional habitat. As their dependency on the fur trade grew, they had less time to live off the rich environment they had inhabited before Europeans came to the bay. Their position was exacerbated by 1776 as the HBC moved inland, leaving their own role in the fur trade less significant. The band was still the social unit of the Cree at this time. This division could be maintained because there were few enemies to threaten it.

The other group of Cree that moved westward were those who eventually became the Plains Cree. They moved down the Saskatchewan River system, which they followed to the west. During this move, the Cree allied themselves with the Blackfoot and Mandan against their common enemy, the Dakota. The Cree traded with both of these allies, as they were among the first to obtain the coveted European guns for trade with plains tribes. The trade-in-arms to the Blackfoot was particularly intense during the years 1732-54. This period, characterized by Milloy as the wars of migration and territorial domination,[11] ended by the turn of the century as the inland posts of the HBC became more accessible to other Natives. Thus, the Cree were no longer needed as the suppliers of European goods. From 1680 to the 1720s, the Cree and Blackfoot lived peacefully next to each other and fought as allies against the Kootenay and Gros Ventre peoples.

Horse Wars, 1800-1850

As the southern Cree were now less significant as middlemen in the fur trade, they began their adaptation to plains life. They became dependent on hunting buffalo for their survival, but were also suppliers of pemmican to other traders. This plains life necessitated the use of the horse, so the Cree forged an alliance with the Mandan to the south. The trade in horses had gradually moved north from the Gulf of Mexico where the Spaniards first introduced them in the seventeenth century. The Cree continued to supply the Mandan with European goods, such as kettles, axes, muskets and powder. In return, the Mandan supplied the Cree with agricultural products: corn, beans and tobacco. By the mid-nineteenth century the Cree had lost their position as primary suppliers of European goods to the Mandan, as the latter were now able to trade directly with the inland posts being established in their territories. With the Mandan trade crumbling, the Cree were forced to look elsewhere for a supply of horses. They had to make careful, rational decisions as they moved west and south in search of horses. Inevitably, they came into conflict with the horse suppliers to the south, especially the Gros Ventre. During the period from 1790 to 1810, there was much fighting on the plains as new alliances were sought. The Cree took to raiding horses from their previous allies, the Mandan. Much of this happened as a result of the move inland by the Hudson's Bay Company and the subsequent displacement of the Cree as middlemen in the fur trade.

The wars with the Gros Ventre occurred as the Cree attempted to gain more direct access to the horses being traded onto the plains by the Arapaho to the south. This could only be accomplished by taking control of territory traditionally held by the Gros Ventre. The Blackfoot, traditional allies of both the Gros Ventre and the Cree, were called upon to assist the Gros Ventre in defending their territory from the Cree. These were the same Blackfoot tribes the Cree had once helped to drive the feared Kootenay and Gros Ventre peoples across the Rockies. Guns obtained by the Blackfoot from the Cree had given them a decided edge in these conflicts.

The new allies for the Cree during this time became the Flathead Indians, who supplied them with horses. In return, the Flathead received European goods the Cree were still obtaining from the HBC. From approximately 1800 to 1850, the Cree consolidated their power on the plains but did not decentralize as the Blackfoot did. In the span of time since the company had moved inland, much had changed. The old alliances with the Mandan and Blackfoot had dissolved. Yet, with great ingenuity and an ability to adapt and forge new alliances, the Cree not only survived but prospered on the plains.

During the early nineteenth century, the Cree were able to exist in their centralized tribal way of life because they maintained many of their traditional social and cultural values. Status was still gained by common activities within the tribe and not by individual conquest or accumulation of wealth. They kept the tradition of distribution through gift giving and a "disdain for material possessions."[12] This was in contrast to the Blackfoot, who were growing more towards a social system based upon status through accumulation of wealth and a decentralized power structure. The gun and horse were absorbed into Cree society without drastic changes to their social structure, although some adjustment had to take place. Tribalism remained the strongest bond for the Cree during the years up to 1850. At the end of this period, they were one of the strongest tribes on the plains.

The once-powerful Blackfoot were enemies not only of the Kootenay, Gros Ventre and Crow, but now also of the Cree.

Buffalo Wars, 1850-1870

The years 1850-70 were characterized by dwindling buffalo herds. The Cree blamed the Métis and whites for the decline, but did not openly clash with them since they still relied on their trade goods. The Cree partnership with the whites was no longer as useful as it had once been. The Cree made their own choices based on what was in their best interest; buffalo were most important to them in the mid-1800s.

The Cree often fought with the Blackfoot during this period. By the late 1870s, buffalo came into Cree territory less frequently but were still found regularly on Blackfoot land. The Cree therefore clashed with the Blackfoot in their quest for territory where the buffalo still roamed. In 1869, during one of the frequent battles with the Blackfoot, one of the Cree head chiefs, Maskepetoon, was killed. It was partially in revenge for his death that the Cree undertook a large campaign against the Blackfoot in 1870-71. One of the last major battles was fought along the Oldman River in present-day Alberta. The Cree lost both the battle and the larger goal of driving the Blackfoot out of buffalo territory.

In the late 1870s, the buffalo rarely came far onto the Canadian prairies and the herds were soon to be depleted even more rapidly as the hide hunters from the United States slaughtered the animals in large numbers. These hides were sold to merchants in Montana who shipped them east, where they were made into large leather belts which were used for pullies in factory machinery at St. Louis, New York and Chicago. Buffalo leather was in great demand as it made the best belts for these purposes.

The era of this trade in buffalo hides was to be short-lived. It ended only a few years after it had begun with the Cypress Hills Massacre in 1873, when a group of American desperados killed thirty Assiniboine in the Cypress Hills.[13] The massacre brought out the NWMP, who established Canadian authority in the area just north of the Canadian-American border, putting an end to the forays of American hunters onto Canadian lands.

Decline of the Fur Trade and Buffalo Culture

In the early 1870s there was no one the Cree could turn to for assistance but the Canadian government, which was offering to settle them on reserves in return for title to their lands. Some Natives had turned to agriculture in an attempt to alleviate starvation, but crop failure, government regulation and the elements made these attempts difficult. More frequently, the Aboriginal traders sold furs to independent American traders who had established their posts across the southern Canadian prairies. Some of these traders remained in the territory and continued their trade even after the arrival of the NWMP, but the Aboriginal hunters found fewer pelts and hides to trade with them. The Natives' options for survival were running out as Prime Minister John A. Macdonald's National Policy, with its aim of a West settled by Euro-Canadians, closed in on them.

What is clearly evident from accounts of Cree life is that they remained a functioning and vital people. They were never directly the victims of white people or

10

other tribes, but consciously and rationally adjusted to new circumstances. However, over the years their conditions increasingly presented them with new problems. By 1870, the Cree were as powerful as they had ever been and were in a strong position to meet any challenges put to them.[14] They had an enviable military and diplomatic record as they faced the Canadian state that was moving westward. In the past, they had often faced new economic and military situations and had come through each crisis: from their life in the woodlands, to the first contact with Europeans, from their adaptation to the gun and horse, to their role as middlemen in the fur trade where they traded with whites and Aboriginals alike, and finally as plains buffalo hunters. None of these changes had dramatically affected their internal social dynamic.

In the eyes of Euro-Canadians, the ironic tragedy for the Cree in the 1880s was not their new dependence on white people, but that they had not internally changed to become the materialistic, acquisitive people that would have adapted well to the capitalistic society they now had to live in. The social system that had served them so well for hundreds of years would now be restricted. "What was led into the bondage of the reserves was not the ruin of a political and social system, but rather a healthy organism which had taken root and grown strong on the plains. The fate of the Plains Cree nation followed that of the buffalo — not to death, but into a white man's pound, the reserve."[15] The 1870s were years of dramatic change for the Cree as well as for the white people in the West, especially with the creation of the province of Manitoba. The new political divisions and institutions were harbingers of change that many Aboriginal people had witnessed on the American frontier. These were transitional years where the Cree would move from a life based on migrating herds of buffalo to a sedentary life on reserves: when European concepts of time and landholding became dominant on the prairies and when the idea of landholding "in common" would change to land ownership based on private property.[16] These were also the years when the Aboriginal idea of time, which was based on a close and synchronized relationship with nature, would be lost as they moved onto reserves. There they were faced with the whites' Newtonian sense of absolute and progressing time as well as the related concept of "wasted time."[17]

The European Worldview

The ideology of the Christian worldview brought to the plains by the European missionaries and traders stood in stark contrast to that of the plains tribes. Christian attitudes toward nature differed markedly from those of the Natives. They did not live in the same proximity to nature and did not feel the same communion with nature as the Natives did. European Christians adopted an adversarial attitude towards nature and viewed it with suspicion and fear. Nature was something to be conquered or overcome, as were their own emotional and physical desires.[18] The Christian worldview was person-centred and only incidentally concerned itself with living in concert with nature or its seasonal cycles. Their god was one to be feared. According to some missionaries, in order to appease this god people would need to toil on earth and prove their worth to avoid the damnation of burning for eternity in hell, a concept alien to Native religion. In Indian belief, an individual might be denied the fruits of a pursuit because spirit powers were not properly appeased, but the consequence was not the drastic punishment the Christian god was supposed to hand out.

The Natives were familiar with Christian concepts through their fur-trade contacts. The European traders did not, however, make any attempt to convert them. As missionaries began arriving, it was soon apparent that they they saw it as their role to try to convert what they regarded as a "heathen savage" people to Christianity. These Christian missionaries, unlike Native religious people or shamans, had what has been described as a compulsive need to convert Natives to Christianity.[19] The missionaries felt threatened by the unknown.

These agents of European culture were represented by Roman Catholic, Anglican, Methodist and Presbyterian missionaries. The first missionaries to the plains in the mid-eighteenth century were French Jesuits led by Father Merenerie, coming west with Pierre de La Vérendrye. Other French Oblate missionaries who arrived in the Red River area at this time included Fathers Taché and Aubert. Some of these Oblate priests, such as Father Scollen, worked among the Blackfoot in the nineteenth century. Other Catholic priests, such as Father Thibault, made frequent journeys across the prairies, spreading the Christian message. By the 1860s, the Grey Nuns had established mission schools at Lac St. Anne, Île à la Crosse, St. Albert and Athabaska. In 1888 a mission was established at St. Boniface by Father Joseph Provencher.

Anglican missionaries were also among the first to arrive in the West. Under the auspices of the Church Missionary Society, Reverend John West established a school aimed at educating Native boys in the ways of European society. Several other missionaries arrived to expand the program in the Red River area and to assist West in his mission, with additional schools being built across the prairies for similar purposes. In 1840 Henry Budd, a Cree and a Christian convert, established a mission at The Pas, and soon more schools like his were begun by other converts among the indigenous peoples. Like the Catholic missionaries, the Church of England missionaries moved westward by the 1860s into what is now Alberta.

Although they arrived later than the Catholics and Anglicans, the Methodist missionaries were no less enthusiastic in bringing the message of the Bible to the Natives. Among the Wesleyan Methodists were some of the more prolific authors who published accounts of their life on the prairies and their experiences with the Natives. The most famous were Reverends Robert Rundle, John McLean, Egerton Ryerson Young, and the renowned father and son team of George and John McDougall. John McDougall published many books describing his early experiences on the plains and perhaps more than the others he tried to understand the Natives' way of life. In spite of his many years among the plains tribes, however, he could not rid himself of the belief that the way of life of the society and culture he was promoting was superior to that of Native peoples.[20] McDougall, despite his attempts to overcome his biases, left the overall impression that the Natives were a feeble, backward race, and as a consequence he argued that the land should eventually be occupied by his own people, whom he believed were stronger and more industrious. The biblical injunctions that informed and directed the missionaries compelled them to reject Aboriginal culture and society. At the cornerstone stood the dictum from Genesis 1:28: "Be fruitful, and multiply, and replenish the earth, and subdue it; and have dominion over the fish of the sea, and over the fowl of the air, and over every living thing that moveth upon the earth." This was the directive for the Christian "sodbuster" to break the land.

The European Critique of Aboriginal Life

Though they had often adjusted to changing circumstances, the plains tribes still lived in close proximity to nature. The seasonal cycles and pulse of nature, not the Newtonian clock of absolute time ticking by the second, dictated their movements. These contrasting concepts of time made it easy for the Europeans to criticize what appeared to them as laziness, since their unit for measuring the time by which tasks were to be accomplished, the "second," was much smaller than that of the Natives. The Europeans seemed to race against time in order to harvest what they saw as the vast potential for power around them.

There were other characteristics of Aboriginal society that made Victorian Canadians critical of Native life. The Aboriginals' apparently casual attitude towards private property was quite alien to the European, whose idea of worth was based upon the concept of accumulation of individual wealth. The European concept of private property eventually destroyed the Natives' claims to the use of the western prairie, and it was the consequences of implementing this idea that ultimately would erode the Aboriginal way of life. The concept of property title for land ownership was alien to Native peoples. The movement of Natives across the plains without an easily perceptible purpose was seen as evidence of a shiftless people, ill-equipped by religion and unprepared by culture to recognize the value of property ownership. Victorians saw private property as a necessary requisite in establishing a habit of work and the desire to strive for improvement. Hunting was not a respected pursuit to the Victorian frame of mind unless as a sport or pastime. Such a lifestyle, based on a feast-or-famine cycle, was thought to be "improvident" and evidence that the Aboriginal, whose economy was based on hunting, was incapable of careful planning for the future. To live so close to nature and be virtually at its mercy was an indication of a "primitive" society; not to accumulate a surplus proved a lack of mastery over nature.

By the 1880s, as the Natives became more destitute and dependent upon the whites, many Canadians believed they had been proven right. To them, the Natives' inability to make the land fruitful by settling rather than wandering in pursuit of game was evidence of a people that did not live correctly. Indeed, their own way of life seemed to flourish next to that of the Native.

Attitudes toward "land use" changed on the prairies during the 1870s and 1880s. The transition (some would say the progression) went from the enjoyment of land in common (that is, to be used by all) to "open access," where land is claimed, but can still be used by others, to entrenchment of land held legally as private property. Prior to the systematic settlement of the prairies, Native society functioned on and perhaps survived through communal cooperation. Natives did not believe that anyone had sole rights to resources: "game was the common property of all, and everyone had a chance to share in this gift of nature."[21]

When passing through occupied Aboriginal territory, individuals were free to take or use any resources needed, whether that be game, water or fuel. The plains tribes were "a people who had no notion of exclusive and permanent property rights in land or the other gifts of the Great Spirit."[22] Those with a wealth of resources in band or tribal society would share with those less fortunate; it was considered to be a matter of pride and an indication of status to be able to give to those who were in need.

The plains tribes were in fact living amid wealth, and by the nature of their culture did not need to be conspicuous consumers. Their environment was rich with resources: wood, water, forage, game, fish, berries, honey, wild rice, clothing, housing, weapons, implements, toys and thread. However, in order to have access to all this, a great freedom of movement was required. Farming, which entailed a more sedentary life, was only incidental to plains consumption, and agricultural products were usually obtained by trade. The tribes thus moved with the seasons as they knew the migrations and cycles of plains wildlife.

Most obviously disruptive to this lifestyle was the disappearance of the buffalo herds, which led to a greater dependence on other food sources and increased agriculture. Their movements were not only restricted by his development, but by the increasing settlement of the plains. At first, through the 1870s, those tribes who had not yet signed a treaty protested against white settlers and interlopers who simply occupied territory and gave nothing back in return. It is not clear if they understood the settlers were actually claiming the land. "[E]mphasis was on the use of the lands — indeed, it seems probable that the Indians thought of the problem as that of the right to *use* their lands ... [t]he outright *sale* of those lands was a concept entirely unfamiliar to them."[23]

Gradually, more of their resources such as wood for fuel and game were not only being depleted, but exploited. Several American companies began fishing in Lake Winnipeg, exporting the catch back to Detroit where demand was high. Throughout Whoop-Up Country, the buffalo were being shot in disturbingly large numbers for leather-machine-belt production. At the time, buffalo leather was the best material available for belts used in factories of the rapidly growing industries of eastern cities like St. Louis, Chicago, and New York. By the late 1870s, only a few major buffalo hunts were being reported, the last one occurring on Canadian soil in 1879. As a result, the plains tribes were without the staple they depended upon for survival. As land was used up and movement restricted or no longer of any purpose, their options diminished:

> The old balance between a limited human use of the gifts of nature held as common property by each tribe and natural regeneration of those gifts was finally destroyed when they were thrown open to all comers including those intent on commercial exploitation. The disappearance of the buffalo was a classic instance of the "tragedy of the commons," when a common-property resource was transferred into an open-access resource.[24]

Increased settlement occurred almost simultaneously throughout the 1880s. Resources such as hay and wood were now pursued and harvested as never before. Even the open-access system was being eroded as "private property" was increasingly being claimed and occupied. In a sense, the loss of the buffalo overshadowed the disastrous "impact on the native peoples of the new order based on private ownership of all natural resources."[25] As plains tribes began to claim and settle on their reserves, they were perhaps unaware that they would no longer be allowed the free movement they had once enjoyed over the vast plains. Now the real significance of the reserves became apparent. Before the 1870s the society was relatively egalitarian,

> in which all had access to common riches provided by nature, and [one] in which, if disparities in skill, strength, and luck gave some more wealth than others, the difference had been to a considerable extent offset by sharing by the more

fortunate of their material means with those in need, in accordance with the strong native tradition. Now they were shouldered aside by wealth-accumulating newcomers, sinking to the lowest position in an unfamiliar order characterized by wide disparities in economic and social status.[26]

The Treaty Process

The treaties were a last attempt to protect the resources the Cree used and shared with others. The treaties restricted their way of life but they believed they could move on the plains as they always had. Their protest against regulations that attempted to prevent their movement was perhaps best expressed in 1885, when they saw the treaties being used to isolate them. Big Bear and his followers were among the last to have any hope that the new order could be resisted. With the common land gone, the Natives had little choice but to move onto reserves.

The treaties signed in the Canadian West between the government and the plains tribes followed from British practice and were similar to the American tradition of settling claims of dispute. Negotiated settlement was usually preferable. It is generally agreed that the treaties were negotiated and not imposed, but whether they were negotiated between equals remains to be determined and is presently a point of contention among scholars. Each side had its own end in mind. The Natives wanted two goals realized: to ensure the physical and cultural survival of their people, and to improve their material position. In most cases, it was expected this would be achieved through a change in lifestyle from the plains buffalo culture to the agricultural life once Natives were relocated on the reserves.

Before 1830, the British government policy was to keep the Natives content so they would not join in alliances with the Americans. To achieve this, presents were given in an effort to keep these Natives loyal; however, after the 1830s, the motives of the colonial and imperial governments changed. Increasingly, the efforts of the government and its agents focussed on "civilizing" the Natives. Although it was an altruistic goal which was in the best interests of the Natives, it was ultimately generated out of self-interest.

By the 1870s, the desire was to remove the tribes as an obstacle to settlement. Large numbers of hungry and unpredictable Indians were seen as a hindrance to the massive prairie immigration envisaged by Ottawa. The attitude at the time was that the Natives would be much more controllable on reserves. Under the administration of a government department, they could be socially and economically controlled, and scrutinized and channelled through regulation into areas of economic enterprises agreeable to the authorities. It was hoped that over time, when "civilized," the Natives could be absorbed into the society being ushered onto the plains.

As was the case elsewhere, immigrants drove the indigenous people back, sometimes using them as labour when needed. Then, as immigration increased, their labour was no longer needed and they were moved out of the way onto reserves.[27] The government encouraged immigration to the West, and, as subsequent events were to show, it was far more interested in obtaining Aboriginal lands than it was with assisting these Native prairie dwellers to a new economic livelihood.

There is evidence in all the numbered treaties in the West that the Natives were willing and in some cases anxious to adapt to a new way of life. Most understood the inevitability of losing their former lifestyle and negotiated hard to wrestle what they could from the commissioners who bargained with them. Of scholars who have written about the treaties, only George Stanley argues that they were not really negotiated.[28] He suggests that the Indians were only able to accept or reject what was presented to them and were unable to change or negotiate terms. He states that the Natives did not understand what was happening and had a different interpretation of what the land-ownership clauses of the treaties meant. While the latter point might be conceded, Stanley's position generally implies that the Natives were not capable of bargaining for their own interests. There is considerable evidence to the contrary, as each treaty in its own way reflects different concerns and terms. While starving tribes who had lost their way of life can hardly be seen to be negotiating as equals, it cannot be assumed they did not negotiate at all. The evidence, especially for Treaties 3 and 6, indicates they were astute bargainers getting what they could from an otherwise difficult situation.

In the mid-1860s, the Canadian government began negotiations with Natives in the Fort Francis-Rainy River area, a place referred to as the North-West Angle of Lake of the Woods.[29] The treaty signings proceeded through Manitoba and into the North-West. At Treaty 6, signed at Forts Pitt and Carlton, all of the Natives bargained hard for better terms and made every effort short of not signing. They did this even though they had been presented with an ultimatum by Lieutenant Governor Morris: there would be little change to the treaty as it was being offered, and the Natives could take it or leave it. Though in a difficult position, the Natives were determined to bargain hard. They knew what they wanted and would not easily give up the 121,000 square miles under negotiation.

At Treaty 6, after many impassioned speeches by the major leaders of the Wood and Plains Cree tribes and many days of bargaining, the chiefs came to an agreement with the government officials. While maintaining the major features of the previous numbered treaties, they won three new concessions. First was a clause to assist the Natives in case of famine and pestilence; second, a medicine chest was to be given under the treaty and kept by the Indian agent; third, the Natives were to receive extra provisions to assist them in crop cultivation for the first three years of the treaty. They also got a greater number of cattle and agricultural implements than had been negotiated in other treaties.

Treaty 6 shows that the Cree wanted to make the transition to an agricultural way of life and bargained as hard as they could for provisions that would allow them to do so. The government may have been forced to give some concessions to the Cree, who were perceived to be among the most volatile and potentially violent of the plains tribes. The government was also anxious to have the agriculturally rich plains of the southern grain belt opened for settlers.

With the treaties for the plains tribes signed by the 1880s, attention turned to administration. Many of the Aboriginal signatories were anxious to adopt a new livelihood, but the government would need to live up to its part of the treaty by assisting in this transition. As historian Sarah Carter has argued, the Cree leadership was persistent in demanding assistance towards establishing agricultural economies and was equally persistent in reminding the government of its promises after the treaty was signed.[30]

By this time, Edgar Dewdney had replaced David Laird as Indian commissioner. Dewdney was faced with formidable challenges in the 1880s. He would need to reorganize his department to facilitate the agricultural society the government wanted the Natives to adopt. He would also have to establish a policy for the distribution of relief, especially in Treaty 6 where a particular provision had been made for such a circumstance.

The Aboriginal position had weakened by the 1880s. While at the start of the negotiations they had only wanted to give up a small part of their lands (in Treaty 1 they wanted two-thirds of Manitoba), by the time Treaty 7 was made, there was less and less territory granted to them by the formula the government used to determine the size of reserves. Indeed, it remains unclear whether the government officials ever explained what the reserve system would be like to the chiefs present at Treaties 6 and 7. Most chiefs at Treaties 6 and 7 thought they had agreed to share the land in return for annuities, education, medical and famine assistance, as well as a commitment to establish ranching and farm economies. The Natives were still left with the understanding that they were free to hunt and fish where they saw fit and were not restricted by the boundaries of their reserves. Big Bear was still demanding hunting privileges into the 1880s, but the detailed position of the government on land surrender had not been made clear to the Natives. These provisions were perhaps deliberately kept vague, possibly to avoid a serious point of contention during the negotiations. In spite of this, it was clear that the Natives had little alternative. They did not want war; indeed, they were not united enough to provide a front against the threatened settlement of their land, and the military presence at the treaty negotiations showed them that any resistance would be met by force. Most of the tribes preferred to settle on the Canadian side of the border and were no doubt lured by the attraction of the initial payment the government offered. If they did not sign, they knew they would be left with nothing. In the final analysis of the treaty process, they did more than merely sign to share land. Through their negotiations they were hoping to establish themselves with a new economy, and they committed the government to assist them in their transition to an agricultural society. Whether that society was to be merely for subsistence or one that would participate fully in the market economy of the grain trade along with other settlers was a question yet to be answered.

TWO

The Material Culture of Fort Battleford

The Herald's Song

I was born without pomp or glory,
Unfettered but uncaressed,
Amid hills eternal and hoary,
In the land of the golden West.

Till the red man's wild traditions
Lose their triumphant sway —
Till errors, and superstitions
Be scattered and swept away.

Thus amid wild turmoiling
I will live to a good old age,
And the deeds of a ceaseless toiling
Shall shine in a deathless page.

When my works from the nation's records
Shall gleam without shade of strain,
I shall feel with a thrill triumphant
That I have not lived in vain.

And perchance, in the long, long future,
E'er the star of my life goes down,
I shall know that this land shines the brightest
Of the gems in the British crown.

That I was her proud defender
Till she bore a victorious sway,
In her robings of matchless splendor
That never will fade away.

P.G. Laurie
(from the inaugural issue of the *Saskatchewan Herald*, 1878)

The material culture at Fort Battleford is the most extensive record that remains for understanding the society that was established there in the late nineteenth century. The buildings, along with the associated furniture, instruments, tools and utensils, art and decoration provide the most significant, conscious (even self-conscious) expressions of Victorian culture and ideology of the late 1800s. They are the concrete evidence that allows us to analyze the nature of cultural values at the time these objects were created. They reflect "the beliefs of the individuals who made, commissioned, purchased, or used them, and by extension the beliefs of the larger society to which they belong."[1]

The agents of Anglo-Canadian culture carried instruments to the North-West for measuring and classifying the land. Other items helped them to survive materially and spiritually as well as physically and psychologically. The stoves for warmth, the pots for cooking, the lamps for light were artifacts necessary for physical survival. For aesthetic survival they hung pictures and posters that conformed to their inherited ideas of familiarity, beauty and comfort. Their spiritual survival was provided through the Christian symbols and literature at the fort.

The attitudes of the police towards other inhabitants in the North-West and to the world in general were reflected by the fort itself. The structure represented what the Mounties feared as well as what they wanted to establish. There were basically two groups of buildings: those which were self-conscious symbols of their culture intended to impress viewers, and those which were strictly functional. There were no obvious frills or symbols included on these latter buildings, which were the most common at the fort. They included barracks buildings, stables, storage buildings, artisan shops and commissariat buildings. Structures that were intended to be aesthetically remarkable included houses for officers and buildings used for official functions. The building distribution reflected in microcosm the importance of the class nature of Victorian society: most were ordinary, only a few were adorned.

The major buildings, built between 1876 and 1900, were designed by the Department of Public Works in Ottawa. They reflect the influence of Victorian architectural trends popular during the nineteenth century in eastern Canada, Britain and the United States. Among the earliest public edifices in the North-West, they were significant because they stood as symbols of the Anglo-Canadian elite which was then emerging as the dominant force in western Canada. The sophistication of this new architecture provided a startling contrast on a frontier where previously Native lodges and log buildings had provided only the barest of shelter.

The Tradition of Forts in Canada

The palisade was one of the first defensive structures used by Europeans when they arrived in North America. In 1876 the NWMP erected a rather primitive palisade at Fort Battleford, just after the fort was established. Fort Battleford was an extension of an established tradition in a land "dotted with old forts."[2] Canada was a place of conquest, and the forts had to protect armies, explorers and traders from those thought to be hostile to them. The builders of forts could not rely on the leisurely process of trial and error that settlers and traders often adopted; they had to work within the constraints of a particular environment. They simply built forts as they knew them from their inherited traditions.

Forts differed one from another within the basic form, yet they all evolved from a common European tradition beginning in the fifteenth century when the cannon introduced a new offensive warfare that could be launched from a fort. In the sixteenth century, bastions were an important feature that allowed more flexible firepower against aggressors. By the seventeenth century, large fortresses housing substantial armies were designed to withstand the new strategy of siege warfare. Changes in technology produced new concepts of fighting, shaped the form of cities, and determined the character of warfare.

Fort Battleford was an example of the "detached fort" that emerged at the end of eighteenth-century warfare. The days of long and elaborate siege wars were gone. Artillery had become too mobile for that. Fortresses were no longer central in warfare but were, in Napoleon's words, excellent support for war. They remained important, but mainly as supply depots. Loopholes in walls replaced the elaborate earthworks of the *enceinte*. Thus, detached posts or fortresses served the centre militarily, and represented a new form of mobile warfare that appeared on the prairies with the forts of the North West Mounted Police. Battleford and other NWMP forts, as ramshackle as they may have appeared, were examples of the evolving use of the fort as an effective form of defence when moving into an unknown frontier.

Beyond the most obvious military reasons for fort building, there were psychological and cultural reasons for constructing garrisons in the New World. These reasons give important insights into the ideology of the European culture that was extending into the North-West. New technologies gave armies more mobility and allowed the European powers greater maneuverability as they expanded into the frontiers at the edge of their empires. However, the need for fortification remained. In spite of the new technology, men and armies still needed fortifications for psychological as well as physical security.

The NWMP moved into the North-West in the wake of the Cypress Hills Massacre in 1873, becoming agents of the culture that first appeared in the West through the fur trader and was entrenched by the homesteader. Like their predecessors, the police arrived to claim possession of the land for a society based in the East; they did not come to live in harmony with it or feel a part of it. Their forts were garrisons in a more direct sense than either those of the fur trader or homesteader. The NWMP was therefore a significant force in extending the cultural values the fur trade companies had begun to establish for those who came to populate the West under Macdonald's National Policy.

In the period 1877-84, Troops A to F were distributed between Fort Macleod, Fort Walsh, Fort Calgary, Fort Edmonton, Fort Battleford and Regina. Each of these main forts also had outposts which became part of the patrol system. Fort Battleford, for example, had outposts at Onion Lake, Bresaylor, Sounding Lake and Sixty Mile Bush. Each of these depots consisted of a rough log structure at which a small detachment of men could spend time. These outposts, strung across the country from the Rockies to Manitoba, were particularly important in the southern portion of the Canadian prairies in the early years of the force. As the flow of whiskey was curtailed and most Natives were consigned to reserves, the forts and outposts in the south were no longer as significant and attention was increasingly paid to the northern plains where most Natives had been encouraged to establish reserves. This distribution of Mounties clearly shows a gradual shift in the period 1876-85. Fort Battleford, with its many surrounding Cree reserves, was the most significant focal point for police activities in the years immediately preceding 1885.

Evolution of Fort Battleford's Layout

Like other early police forts, Battleford's layout was organized around a military square with a rough stockade to protect the forces. Quarters for the superintendent and officers were the most elaborate and were set off from the rest of the force. Stables and enlisted men's barracks were situated across the square away from the officers. Next to these facilities were quartermasters' stores, artificer shops, and hospital buildings or rooms. Often many of these functions were combined in one long building. This arrangement was typical of almost all of the early forts. There were also smaller separate buildings for the magazine, icehouse, blacksmith shops and guardhouses.

Fort Battleford's beginnings as an outpost were typical of other NWMP forts. It gradually evolved to accommodate itself to the surrounding community by adopting a less military appearance. In the first years, the fort was significant as the place that housed enforcement and reflected the administrative authority of the Canadian government through the territorial capital established in 1876. Unlike Fort Walsh and other prairie forts, a stockade was not immediately constructed (perhaps due to the lack of proper logs); instead, fairly elaborate buildings were raised that displayed symbols of Victorian Canada to the indigenous prairie peoples. Thus, though perhaps less militaristic in appearance than forts like Walsh, the authority of Victorian culture was obviously represented in the Gothic Revival of the commanding officer's residence. The military square was clearly established early in the layout of the fort.

There were three distinct phases of the fort's physical life: 1876-85, 1885-1914, and 1914 to the present. Eighteen to twenty buildings were erected in the period 1876-85, one-third of which were constructed in the first year. Three of these early buildings were living quarters for officers and enlisted men, while an artificer's shop, storehouse and stables were also built. Over the years, a number of other service buildings were added, such as a hospital and the Native department store, as well as more living quarters. An icehouse and dry kiln were constructed for keeping ice during the hot summer months and making bricks respectively. A rough stockade was also raised to protect the police grounds. The most remarkable feature of this layout was its militaristic character, most evident in the parade grounds and square, stockade and military arrangement of the buildings. A number of other impressive structures built at this time made clear statements about the kind of culture the police would disseminate in the North-West.

The fort was located on high ground between the Battle and North Saskatchewan rivers. It was isolated from both the town and government buildings and its location guarded against attack from all directions. While the fort had an easily accessible water supply, water had to be hauled up a steep riverbank when the wells did not provide sufficient water. This was to be the source of some embarrassment and inconvenience in 1885 during the "siege," when the 500 people located within the stockade were in dire need of water. On the other hand, the fort was fortuitously surrounded by good hay lands.

Other landscape features of this period included a series of local trails to the fort which led to Government House and the townsite. There were also hayfields and gardens located behind the commanding officer's residence. It was thought that such gardens were commensurate with the civilization that should accompany a commanding officer of the NWMP. A sports field was located to the north, toward the townsite. Thus by the time of the fighting in the spring of 1885, there were approximately fourteen buildings standing around the parade ground inside the stockade; some half dozen others were located immediately outside its protection. During this period, the fort stood as an obvious example of the garrison mentality, with the police huddled within its confines against the unknown forces of nature and the surrounding indigenous populations. Their material culture, especially as it adorned their buildings, shows the need to identify with the culture of the mother country. In these early years the police adopted little of the culture of their neighbours, although their own culture did eventually change as it became necessary for the Mounties to make adaptations to survive in such a vast, unfamiliar territory.

The second distinct phase in the history of the fort's layout was the period 1885-1914. The number of buildings at Battleford increased significantly as did the number of men at the fort. This period was most remarkable for an overall change in the orientation of the layout. It moved away from the strict military square to one that was aligned along the local survey grid of 1884. Thus, the old rigidity of the imposed structures gave way to accommodate local and environmental conditions. As the construction boom period of 1885-90 began, buildings were now located along extensions of the town's streets rather than reinforcing the defensive military features that had characterized the fort to that date. The stockade was replaced by fences and the layout began to meld with the town survey pattern. It was obvious that threats from Native populations were no longer seen as imminent. Perhaps the police knew they had served their purpose and were now able to relax in the new, less formal layout. This reflected, in part, their successful subjugation of the Native population, who were no longer seen as a threat to the incoming white settlers.

In this new alignment, buildings were constructed along the extension of First Avenue. These included the concert hall, mess hall and quartermaster's store. There was also a new hospital located close to the town as well as a surgeon's residence. These buildings represented greater physical contact with the local community as the police were no longer needed in a military capacity. They were also there to serve the needs of the townspeople, if not the Cree residents on the reserves, instead of simply protecting them. The concert hall built along the street was easily accessible to the townspeople and was a good example of the erosion of the military barriers that had once stood. The concert hall housed many social and cultural events and became part of community life. By 1890, only five years after it had so significantly protected the local population, the stockade had fallen into such disrepair that it simply collapsed and was not replaced.

There were new buildings erected inside the stockade as well, most notably a handsome officers' quarters built in the Second Empire style. New stables and a wagon shed appeared, as did a new guardhouse, and a specialized sick horse stable was raised. New improved privies replaced older dilapidated ones, and boardwalks especially useful during wet weather were constructed to facilitate local foot traffic. As older buildings were dismantled new ones appeared, and in 1890 the sergeant's residence was moved onto the grounds along First Avenue to provide a family home for an officer. As new streets were used, the old trails fell into disuse and new fence lines appeared.

Overall the fort resembled a hybrid, a mix of the military square and the new grid layout of the expanding municipality. A new square was created in the mid-1880s, located in an area between the concert hall, mess buildings and stables. After the 1890s, there were few new buildings and gradually the need for a large fort was reduced. By World War I, many of the buildings had collapsed and only a few families of policemen still lived on the property.

The third period, 1914 to the present, was also a period of dramatic change in the layout of the fort. In some ways this period represents the era when the most significant alterations happened. The changes, however, issued more from administrative decisions than from cultural use of the fort by the NWMP. The great majority of alterations occurred after 1926 when the site was declared a place of national significance. These major changes reflect approaches and attitudes of

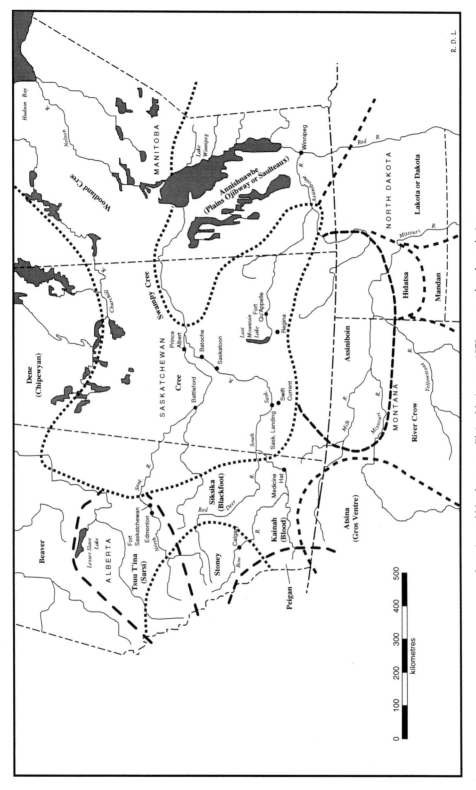

Locations of Northwestern Plains Nations ca. 1870, over modern boundaries.

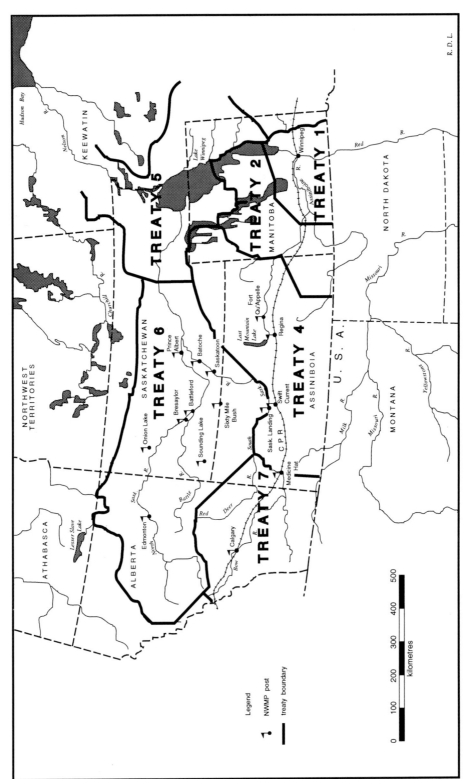

Post-treaty North-West.

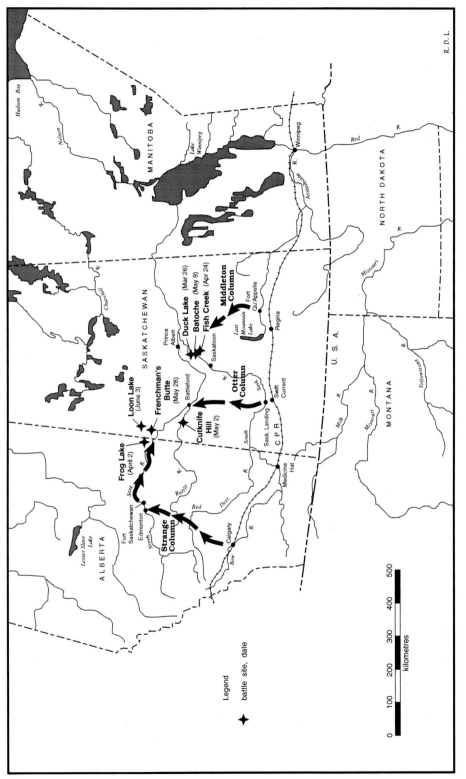

Featues of 1885 battles.

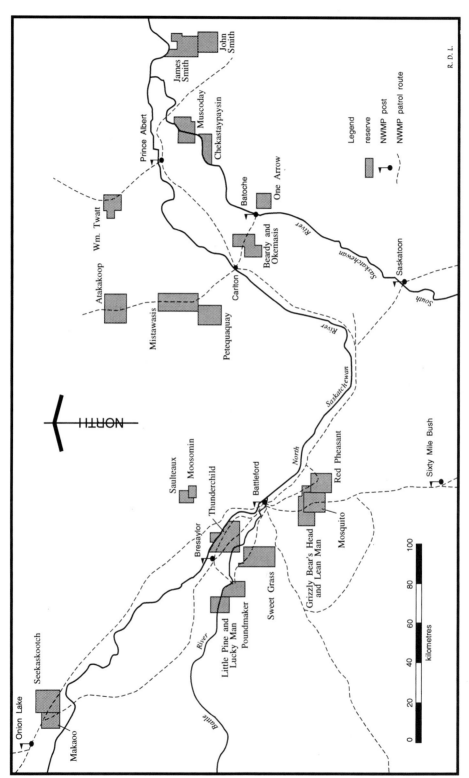

Reserves of the North Saskatchewan and patrols of the North West Mounted Police, 1885.

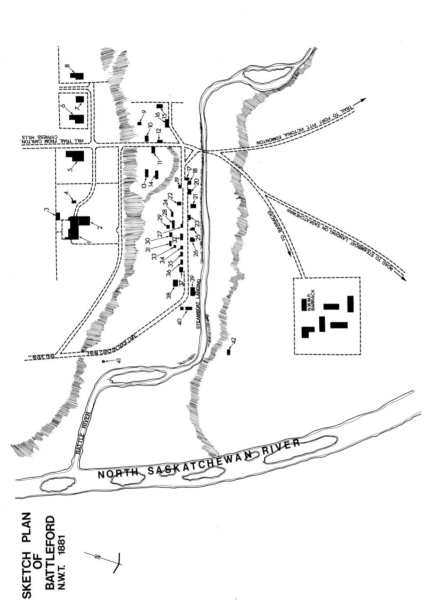

Fort Battleford and surrounding area, 1881 (National Archives of Canada, H2/540).

Legend: 1. residence of Lieutenant Governor; 2. council room; 3. stable; 4. storeroom; 5. residence of registrar; 7. registry (at present Indian) office; 8. residence of clerk of council; 9. jobbing carpenter shop; 10. Methodist mission building; 11. English Church mission and school house; 12. general store; 13. hut; 14. hut; 15. residence of Roman Catholic clergyman; 16. Roman Catholic school room; 17. hut; 18. hut; 19. hut; 20. trader's storehouse; 21. trader's residence; 22. hut; 23. mail station; 24. hut; 25. *Saskatchewan Herald* newspaper office; 26. Roman Catholic mission building; 27. storehouse; 28. hut; 29. hut; 30. hut; 31. hut; 32. general store; 33. hut; 34. storehouse; 35. storehouse; 36. storehouse; 37. general store, Hudson's Bay Company; 38. residence of Hudson's Bay Company officer; 39. Dominion government work and machinery shop; 40. telegraph and post office building; 41. telegraph stable; 42. residence of English Church clergyman.

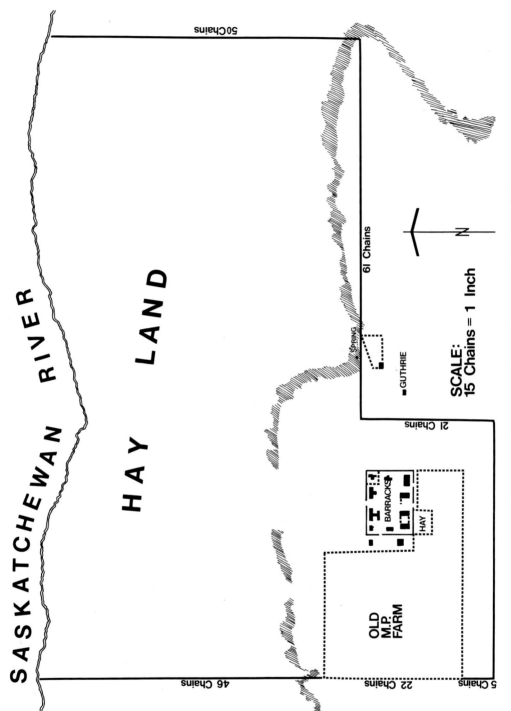

Fort Battleford and surrounding area, 1877 (National Archives of Canada, H3/540).

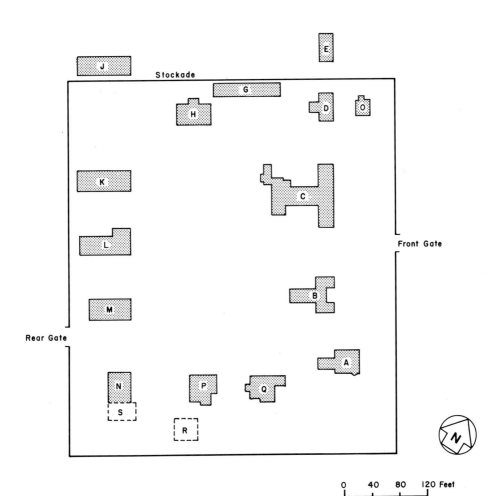

A   Commanding Officers Quarters

B   Orderly Room Etc.

C   Barrack Rooms Etc.

D   Guard Room Etc.

E   Sergeant's Mess Room

F   N° 4 Barrack Room
     (Constructed 1884)

G   Waggon Shed

H   Blacksmith Shop Etc.

I   Hospital
     (Constructed 1884)

J   Q.M. Stores
     (Constructed 1884)

K   N° 3 Stable
     (Constructed 1884)

L   N° 2 Stable

M   N° 1 Stable

N   Indian Department Stores

O   Magazine

P   Officer's Quarters

Q   Present Officer's Quarters Etc.
     (Constructed 1885-6)

R   Present Location of Sick Stable
     (Moved here at time of Renovation)

S   Present Location of Guard Room
     (Moved here at time of Renovation)

"The Log Fort," 1885 period (Fort Battleford NHP Library). This drawing by Harry Tatro was based on an 1884 plan.

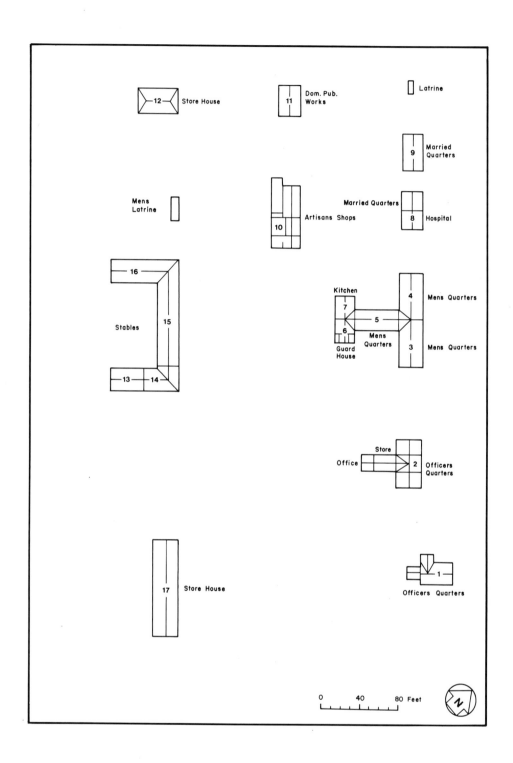

An accurate diagram of Fort Battleford's barracks, 1878 (National Archives of Canada, RG11, vol. 576, file 94).

This is a classic bird's-eye view from the roof of the Commanding Officer's Residence at Battleford. Perspectives such as this, where the viewer looks down at the scene from a position of power along with an agent of the colonizer (in this case a Mountie) were common to art produced by British publishers reporting on events throughout the Empire. Mary Louise Pratt has labelled such views as portraying the colonizer as "monarch-of-all-I-survey." The landscapes typically present the land as virtually empty of any other habitation (other than their own) and when Aboriginal people are presented they are made to appear sinister and threatening (Glenbow Archives, NA-1480-32).

Government House (Fort Battleford NHP Library).

Note the subtle details associated with Gothic Revival architectural styles which include trefoil and quadrefoil designs on the pendants and bargeboards. These designs symbolize the Trinity and the Cross. Gothic Revival was closely associated with Christianity and was the style that most clearly represented the British connection. Government House was the seat of the capital of the North-West Territories from 1876 to 1883, when it was moved to Regina.

The Commanding Officer's Residence as it looked during the "siege" in the spring of 1885. Note the bell tents that helped to house some of the 500 local residents who feared for their lives after the killings at Frog Lake. Fears of attack by the local Cree were lifted with the arrival of Colonel Otter's column later in April (Fort Battleford NHP Library).

The Commanding Officer's Residence with its pendants, finials, bay window and trefoil bargeboard place this building clearly within the Gothic Revival style. The Commanding Officer's Residence along with Government House were designed in Ottawa by prominent architects who worked for the Department of Public Works. These two buildings were the first buildings to display "national styles" in the North-West Territories. Seated in the foreground is Commissioner Irvine (commissioner from 1875 to 1886) who was visiting at Battleford. Note the rather rickety "stockade," that looks nothing like the stockade presently around the fort (Glenbow Archives, NA-659-33).

An early photograph of the Commanding Officer's Residence with the summer kitchen annex as well as a storage shed. To the right is the Officers' Quarters with its mansard roof. To the left are stables and artisans' shops. Note the stockade with planks nailed onto the top to keep the thin poplar posts in place. To the extreme right is the flagpole which was at the south end of the parade square which can be seen in the foreground (Glenbow Archives, NA-936-17).

"Inside the Police Barracks during the siege. Tents of refugees in the Barrack Square," by William R. Rutherford, ca. 1885 (Glenbow Archives, P-1390-8).

Canadian troops entering Battleford, 1885 ((Glenbow Archives, NWR 1.2-8).
Residents of Battleford town were greatly relieved by the arrival of Otter's column. Members of the force are depicted arriving to a heroes' welcome by handkerchief-waving residents.

This is a view of the south side of the Concert Hall. Note the small Gothic windows under the gable. Flourishes such as this were found on a number of the more functional buildings, though most of the style and decoration were reserved for the residences of the officers (Glenbow Archives, NA-779-2).

This photograph from about 1890 shows, from left to right, the Surgeon's Residence, the Commanding Officer's Residence, the Officers' Quarters, the hospital, stables, icehouse, men's barracks, Mess Hall, Concert Hall and Guard House (Glenbow Archives, NA-2235-20).

A good view of the Officers' Quarters taken in the mid-1880s. Note the mansard roof, finials on the dormer windows as well as the decorative bargeboard typical of the Second Empire style popular with official residences during Victorian times (Glenbow Archives, NA-3320-3).

early heritage preservation, especially through the first three decades following the designation of the site. The initial garrison construction of the fort was eroded even further during this period.

There was an initial time of upkeep from 1914-19, when Superintendent C.H. West occupied the command post at Battleford. In 1919, the area headquarters was moved to Prince Albert and the fort was only used as a depot. It was totally abandoned in 1924 when Sergeant Shepard was transferred to North Battleford. At this time, significant deterioration began. Joe Guthrie, a long-time resident of the area who lived in the commanding officer's residence for awhile, remembers 1924-28 as the years when the fort fell into total disrepair:

> But then for the years from 1924-25 there, until about 1928, the place was vacant. It just went to wreck and ruin. Everybody went in there and they ransacked it and they broke windows and sell the rest of it. And then the town took it over, and they rented some of the buildings to Harry Stewart, he had some cattle up there and he also stored grain there. And then the concert hall was sold to Hull, Clink and Quail, I guess Quail bought it not Hull so much, and then he tore it down and made a bunch of cabooses out of it. Well, then some of the older buildings were torn down, it was one of the last ones to be torn down. It was in good shape, the barn. Well, to tell the truth, I don't know why they tore it down. The town sold it but like the big barn, the latest barn that was torn down, it was torn down for the lumber. But then they had what they call the icehouse, and the fire hall and the blacksmith's shop, they were all made of logs, but they gradually deteriorated, the plaster fell off of them and they were getting to be a danger you know of falling over and peoples' kids going in there and one thing and another, so they tore them down. The town sold some of them then they tore them down and just scrapped them.[3]

The Guthrie family moved into the commanding officer's residence in 1928 and helped slow the deterioration of a few of the remaining buildings. This, plus the work of Campbell Innes, a local school teacher, helped to stop the total decay of the buildings at Battleford. Some buildings, like the concert hall, were removed from the fort while others were simply dismantled for lumber and logs. This process was accentuated from 1924-28 but continued throughout the 1930s and 1940s. What was protected were the officers' quarters and commanding officer's residence. The former was turned into a Native museum for awhile, with the latter being restored to contemporary standards.

Road systems, parking lots, fences, hedges and tree lines also altered the shape of the fort's layout throughout these years. The roads increasingly reflected the grid layout of the municipal system, while the hedges and tree lines were examples of the styles thought appropriate for adorning heritage sites. Manchurian elms, caragana, maples and spruce trees were planted at various times to outline specific areas and the site as a whole. Through the 1940s and into the 1950s, gardens and ornamental stones were placed along pathways.

The 1950s was an era of significant change. Most notably, the stockade was reconstructed in conformance with the model of the Fort Langley stockade. However, because little research was available at the time, the reconstruction was more closely suited to the fur trade than to a North West Mounted Police fort. A new entrance changed the prevailing road system once again, and new administrative buildings greeted visitors as they approached the site. Outlying buildings, such as the sick horse stable and guardhouse, were relocated and lined up with the commanding officer's residence and officers' quarters to provide visitors with easier access to the remaining historic structures outside the stockade. Only "Barracks 5" (or the mess hall) was left in its original location. Some ornamental landscape features were added, such as painted stones and gardens, but these were not based on historical research either.

Minor changes occurred through the 1960s. The outlines of building foundations were indicated on the grounds, and maintenance and restoration work to existing buildings also took place during this time. Limited resource allocation for the fort meant that little reliable archaeological and historical research was undertaken. Only in the late 1970s were structural histories written and in the 1980s a contextual history placed the history of the fort in a national and regional context. With the management planning underway in the 1980s, new initiatives were identified and the development of historic resources undertaken.

Victorian Architectural Traditions on the Prairies

For the Victorians, architecture not only provided shelter but served as a means of communication. Architectural forms were often chosen for the buildings' needs. Regionally, the structures erected at Battleford by the Department of Public Works were the first buildings after 1870 to depart from the simple log shelter, and were built with a style and panache to convey messages of this culture to newcomers. Government House at Battleford is an example of this more sophisticated style.

The "picturesque" structures occupied by the North West Mounted Police were instrumental in disseminating Anglo-Canadian ideas to the West. Many immigrants may not have understood the concepts depicted by Victorian styles, but the culture represented by these buildings and the customs of the society they symbolized were firmly passed on by the police.[4]

These Gothic Revival buildings were constructed in the last quarter of the nineteenth century, at a time when the influences of Victorian architecture were dominant in Canada. Two architects, Thomas Fuller, Sr. and Thomas Scott, shared responsibility for imposing the Gothic and Italianate styles upon public building in Canada late in the century.[5] Both were born in Britain, worked on the design and construction of the Parliament Buildings, and had lengthy careers in the public service.[6] Fuller, whose tenure as Canada's chief architect lasted from 1881 to 1897, was particularly influential in determining the style for federally financed buildings in Canada. His tenure ensured that Gothic and Italianate became dominant modes even for relatively insignificant wooden buildings, such as those designed for the North West Mounted Police.[7] The commanding officer's residence at Fort Battleford, built in 1876-77 and still standing, is clearly within the Gothic style of the Romantic Revival. Its vertical lines, originally crowned by a finial, bargeboards, pendants, bay window and "picturesque setting," make it typical of this style.[8]

Details characterizing Christian traditions were included on Gothic structures. Trefoil designs represented the Trinity, and the trefoil pattern carved into the wooden bargeboard beneath the peak of the gable in the commanding officer's residence is a graphic depiction of "carpenter's Gothic." Cruciform plans were used to symbolize the everlasting sacrifice, while pinnacles represented souls seeking their "'finial' in that heaven where alone the soul's consummation 'can' be sought."[9] Although the commanding officer's residence was L-shaped (as was Government House) instead of the cross-shaped floor plan, it did originally display finials (or pinnacles) at the peak of each gable.

The adaptation of the Victorian Gothic to domestic housing led to the introduction of a number of other features such as bay windows (which allowed for a feeling of closeness to nature), chimney stacks, ceilings, and panelled wainscots around interior walls. Both the commanding officer's residence and Government House exhibited these additional features, the most outstanding being the elaborate bay window in the former structure.

Of course, the Greek Revival style was not totally excluded from public buildings in North America, nor was it categorically condemned. As the nineteenth-century American architect H.H. Holly stated:

> For ecclesiastical structures, colleges, etc., the Gothic designs are rapidly superseding the Italian, while for public buildings for government, and other secular purposes, the Grecian is generally regarded as preferable.[10]

Details of the Greek Revival are found in the pedimented window casings in both the commanding officer's residence and Government House.

The interior features of the commanding officer's residence are consistent with those of other Victorian houses.[11] Immediately to the left of the front entrance is a large living room or parlour for public and official occasions. To the right, upon entering the front door, a stairway leads to the private section, making the division between public and private areas of the house immediately apparent. At the back is the winter kitchen and servants' dining room while an ell containing the summer kitchen is attached to the rear of the house. The servants' stairway is another feature common in Victorian housing. The second storey contains three bedrooms and a small landing.

The officers' quarters with its French-style mansard roof, decorative bargeboards, finials and dormer windows is clearly within the Second Empire style popular during the mid-to-late nineteenth century. Even though this fashion originated in France, it was seen as a variation of the Italianate style because of its heavy forms and elaborate ornamentation.[12] It was the addition to the Louvre, commissioned by Napoleon III, that brought the Second Empire style international recognition and most often "focused on notable, newly constructed public buildings."[13] The style did not, however, make its way to North America directly from France, but was introduced through British architects who were designing public buildings in Britain after the Second Empire model. It therefore became part of the broader Victorian architectural tradition in North America through this British connection. The Italianate style as part of the Romantic Revival in Victorian architecture swept North America during the latter part of the nineteenth century.[14]

The officers' quarters, done in the Romantic Revival style of the 1870s, took nearly four years to complete and serves as an example of a building whose construction was significantly influenced by local circumstances. A shortage of materials meant that the walls of the structure had to be built of logs instead of finished lumber. Although porches were initially not part of the building, they were added later because of the effects of extreme temperature on the building. An absence of skilled labour on the Canadian frontier in the 1880s frequently resulted in jerry-built construction, as is evident in the trussing visible in the attic of this building.

Victorian architectural details are also found scattered throughout other buildings at Fort Battleford, for example the cross-shaped floor of the surgeon's residence and its gingerbread gables. The Gothic arch on the concert hall (no longer standing) was an interesting sidelight on an otherwise ordinary building, and an example of late Victorian eclecticism was found in the original pagoda-style cupola on the sick horse stable. This scattering of detail is in itself illustrative of the derivative nature of western building, though the retention of "picturesque" features and asymmetrical designs in the face of the "classical revival" seems more suitable to the plains environment.

Despite the derivative nature of Government House and the commanding officer's residence, these buildings are examples of what has been labelled the "Canadian vernacular."[15] This classification defines those buildings that, though clearly representative of borrowed styles, show adaptation to their setting and environment through structural refinement or the use of local materials. Constructed with logs and often covered by clapboards and stucco, both buildings were built of local timber. The discrete simplicity of the decorative details of these two buildings is more compatible with their environment, especially when compared to the garish, exaggerated styles of the late Victorian period. "The handling of materials aware but abrupt — helps to identify those structures as part of the Canadian vernacular."[16] Government House and the commanding officer's residence readily fall within this definition.

Adaptation was required to cope with unanticipated environmental conditions, such as the extreme cold of winter and the heat and dust of summer. This was best reflected in the addition of porches over main entrances. "In a climate such as this, they [porches] are useful in winter and summer; in the latter season they furnish protection from the constant winds and sand storms that often accompany them."[17] Funds for renovation were frequently requested from Ottawa in order to make the buildings habitable. Invariably the requests fell on deaf ears, despite the often desperate pleas from the frontier where the unseasoned wood shrank, thus cracking the mud and leaving gaps in the walls which allowed the wind to whistle through the buildings. The consequences were sometimes severe. One commanding officer at Battleford reported to the officials in Ottawa:

> I have the honour to make the following report regarding the [commanding officer's residence] I occupy as a quarters and which I consider unfit for such in their present state. During the past winter four stoves were kept going the whole time, the building was not any too warm. At night full pails of water frozen [sic] solid — there is no storm sash — many mornings I have seen my bed covered with snow and rain — one-half of the building has no ceiling, only paper and cotton parts of the logs are rotten and when soaked by rain throws a dampness and has an odour throughout the house. The moulding inside is in between the cotton and wall.[18]

As is evident, the inhabitants of the buildings at Fort Battleford had not been freed enough from the elements to be overly concerned with the aesthetic appeal of uncluttered structures. Such concerns were still a luxury when the environment demanded porches and patchwork for self-preservation. In many cases buildings had to be extended even though funding for new structures was not forthcoming. The result was the appearance of lean-to additions which, like porches, were unforeseeable afterthoughts: makeshift extensions to otherwise completed buildings. There were frequent complaints over the quality of the construction. No storm sashes were provided for Government House, which Lieutenant Governor Laird found most uncomfortable. He wrote to the prime minister: "When the high winds and cold come together we are nearly perished."[19] Superintendent Walker also had reservations about the workmanship and asked for men "who knew something of carpentry work" to complete the structures. Frustrated with the lack of progress, Walker finally wrote to the commissioner: "The Department of Public Works finished here last week but all the buildings are as yet in an unfinished state and could not be finished for want of materials and what work is done does very little credit to those in charge of the works."[20] Thirteen years later continuous shortages of materials and money had left the buildings in a barely habitable state.

There were more complaints from all levels of the police against the extreme conditions of winter and summer than grievances about any other discomfort. The commanding officer's residence could not be protected against the elements any more than the barracks buildings. While differences existed in terms of privacy and living space, the variations between buildings were more a matter of style and ornamentation.

Both the ordinary vernacular structures and the more elaborate, stylistic buildings of the officers eventually had to have porches added and their walls properly chinked to battle the levelling effect of the elements. Thus, both the buildings with Victorian detail and the simple functional buildings tell us as much about frontier life as they do about the class distributions of this Victorian police force.

Both kinds of buildings have their own significance, but there is much that can be understood about the existence of those who lived in what were apparently simple functional buildings occupied by the regular enlisted men. It is important to value the so-called ordinary and challenge the notion that only the monumental is important. "Art historians tend to treat only large ostentatious examples of Victorian architectural styles and relegate to limbo the more commonplace and simple structures of the Vernacular tradition of … building."[21]

Although the buildings at Fort Battleford had to be adapted to their environment, the styles represented a transplanting of traditional British and eastern Canadian values. The North West Mounted Police were Canada's Imperial constabulary whose federal image and national role were more than reinforced by the long arm of the design group of the Department of Public Works. The styles the buildings displayed are a reminder of a culture that imposed structures and institutions on a frontier, leaving little room for the emergence of an indigenous architecture. The police, like the buildings they lived in, had to adapt to unfamiliar conditions. The resultant changes, however, were more a matter of degree than form and issued from a desire for self-preservation rather than a wish to adopt indigenous styles. Many of the policemen retired to settle in the West and helped to perpetuate the culture they had carried with them. An indigenous western architecture of the late nineteenth century could hardly be expected to emerge from what appeared to the police as a sparsely populated frontier.

The Wacousta Syndrome and the Garrison Mentality

Unlike prairie Natives who learned over many hundreds of years to forge a symbiotic relationship with the land, Europeans tended to recoil against the unknown in the natural world around them. Early expression of this attitude of resistance to nature is contained in the novel *Wacousta* by Major John Richardson. The "Wacousta Syndrome" which, it has been argued, typifies a Canadian response to nature, is characterized by the relations between people as they arose out of the pioneer experience in the "wilderness." Central to the definition of this syndrome is the predominantly negative reaction to what was seen as an overwhelmingly threatening and brutal environment. Nature was viewed as harsh, impersonal and uncompromising. Survival for humans in these surroundings was considered a monumental struggle. The Euro-Christian worldview approached nature already feeling besieged. Homesteading or establishing a foothold in these northern regions was seen as dangerous and life threatening. The unpredictable, sinister, chaotic, untamed, limitless, impenetrable, alien landscape produced a fear of nature. The pioneer, soldier and explorer lived in constant fear of nature and recoiled from it whenever possible, heading back into the barricaded fort or the walled-off homestead. The coping mechanism of early European inhabitants tended to be less of overt hostility to the forest, open prairie or vast lake country and more of an attempt to mediate or avoid nature with inherited cultural forms.

Whereas Aboriginal cultures tended to make peace with nature, the Europeans by contrast continued to battle against it in one form or another. The most obvious strategy was simply to avoid nature, replacing its looming presence with a focus on comforting detail and avoidance of context. The result was that Europeans rarely appreciated their place in nature, but found comfort by withdrawing to the protection of the fort and the familiarity of the culture they brought onto the frontier. The NWMP can be seen as a part of the Euro-Canadian reaction to nature that refused to see the indigenous people for what they were; instead, the whites lived in fear of them, threatened by them in the same way they felt threatened by the environment of which the Natives were a part.

The second coping strategy of Euro-Canadians was to impose European forms onto what was found in North America: to see nature with a romantic sensibility as an extension of the pastoral myth they imposed on their image of the western frontier. In this way their culture produced images of the noble savage and landscape paintings that looked like they were painted in European settings. The eventual failure of the vision was that nature remained the same in spite of attempts to use European culture to tame it. Thus, the reliance on European cultural forms exacerbated the problem of not being able to come to terms with nature and the Natives living in accord with that nature.

The fortress thus became the image of security for Canadians, a place from which nature was kept at a distance to allow for mediation. The forts were depots that provided security for those who clung to Old World forms most tenaciously. They were there to disseminate the alien European culture, not to accommodate the indigenous culture already there.

The cultural problem the NWMP faced can be seen with relation to the visual art produced by artists from European cultural traditions. In form, Native art identified with the landscape through its non-perspective style in which the artist could not place him or herself against the landscape, but only feel part of it. In content, it reflected its identification with the landscape through its images — flowers, animals and trees were painted, woven or sewn onto clothing, lodges or rocks. There was a spiritual identification with the environment, and with nature. By contrast, early European art used a privileged perspective where the single artist, outside the landscape, pointed to what he or she stood against. In some cases, the position of the artist even reflected a desire to dominate the scene. In content, the art was focussed on the Imperial culture and tended to depict forts and exploration or feats of discovery, where the explorer's perspective — as opposed to the nature or environment he or she stood in — was highlighted. Thus the Euro-Canadians, through their art and valorization of forts or man-made enclosures, began to determine and lay down new approved forms of expression. Paintings and drawings of NWMP forts became a flourishing art form and included paintings of Fort Battleford by artists such as Richard and Mrs. Lindemere.

These aesthetic forms provide evidence of the ideology behind the European worldview which was brought to the North-West by those who occupied the forts. European paintings seem to be natural, or of nature, but actually are cultural expressions. A comparison of paintings by artists James Isham and Samuel Hearne is instructive: Isham felt a part of the nature he lived in while Hearne stood against the land and felt threatened by it. There is, for example, a clear difference between the perspective of the painting of Prince of Wales Fort by Hearne and a non-perspective painting by Isham. Referring to Hearne's painting, the difference became clear:

> Far from being Natural, Hearne's perspectival technique expresses a cultural or political relationship of power over the land, for it appropriates the land in its own terms just as surely as did the men for whom the visual art was intended... Not only is there nothing natural about this work of Hearne's, but the work is a cultural artifact drawn according to a set of conventions that are themselves based on power and domination, and done so on behalf of a conquering system based on power and domination.[22]

In contrast, Isham's watercolour of Natives hunting beaver reflects no desire to dominate the land. His images are of the natural world with no attempt to create depth of space or man-made regularity. He painted animals and nature in a way that was understood and shared by the Aboriginal people. Hearne's geometric fort is revealing when juxtaposed against Isham's organic representation of nature. Thus the fort and the European style of representation shows how ideology functioned:

> Hearne's work reifies the fort and land by turning them into massively static "things" to be viewed by the isolated individual being. Isham's drawing is not about static things, but about communal life in relation to the land as process. In this it comes very close in technique to modern cartoons, except here the various parts of the sequence of events associated with the beaver are placed within a single frame. In Isham's work there is no privileged viewing position for the beholder, nor are we encouraged to command the space. Hearne's work and space invades our bodies to shape us. We enter Isham's space to share it ... it comes close to the vision and life of the native peoples.[23]

Both the Wacousta Syndrome and the visual analysis of the paintings of Hearne and Isham lead to the more comprehensive formulation of Northrop

Frye's "garrison mentality." This concept has been applied to the western Canadian context by Ian Clarke and Greg Thomas. The authors pose the question of how two landscapes — a fur-trade post and a prairie homestead — reflect the fear of isolation felt by Euro-Canadians:

> The Hudson's Bay Company employees came from the hamlets, villages and towns of Britain and its outer isles. A century and a half later, a number of Ontario farm settlers left their forest clearings of Upper Canada for homestead land on the western plains. How these two groups responded to their new environment is in part reflected in the structures and landscapes which they introduced. But what particular consciousness did the fur traders and Ontario settlers bring to the land?[24]

Clarke and Thomas view the reaction of these two groups to the western Canadian environment as "very conservative." In response to this fearsome environment, the immigrants set about modifying their landscapes as quickly as they could. "The insecurity pervading such locations compelled British settlers to retain a psychological as well as a political and economic connection with Britain."[25] There was little attempt to copy or use those forms already established on the plains by the Métis and plains tribes. The new arrivals were determined instead to shape the West in their own image. Insensitive to existing populations, they created the mould to which existing populations had to conform. Incoming settlers would then be channelled into the established form. Though the new Euro-Canadians did not identify with the landscape they moved into, they nevertheless assumed power rapidly and imposed their cultural visions with great facility. "The societies that flourished within the narrow confines of the fur trade fort and the Ontarian prairie homestead might then be seen as 'garrisons' which manipulated the social and natural landscape to approximate more closely the familiar environment of their traditional cultures."[26]

During the fur-trade period, enclosed fortifications developed quickly and space reminiscent of the "plantation" was cleared. The layout of fur-trade posts was, however, usually a "square" like the stockade fort of the NWMP. When leisure time allowed, gardens were planted, with flower, vegetable and shrub gardens creating an atmosphere of familiarity. Even fruit tree groves were formed. Generally the newcomers had no aesthetic concern with the landscape around them. They simply denuded the trees around the fort without any concern for the resulting aridity this created. However, this action did exaggerate the desolation felt by the Euro-Canadians towards the land. The North West Mounted Police needed the palisade forts for defence purposes as they did indeed fear Indian attacks. Most of their attention was given to the decor of the interior of the forts and shelters. For aesthetic enjoyment and food they kept small gardens; for escape or consolation they maintained libraries of books and journals. Shelter was never just physical. The cultivated gardens of the fur-trade posts stood as a symbol of the inability of the Europeans to accept the surrounding landscape for what it was. They felt a need to cultivate and tame what they viewed as a savage wilderness.

In the settlement period before 1914, change to the landscape was dramatic in form if not in scope. Farmers like W.R. Motherwell transplanted their own cultural forms and institutions onto the prairies rather than trying to merge with what was found. The environment was still to be feared, and windbreaks not only provided physical protection from dust and snowstorms but stood as a spiritual sanctuary away from the environment around them. Houses that were built by predominantly Anglo-Canadian settlers resembled fortresses against the land, especially when compared to the vernacular architecture of the Métis and Native inhabitants. In the settlers' houses, a material culture was displayed not unlike that of the NWMP, with art and artifacts that could have been found in many Victorian homes throughout the British Empire. Though the first homes were simple log or wood frame, one of the first general improvements made by early homesteaders was to build a field-stone house like the ones back East. These homes were invariably surrounded by hedges of caragana, maple, spruce or willow. These shelterbelts kept nature out and betrayed a culture afraid of its environment. Unlike the Native people of the prairies, the openness of the plains was oppressive for white homesteaders. Even in pioneering days many immigrants built tennis courts and formal walkways to create the atmosphere of a British garden. This was done with great physical exertion and expense since the levelling effect of the prairie environment was hostile to these constructions. Most of these features can be seen as extensions of the Wacousta Syndrome or garrison mentality.[27]

THREE

Administration of the Law at Fort Battleford: 1876-1885

Thanks to the North-West Mounted Police, settlers in Canada found a country free from desperadoes, vigilance committees and scalping Indians.

J.P. Turner

Maintenance of law and order is the most common theme in early histories of the NWMP. Histories of the North-West written prior to and immediately after World War I focussed on what was viewed as the problem of establishing civilization amid what was still characterized as threatening Métis and Native populations. These accounts reflected the times and preoccupations of the authors, who were almost exclusively male and Anglo-Canadian. The law-and-order theme in the official records was an extension of, or mirrored, the justification for the use of force and physical violence against Aboriginal populations. Natives, it was thought, threatened the establishment of an agricultural base for the white immigrants who were being encouraged to settle in the West. It is evident from early histories like Edmund H. Oliver's contribution to Shortt and Doughty's *Canada and Its Provinces*, and John Hawkes' *The Story of Saskatchewan and Its People*[1] that it was important for white settlers to feel confident in the ability of the police to make the West safe for settlement. Victorian Canadians also felt a need to be protected from the threatening forces of untamed nature and those who, in their minds, lived close to nature.

Over time, the law-and-order theme gave way in historical accounts to the image of the NWMP as agents of the National Policy; the Mounties were portrayed less as military enforcers of British and Canadian law and more as a police force ushering in the newcomers.[2] With Aboriginal populations no longer a threat, historians did not have to emphasize the necessity of using physical or military power to gain the respect of local Native people. Histories written since World War II were more "liberal" in their outlook, but paid scant attention to Native populations. Historians increasingly saw the Mounties as policemen for the large white populations that were increasingly occupying the plains as the National Policy blossomed under the Laurier Liberals. This view reflects the transformation of law enforcement in a society moving from a reliance on *dominio* (or force) to one in which hegemony (or cultural persuasion) directed the authorities responsible for social control. With the establishment of Anglo-Canadian culture and its legal systems, the use of physical force was no longer as urgent and Aboriginal populations could be controlled by less crude means. As the ideology of those who held power began to permeate educational and social institutions, the images and models for acceptable behaviour were reproduced and disseminated in books and through teaching in schools and churches. Thus, the tools for controlling behaviour effectively became cultural and the reliance on overt presence of force decreased.

Only recently have historians looked again at events in the Canadian West that involve relations between white and Native populations, and have begun asking questions about the nature of the power relations between them in the period of North West Mounted Police administration.[3]

The Mission of Law and Order

It is difficult to find a balanced history of the NWMP, largely because of the many previous laudatory accounts that have mythologized their mission. The lasting success of the generic Mountie as collective hero of Canada's national consciousness has led some to express concern about the country's penchant for authority.[4] Early popular studies such as A.L. Haydon's *Riders of the Plains* did much to entrench the image of the undaunted Mountie faithfully serving the Crown. It is obvious from the opening sentences of his book that the police were not stationed in the West primarily to serve the local people, but were given power to enforce and transplant a way of life onto the prairies. Haydon reflected the aspirations of his own generation when he wrote of the traditions of the "British race" being carried west by the Mounties, who to his mind were not sufficiently valorized:

> It is a characteristic of the Rider of the Plains that he does not waste words upon his deeds; to this is due the general ignorance of his solid achievements... It is time that an authoritative history of the Royal North-West Mounted Police should be added to the regimental records of the British Empire.[5]

Instead of pointing out that the police became part of a greater coercive treatment of Native populations after 1885 (through the pass system, for example), Haydon says that the Mounties' role became more difficult after 1885.[6] He argues, against the evidence, that Natives continued to be lawless, thieving, killing and generally threatening toward the peaceful settlers. Were it not for the stalwart role of the Mounties, Haydon thinks that their defiant and aggressive attitudes would have led to "far more serious consequences."

Today such writing is no longer in the mainstream, but such views toward Aboriginal people were not uncommon or isolated. In a very significant way, the "Indian problem" was perceived by the fledgling police force as its most important obstacle to establishing law and order. They maintained their reputation by their manner of treating the Aboriginal people; it was this treatment that set standards against which others yet to arrive in the territories would be judged and measured. All new arrivals would be instructed in what constituted acceptable behaviour. Thus the legendary stories of the Mounties began.

Of the same generation, yet less emotional in tone (if not in content) is the work of historian Edmund Oliver. Oliver was a contributor to the prestigious twenty-three-volume series, *Canada and Its Provinces: A History of the Canadian People and Their Institutions by One Hundred Associates*, published in 1914.[7] Those who wrote this history were mostly from an Anglo-Celtic background and did little primary research. Oliver, a professor of history at the University of Saskatchewan, contributed the sections related to the West. He was familiar with Haydon's book and used it as the major reference for his sections on the North West Mounted Police. Like Haydon, he presented the police as officers of law and order, but defined their role more broadly, showing the Mounties to be not only enforcers of the laws but men who made the law as well. "The officers of the force not only maintained order throughout the country, but they also suggested legislation. The early territorial ordinances governing irrigation, branding of stock and marriages by justices of the peace have their origin in that knowledge of local conditions which the police alone possessed."[8] Like Haydon, Oliver also saw the local Aboriginal population as the major concern for the police up to 1900.[9] Aggressive attitudes would have led to "far more serious consequences."

What emerges from such interpretations is that the main concern of the early NWMP administration was to deal with the pacification of Natives in what Prime Minister Macdonald referred to as "that fretful realm." The institutions to establish systems of education, legislation, municipal and judicial tribunals were to constitute a Canadian presence, and Aboriginal populations were expected to assimilate into the Anglo-Canadian society. The link with the East was to be through the Canadian Pacific Railway's transcontinental system, which was to herald the inauguration of a "new order for the white settlers."[10] The Aboriginal and Métis presence was the main obstacle of the police up to the turn of the century. In this sense, the Mounties were established primarily to deal with a Native threat to new white settlement. In fact, the police were originally intended to disband after their function had been completed; they were not meant to be a permanent force.

The broad authority given to the police in the era of the National Policy enabled them to carry out a wide range of administrative activities. They had the power to administer and enforce British and Canadian law in the territories, but that law was not the law of those already living in the West. The NWMP powers referred to laws contained in the act of 1873. Oliver mentions only Canadian and British law in his section on "Law and Justice on the Prairies"; these were the laws he hoped would lead to the Canadianization of the territories. The laws and traditions of the Aboriginal peoples were ignored. The culture to be nourished was to be Anglo-Canadian; the culture to be denied was that of the Native groups.

Few laws were enacted to aid the Native or Métis populations in making adjustments to the changing realities they faced in the 1870s. Big Bear had asked for laws that might have helped to conserve the diminishing buffalo herds. But most of the laws and regulations, especially in the Indian Act, were made to restrict and contain Aboriginal activity. Nor was much done to give them any power in the established Territorial Council which ended up being dominated by eastern Canadians. Indeed, the early ordinances passed by the Council dealt with fires, irrigation, stock branding, marriages and licensing. The West functioned as a colony administered from Ottawa. Officials recorded in glowing terms the accomplishments brought about by the colonization of the prairies. Even in 1964 the commissioner of the Royal Canadian Mounted Police could write in an introduction to a new edition of *Riders of the Plains*:

> Great cities now stand where log forts of the company stood one hundred years ago. Take nothing away from the missionaries, the explorers and the traders who first ventured into this land of nomadic Indian nations, but realize that it was the police who made it possible for the pioneer settler to bring his women and his children into this great lone land in safety. It was the presence of the police that permitted him to dip his plow into the prairie's beneficent earth and garner its rich rewards. Seldom in the history of man has such a fantastic empire of new land been opened to peaceful settlement with so little turmoil, so little corruption and, except for 1885, so little of the violence and bloodshed that followed the passage of other great historic migrations.[11]

This legacy of police administration has been so influential that even one hundred years later their history is still written from a single perspective — one that only presents the viewpoint of the colonizer. It is a voice unable to show sympathy for the aspirations of those peoples who lived in the West before the police arrived. The political culture that the force represented was one deferential to imposed authority. It was a tradition which, with the exception of the 1837 revolution in the old provinces of Canada, lacked a sense of people's democracy in a country much devoted to law and order. The force was answerable to an authority that was far away, and the police bore little relationship to the Natives in spite of claims in their own histories to the contrary. The great powers of the police put them in the position where they were the law, not merely its enforcers. The commissioner of the NWMP automatically held a seat on the Territorial Council, which was the lawmaking arm of the legal system then emerging in the West.

As well as potential makers and enforcers of their own laws, the police were given powers as magistrates so they could administer the same laws. The NWMP and Royal Canadian Mounted Police have always been in this extralegal position. The NWMP were not simply a state police force organized along military lines but were equivalent to colonial police forces in the old British Empire. In fact, the NWMP were directly modelled on the Royal Irish Constabulary.[12]

Culturally the force represented the narrow interests of the colonizer:

> The RCMP's conception of 'upholding the law' has always been an imperial and material conception... The English-dominated force ... marched off into the sunset to bring civilization to the Canadian prairies, taking charge of dealing with all kinds of matters: from insurrection and railroad workers' strikes, from murder to playing billiards on Sunday, from control over native Canadians and the British and French Métis, to the regulation of liquor, gambling, and blasphemy.[13]

The law and order was then culturally determined by the customs and standards of Victorian Canada. Vague concepts that refer to absolute forms of justice mean little without appreciating the context within which the police functioned.

The NWMP as Agents of the National Policy

It has been argued that police administration of the law was fair and the term "benevolent despotism" has been used to describe its function; however, a closer examination of Aboriginal-NWMP relations, especially after 1885 and culminating in the case of Almighty Voice, suggests a revision may be necessary. By the late nineteenth century, the police no longer showed sympathy to the Natives but saw them as the enemy. The NWMP were armed with broad powers to introduce "law and order" and ensure that an Anglo-Canadian way of life would be established in the West. R.C. Macleod, NWMP historian, censures academic traditions that suggest a repressive police state in the West. Macleod maintains that structure does not dictate function and that, even though the police enjoyed broad powers, these powers need not of necessity be abused. Macleod maintains that an examination of the police record suggests a fair treatment of minority groups by the Mounties and an equitable and fair execution to enforce the liquor laws in the North-West:

> This last point is stressed rather heavily ... among academics and other social critics to assume that structure dictates function; that because an institution enjoys wide powers, those powers must necessarily be abused. An examination of

the treatment of minority groups by the police, of their handling of criminals of all types and of their approach to one particular problem, enforcement of the liquor laws of the North-West Territories, provide abundant evidence that the Mounted Police almost invariably used their authority wisely and well.[14]

Here the limits in place for the police were to be found in "informal controls. ... in the political system and tradition within which the police operated, in the semi-military tradition of the force, and in the social structure of late nineteenth-century Canada."[15] Though there is evidence of the fair treatment of Aboriginal people by the NWMP, it may be too sanguine to suggest that the police were inherently fairer than other members of the same Victorian society from which they were recruited, or that they were more tolerant than any other force armed with broad powers which bore the burden of bringing civilization to Aboriginal people. A careful examination of the acculturation process shows the police involved in both overt and subtle forms of cultural subjugation that reflected their belief in the superiority of the culture they represented and were to impose. They remained agents of Anglo-Canadian hegemony over the West, often treating the local people as inferiors and sneering at their culture. This they did as much by ignoring the Native community as through overt acts of physical force.

The forms of discrimination and subjugation the Native people had to endure were not only the fault of the police, but also of the attitudes and intolerance of the culture the police represented. No matter to what lengths academic scholars go to document that police despotism was benevolent, they cannot erase the fundamental prejudice entrenched in Victorian attitudes to race: that Aboriginal peoples are relegated to an inferior status. It was the "us (white 'civilization') against them ('savagery')" attitude that completed the basic binary oppositions that constituted the culture of the late nineteenth century. The paternalistic mission was clear:

> The force was to be a civil one under military discipline. The Prime Minister had stated that he wanted as "little gold lace, fuss and feathers as possible" in the North-West Mounted Police. He did not want a crack cavalry regiment, but an efficient police force for the enforcement of law and order in a rough and ready country. The outstanding objectives were: to stop the liquor traffic among the Indians by whites, to gain the respect and confidence of the Indians, to teach them respect for the law while acquainting them with the great changes pending to break them of many of their old practices by tact and patience, to collect customs dues and to perform all duties such as a police force might be called upon to carry out.[16]

Thus the goal of the Mounties could eventually be described as a cultural one — to gain the trust of the Natives and then wean them from their customs and beliefs by enforcing laws intended to diminish the Native culture. This was also to be done by example, persuasion, government programs and education.

Macleod was confident that "Canadianization" of the West was of the greatest benefit to the greatest number of individuals. Its optimism firmly presented the history of material progress in the West. Indeed, there was virtually no mention of the police role in enforcing the pass laws, the permit system, or aiding government policies such as the severalty laws designed to make lands negotiated by the Natives under the treaties more vulnerable.[17] He replaced the image of the police as physical enforcers of law and order with an image that portrayed the police as agents of a new society and the final triumph of the hegemony of an Anglo-Canadian way of life for the prairies. In his estimation, it was Native culture that prevented them from benefiting from the wealth generated by the National Policy, and he slipped into the civilization/savagery paradigm of earlier historians when he wrote, "Had the Canadian government poured massive quantities of money and effort into the reserves [as they were obliged to under the Treaties,] it would not have made a great deal of difference. Even today, as the experience of aid to underdeveloped nations and the literature on the subject demonstrate, no one is even close to understanding how to use the resources available to change a primitive society into a modern one."[18]

Macleod's explanation of the police function in pacifying the West remains as unsatisfactory as those of earlier generations of police historians. More recently, new research suggests other explanations for the failure of the National Policy to include all people in the development of western Canada, explanations that go beyond blaming the victim.

The Relationship Between the NWMP and the
Aboriginal Peoples Through the Acculturation Process

The police, as representatives of official authority for the Crown, acted as agents on behalf of the Canadian government and were instrumental in negotiating the treaties on the prairies. Their presence at the negotiations was more in terms of military (*dominio*) authority than in a policing capacity; they were a ceremonial extension of the Canadian governmental authority. In a sense, the treaties were the culmination of the move by British and Canadian colonizers to gain possessory rights to Native lands.

NWMP attendance at the treaty negotiations coincided with the establishment of the Battleford post at the confluence of the Battle and North Saskatchewan rivers. Superintendent Walker, with his troops (made up primarily of "E" Division), had travelled northwest to the Battleford area and had chosen a height of land for a fort. After the construction of the outpost, begun under Sub-Inspector Frechette, Walker and his group continued to Carlton with the main portion of the troop. At this point the Mounties were to provide a military function by escorting the treaty commissioners who were to arrive at Carlton, but a rumour circulated at Carlton that Chief Beardy intended to stop the government party at a site along the south branch of the Saskatchewan River with the apparent purpose of signing a separate treaty with them. Walker immediately marched his men southwards to investigate and found Beardy's Cree. No problems were encountered between the two groups. The official history of the force suggests it was the very presence of the Mounties in their orderly, military attitude that overawed the Cree.

The police trotted past the Cree in their smartly polished uniforms and in military attitude: "On that day a lasting impression sank into many a redskin's mind, and the scheme to block the governor's passage was promptly abandoned."[19] The police role in these early contacts was clearly to establish the authority of the government party, and to show the Natives who was in control and who held ultimate power.

The large commission party made up of more than one hundred Red River carts reached Fort Carlton in mid-August 1876. The officials included Lieutenant Governor Morris; Chief Factor William Christie; the Honourable James McKay; Dr. A.G. Jackes, secretary to the commission, and Pierre Laveille, NWMP guide and interpreter. After some preliminary negotiations with the Cree, it was agreed that treaty negotiations would begin on 18 August 1876.

It was important for the commission to have a military aura accompanying the negotiations in order to present an image of control and authority. It was primarily in this role that police participation was indispensable. The atmosphere of significant ceremony was created by the government party to establish itself in a position of power. The negotiations began with the Cree conducting their own ceremonies before meeting the government men. The official history describes the ceremony with the lingering ethnocentrism of the 1950s:

> The Indians drew together amid a bedlam of gun firing, beating of drums, yelling and chanting. Turning towards the headquarters marquee, with their mounted warriors in front, they advanced *en masse*. After a display of barbaric horsemanship by painted and feathered riders, the chiefs, medicine men, councillors and musicians moved closer and sat down on buffalo robes and blankets.[20]

On this first day the Natives consisted of 250 lodges — about 2,000 people. The introductions of the chiefs were made by Peter Erasmus, the interpreter chosen by the Natives. The government then proceeded to describe what it was offering. Morris explained his position as a "servant" of the Queen with a brief history of the negotiations of other treaties. Morris spoke at some length of his intentions:

> We are not here as traders, I do not come as to buy or sell horses or goods, I come to you, children of the Queen, to try to help you; when I say yes, I mean it, and when I say no, I mean it too.

> I want you to think of my words, I want to tell you that what we talk about is very important. What I trust and hope we will do is not for to-day and to-morrow only; what I will promise, and what I believe and hope you will take, is to last as long as that sun shines and yonder river flows.

> You have to think of those who will come after you, and it will be a remembrance for me as long as I live, if I can go away feeling that I have done well for you. I believe we can understand each other, if not it will be the first occasion on which the Indians have not done so. If you are as anxious for your own welfare as I am, I am certain of what will happen.

> The day is passing. I thank you for the respectful reception you have given me. I will do here as I have done on former occasions. I hope you will speak your minds as fully and as plainly as if I was one of yourselves.[21]

The first day ended with the arrival of more Mounties from Fort Saskatchewan under the command of Superintendent W.D. Jarvis. This increased the number of police support to about one hundred men. On the second day the two groups continued their discussions. It was the Natives' turn to speak, beginning with Mistowasis, Atakoop, James Smith, John Smith, Chipewyan and others. They generally pledged their loyalty to the Queen and outlined their wishes for the treaty. (One problem emerged to interrupt the negotiations. This was Chief Beardy's initial request to meet with the governor at Duck Lake. The governor, having refused, later invited Beardy to join the others at Carlton.) Then Morris spoke and outlined in some detail the provisions he would include in the treaty, such as schools and agricultural assistance. During this process, another request came from Beardy. He wanted to be informed of the terms of the treaty and given material provisions which the commissioners supplied to members of the negotiating parties. The provisions were offered to Beardy as an enticement if he came to negotiate. The chiefs then asked for time to consider the government's proposal. According to the official police history, there was a delay after these initial meetings. This was interpreted as the Cree stalling for more supplies. The chiefs all outlined the needs of their bands and spoke of loyalty to the White Mother. After their speeches, they asked for time to confer with their people and retired to their lodges. One historian suggested that they were in no hurry to strike a deal since the government rations supplied while negotiations were going on were "to their liking."[22] After the request for time, Morris responded with a short statement:

> This is a great day for us all. I have proposed on behalf of the Queen what I believe to be for your good, and not for yours only, but for that of your children's children, and when you go away think of my words. Try to understand what my heart is towards you. I trust that we may come together, hand to hand and heart to heart again. I trust that God will bless this bright day for our good, and give your Chiefs and Councillors wisdom so that you will accept the words of your Governor. I have said.[23]

On the third day Morris indicated his impatience with the slow response from the Cree, and it was Poundmaker who replied:

> We have heard your words that you had to say to us as the representative of the Queen. We were glad to hear what you had to say, and have gathered together in council and thought the words over amongst us, we were glad to hear you tell us how we might live by our own work. When I commence to settle on the lands to make a living for myself and my children, I beg of you to assist me in every way possible — when I am at a loss how to proceed I want the advice and assistance of the Government; the children yet unborn, I wish you to treat them in like manner as they advance in civilization like the white man. This is all I have been told to say now, if I have not said anything in a right manner I wish to be excused; this is the voice of the people.[24]

Morris answered by saying the Cree must trust the Queen and her promise to help future generations.

The last day of the negotiations was the most intense with the Cree again putting forward a list of requests to which Morris promised some additional provisions. At the end of the exchanges between the governor, Poundmaker and Red Pheasant, a general agreement was struck over the provisions. On 24 August 1876, the treaty was presented and signed:

> the governor invested each chief with his uniform, flag and medal. The uniform consisted of a scarlet coat decorated with gold lace and a top hat with gold band. In the evening, the councillors were presented with blue coats and hats similar to those given to their chiefs. The medal bore an etching of the Queen's head and an appropriate inscription. ...

> On August 26 the Indians assembled at "Carlton House," their chiefs, and councillors proudly decked in the new uniforms. They had come to say farewell. They shook hands with the commissioners, well pleased with the way things had turned out and profuse in their gratitude for what had been granted them. They all joined in three cheers for the Queen, Governor Morris, the Mounted Police and Chief Factor Lawrence Clarke. Firing the guns in the air, they gradually dispersed.[25]

The commission then moved to Duck Lake where it was able to come to an agreement with Chief Beardy as well. On 5 September, three days after Beardy signed Treaty 6, the commissioners' retinue moved on to Fort Pitt. Superintendent Jarvis and his men had travelled ahead of the main party and, with a band playing, the Cree were escorted into the HBC post to meet with the commission. The police performance in this ceremonialism brought a great crowd of Natives to witness the "unusual" activities of the government commission. Negotiations similar to those at Carlton took place from 5 to 7 September between Morris and the leading chiefs, Sweet Grass and Yellow Sky. As at Carlton, the Cree asked for more time to consider the nature of the treaty and met again on the ninth to have matters clarified. After the majority of the Cree signed, speeches were made. Little Hunter spoke on behalf of his people:

> I am here alone just now; if I am spared to see next spring, then I will select my Councillors, those that I think worthy I will choose. I am glad from my very heart. I feel in taking the Governor's hand as if I was taking the Queen's. When I hear her words that she is going to put to rights this country, it is the help of God that has put it in her heart to come to our assistance. In sending her bounty to us I wish an everlasting grasp of her hand, as long as the sun moves and the river flows. I am glad that the truth and all good things have been opened to us. I am thankful for the children for they will prosper. All the children who are sitting here in hope that the Great Spirit will look down upon us as one.[26]

One major problem that developed for the commission was the arrival of Big Bear on 13 September. Big Bear told the commission he could not sign without consulting his people and had not known the date of the negotiations. He also expressed his concerns about the preservation of the buffalo. Sweet Grass and Red Pheasant tried to persuade Big Bear to sign the treaty, but to no avail. Big Bear met with Morris and told him he did not want to be disloyal, but did not feel he could sign without his people being present. He then agreed to meet with treaty negotiators again the next year. In retrospect, the refusal of Big Bear to sign was prophetic, for, throughout the next decade, the government commitment to aid the Natives in making the transition to an agricultural economy proved to be an abysmal failure. This was not so much due to the Cree, whose willingness to farm has been solidly documented, but more to government ineptitude, neglect and the inability to keep its financial promises. The reasons for ignoring Big Bear during the bargaining are not clear, but it has been proposed that the government deliberately chose to sign treaties as early as possible with the Christianized chiefs who were under the influence of their priests and ministers. This, it was thought, would encourage others who had doubts about signing and convince them to adhere to the treaty promptly for fear of being excluded from the supplies granted to the signatories. To allow Big Bear, a powerful orator and leader of other non-Christian chiefs, a high profile in the negotiations might have swayed the doubters away from agreeing to take reserves and to begin the settlement process:

> Because Big Bear had arrived after the treaty was concluded, he had no chance to negotiate and discovered that the door seemed closed to further discussion. He knew, however, that the Indians who had signed Treaties One and Two had become dissatisfied and that the government had altered the terms four years later. If the government could renegotiate those treaties, he saw no reason why they could not do so with Treaty Six, particularly if all the Plains Crees could speak with a unified voice. Stubborn and intractable when he believed he was right, Big Bear was not willing to meekly accept what the Christian chiefs had taken. He would try, with determination, to get a better deal for his people.[27]

Most importantly, what had been agreed to in the treaties in the Battleford area was a commitment by the government to assist the Cree in the transition to an economy based on agriculture. Distinctive to Treaty 6 was the procurement of the starvation and medicine-chest clauses. It was provisions such as these that allowed Big Bear correctly to believe that the treaties were more flexible than Morris would let on and that changes could be made through continued negotiations.

Without doubt, the majority of the NWMP concerns in the period between the signing of the treaties and 1885 were with the Native population. This is especially clear when looking through the *Sessional Papers*, where the annual reports of the police reflect their preoccupation with Native peoples. Immediately after the treaty signing, the police were most concerned with those who had still not signed Treaty 6 and those who had signed reluctantly and perhaps without a sound understanding of how the treaties would be administered. Two such leaders were Big Bear, who did not sign an adhesion to Treaty 6 until 1882, and Beardy, who signed in 1876. The gradual increase of the police numbers from 1876 to 1885, when Fort Battleford became the biggest force in the West, shows the great concern of the Mounties with the Battleford Cree.

According to the official police history, the problem with Chief Beardy was that he claimed to have signed a treaty that gave him better conditions than those who had signed at Carlton or Pitt. Beardy apparently told the police that Morris, by coming to Duck Lake, had given him a better deal. By 1878, Beardy and his band were still demanding more, and Superintendent Walker finally intimidated the band into accepting their supplies under the threat of getting no goods at all. Then, in 1880, Beardy ordered three head of cattle killed for a celebration, which was done against the wishes of the farm instructor. The Mounties arrested the Natives named in the warrant and escorted them to Prince Albert. There was little or no recorded protest from Beardy's band after their men had been sentenced and their leaders imprisoned and humiliated.

The almost constant concern of the police with the Natives of the area can also be seen through their duties in supervising and distributing annuity payments. In some instances, these meetings were an occasion for other Natives to appear and sign adhesions to Treaty 6. It was also a time when those who still refused to sign would appear to ask more questions about the treaties — in a sense, to continue to negotiate. It was this kind of behaviour that has been used as an example of the Treaty Rights movement which was a continuing process in the minds of the Cree who had signed the original treaties. Many Aboriginal leaders did not view the treaty as a once-and-for-all agreement but saw the treaty as the beginning of a process of negotiations that has continued to the present day. According to the police, the treaty payments required strict vigilance and tact in dealing with the large number of Natives in the area. The Mounties were now escorts and pay clerks in addition to their role as keepers of order. Administration of payments and transportation to the sites were very time-consuming processes:

> In the Battleford district, "non-coms" and men were detailed to make payments at Fort Pitt, also on the reserves along Battle River and in the neighbourhood of the lakes to the west and north. The Force also assisted at other payments made on the several reserves in the Eagle Hills south-east of Battleford, and at Cumberland House on the Saskatchewan.[28]

To the NWMP, the spectre of Big Bear always loomed over their efforts to secure a prairie safe for white settlers. Each year his movements were reported to the force until 1882, when he finally signed Treaty 6. The police reports claim that he had at one time threatened to use force to feed his starving followers:

> About 150 of Big Bear's warriors, all armed and mounted, appeared. Messengers accompanied them with summary demands from Big Bear for food — which was flatly refused. They were told that: no assistance of any kind would be given to non-treaty Indians; they need not seek help from the Mounted Police or the Indian Department; any attempt to force the issue would be disastrous to them. ... presently Big Bear and his collection of outlaws drifted away. The last seen of them was a motley group slinking towards the plains on what was said to be a horse stealing expedition.[29]

After Big Bear signed, police efforts were concentrated on getting him to take a reserve in the North Saskatchewan area.

The negative image of Big Bear in the official record was not deserved. In more recent histories written of the Cree, evidence is presented that there was substance to his complaints regarding government policy towards the Treaty 6 Natives. Prior to these studies, the record had been dominated by the image of Big Bear the troublemaker, rather than the diplomat and politician. His agitation for changes to government policy and a more responsive bureaucracy was quite wrongly labelled as "radical" by observers of the day, including the police. In some instances, after admitting the failure of government policy, the police were still able to write, "All [the Cree] were prone to exaggerate their shortcomings despite the fact that in many instances the government had done more for them than the treaty called for. Nevertheless it was self-evident that not enough was being done to meet their needs."[30]

Sadly, it was Big Bear's arrest after the events of 1885 and his subsequent imprisonment that was to end his leadership of the dissenting Plains Cree. It was an arrest and imprisonment that was questionable even by the standards of that time, but it appeared to be the policy of the government to remove the leadership of the Plains Cree, however that might be accomplished.[31]

Even though the police tried to be optimistic about their success in moving Aboriginals onto reserves and making the West a safe place to settle, there was one problem that came up again and again in their reports that could not be ignored. This was the problem of starvation both on and off the reserves. Indeed, as early as 1878 at Battleford, a stockade was erected for fear that starving Natives might attack the fort where supplies were held. This not only led to the increased deployment of troops, but also to the establishment of sub-posts at Duck Lake, Prince Albert and Carlton, all administered from Battleford. In 1881, the Natives were in such a state of destitution that they even brought their horses into police posts to trade for two or three sacks of flour. Warnings by the NWMP to the government took on an urgent tone, especially in the late 1870s. With dissatisfied Natives not yet on reserves, the famine was viewed as a potential tinderbox that threatened the security of both police posts and settlers. Superintendent Walker was in a constant state of alert: "They [the police] knew that hunger-maddened men were dangerous..."[32] The great hunger in the Battleford area was presented ominously by the NWMP:

> During the past year there has been great distress and suffering from hunger among the Indians of this district, owing to the scarcity of game, the buffalo having entirely disappeared from this section.

I have experienced great difficulty with this matter, applications for relief being constantly made to me by starving bands of Indians.

Owing to the scarcity of flour and the uncertainty of the arrival of further supplies, I was able to afford but comparatively small assistance to the many thousands of starving Indians.[33]

Battleford was even assisting beyond its jurisdiction:

I dispatched Inspectors McIlree and Frechette, at different intervals to the camp at the Blackfoot Crossing, with such provisions as I was able to get, to their relief, and to the extent I was able to spare from my limited quantity of stores; at one time I was reduced down to six bags of flour on hand. At this time (June) from 1,200 to 1,500 Indians, Bloods, Piegans and Sarcees, encamped around the Fort, were being fed, and later on as many as 7,000 men, women and children, all in a destitute condition, applied for relief; beef and flour were distributed every other day in small quantities to each family.[34]

And the ominous report from the south:

Not only the Sioux, lately arrived, but the local Crees and Assiniboines suffered from the general threat of famine. In the various camps the rawhide drums could be heard day and night. Ceremony followed ceremony in the pagan belief that the happiness of other days could be thus invoked to return to the children of the Great Spirit. The younger generation continually displayed suppressed desperation, the elders made long speeches telling of days of war and plenty.[35]

To these concerns was added the burden of official visits to the West. The 1881 visit from the Governor General — the Marquis of Lorne — required one-fifth of the strength of the force for escort and surveillance of the local Native population that was perceived as potentially "dangerous." No incidents were reported and the plains tribes fully participated in the events during the visit that took the Governor General throughout the West. At Battleford he attended a grand powwow and inspected the police fort, reportedly "commenting highly" on the condition of the buildings. (On occasion, members of the Anglo-Canadian establishment would participate in Native celebrations, but this was rare and was reserved for "official" ceremonies and functions when it was important to communicate the appearance of harmonious relations to eastern constituents.) The Governor General was then joined by Indian Commissioner Dewdney at Battleford as the entourage proceeded towards Calgary.

The "Indian problem" required increased manpower. From the twelve men and sixteen horses at Battleford in 1876, the force grew dramatically by the spring of 1885. At that time, 200 men of their total force of 557 were stationed in the Battleford Division; 107 horses from a total of 200 were being used there.[36] These numbers are the best indication of the importance of NWMP administration in the Battleford area up to 1885.

It is evident that in this first decade the function of the NWMP force was a military one. Their actions in protecting Aboriginal culture have perhaps been overestimated, as it is evident from recent scholarship that the Mounties were agents of the National Policy and an eastern Canadian image of the West. Whether their legacy of despotism was benevolent is now open to re-examination and closer scrutiny.

The Emergence of Government Aboriginal Policy

As a signatory of the numbered treaties, the government assumed responsibility under its obligation to provide seed and materials for farming the land, but in the early years of 1876-79, this was not enough. There was malnutrition and even starvation on many plains reserves. During this period, the government failed to provide a minimally adequate administrative structure.[37] Often materials and seed stipulated in the contract were not sent. Many problems were also due to a distant government in Ottawa that did not understand the problems and conditions in the West. For example, in 1876 it was still possible for the Minister of the Interior, David Mills, to think that all Natives were on reserves. This frequently led to policy decisions that did not relate to actual problems. However, it may be that the solution to the very difficult problems faced by the Natives was beyond the insights and resources available to that generation.[38] These problems were compounded when those starving tribes who had not initially signed treaties began to turn to the reserves as their hopes for subsistence from game on the plains waned.

Aboriginal policy and the administration put in place to implement it originated in Ottawa. The first policies from the early 1870s were part of a process intended to settle Natives on reserves. The main task of the first two Boards of Commissions was to sign treaties with the Natives, especially in the fertile belt where settlers were expected and encouraged to take up lands according to the National Policy.

By 1876, with the treaty-making completed, changes were made to correspond to the duties that emerged. The Board of Commissions was replaced by a system of Indian superintendents with two or more Indian agents in each superintendency. Under this arrangement, there were four superintendencies for the area east of the Pacific Coast to the Ontario-Manitoba border: the Victoria, Fraser, North-West and Manitoba superintendencies. The arrangement was articulated by David Laird, Mills' predecessor as Minister of the Interior.[39] The agents were first to distribute annuities, then instruct the Natives in farming, and finally advise them in the transition to proposed agricultural life that was to be established on the reserves. It was, to say the least, a vast task for a handful of agents. In the North-West Superintendency alone, there were 17,000 Treaty Natives to administer. The Indian agents had the least amount of time for farm instruction which, ironically, was the task that the Natives required most. Many of the farm instructors hired to assist in developing agriculture proved to be sadly inept. Most had little farm experience and were unsuitable for dealing with a society that was so different from their own. Much tension and misunderstanding resulted from this situation.

This administration proved disastrous. The Natives had been encouraged to settle on reserves, but the agricultural policy the government was proposing was not able to provide them with enough food for subsistence. It forced many Natives who were willing to farm to return to hunting in order to survive — precisely what the government wanted to avoid. Money granted by the treaties proved to be grossly inadequate to purchase enough food to provide basic nutrition. The absence of farm equipment also prevented farming beyond the very primitive level. When provided, equipment usually lacked adequate and proper instruction for its operation. When broken, there was no means for repair and much of the machinery remained virtually useless. The Natives were interested in learning about mechanized farming practices, but complained that little teaching was available. Instead, they actually provided the farm instructors with free manual labour, while the profits did not even go to the workers.

The instructors were also directed by Ottawa to implement a policy of "work for rations" which the Natives resented. They thought the rations were a right, not something to be earned. In Treaty 6, they pointed to the famine clause, as Native culture demanded sharing with those in need and assistance to the sick. While the policy was intended to instill in the Natives the idea that rations could not be handed out, but had to be earned by completing tasks, the Natives found this to be humiliating and menial. They also saw little use in the busy work demanded of them.

With no solution from the starvation on reserves in sight, the government recognized the need to revise its policies. In 1879, it began the Home Farm Plan, which was to provide examples of proper farming practices on model farms. Under the direction of the farm instructor, Natives were expected to work on these farms for nothing and then use the experience gained to manage their own farms. Besides receiving education, the farms were meant to provide them with enough food to stave off starvation and to supply seeds for future crops. The program proved to be a failure as the Natives resented the free labour demanded of them. They wanted wages.

By 1882, Macdonald's government had begun to cut back all government programs, and the Home Farm Plan was one of the first casualties. This attempt at using model farms fizzled dismally. Proper and competent administration was lacking, as were adequate resources. The problems of farming on reserves were a concern to government officials throughout the early 1880s, but the only solution provided was to send more farm instructors and Indian agents. In areas where there were no model farms, little was done to provide instruction in agricultural practices beyond the presence of a farming instructor, if one was available. These were poorly conceived solutions to what were becoming increasingly complex problems that would require more comprehensive remedies to solve. The Natives were beginning to give up on a government that during the treaties seemed so anxious to assist them to adapt to agricultural life on the reserve.[40]

The NWMP as Enforcers of Government Policy

By the mid-1880s, the NWMP were called upon more often to deal with problems arising from decisions made in Ottawa. It was clear that the policy for assisting the Natives to make the transition to an agricultural way of life was not working. This is demonstrated by two incidents involving the NWMP: the Yellow Calf Incident in the Qu'Appelle district and the Craig Incident in the Battleford area. The police who had worked for many years to earn and gain the respect of the Natives were now called upon to deal with eruptions of violence resulting from ineffective government policies. They were becoming enforcers of unpopular legislation in contrast to earlier times when much of their activity, from the Cypress Hills Massacre onward, had been to assist in the protection of the Natives from aggression.

By 1884, the government was still enforcing the policy of "work for rations" among the Aboriginal members of the numbered treaties. The only exceptions made were for the sick or disabled, even though on most reserves there was less and less to work for, and the Natives resented jobs that were merely to give them something to do. They felt humiliated doing work they saw as pointless. Even Indian Commissioner Edgar Dewdney admitted that "the tools and implements provided at the time the treaties were made, go but a small way to keep so many employed."[41] Thus, tension grew on the reserves as food shortages became more acute and agriculture was failing to provide even a subsistence-level supply. The Craig Incident occurred on the Little Pine Reserve ten miles from Battleford in the spring of 1884.

Members of Big Bear's band had still not taken reserves and became the focal point for those who had doubts about signing the treaties. In 1882, these Natives were still looking for buffalo to survive on. In 1883, they had been escorted by the police onto a reserve near Fort Pitt. They stayed the winter but, in the spring, made ready to move to Poundmaker's reserve where the Cree said they had been invited. They did not like working for the instructors:

> On Poundmaker's Reserve were about two hundred and fifty Indians, with a very large proportion of able-bodied men among them, fair workers, but resenting all, even advisory interference, and with an undisguised truculence of manner; showing pretty plainly that it was only the dire pressure of circumstances that had brought them to accept the restraint of Reserve life, and further that they were prepared to resist anything that looked like an encroachment on their free will, either as to what they should do, or how they should do it.[42]

Robert Jefferson, the farm instructor on Poundmaker's reserve, thought the chief was attempting to increase rations and hasten the delivery of farming supplies and agricultural equipment. Poundmaker hoped to "constrain the authorities to make better terms and so to give the Natives a more hopeful outlook on the future."[43] Jefferson, who was usually sympathetic with the Natives, said:

> Had the Indians known the term, they might have called this "patriotism." The Indian Department called it insubordination and contumacy, and all sorts of bad names, for all their policy had been directed to precluding such an event by closing every avenue that might lead towards it.[44]

It was June, and Poundmaker's band had just completed seeding and was making preparations for its Thirst Dance. It was presumably to this that Big Bear had been invited. Thus, there were many Natives in the area who had come to join in this traditional celebration of the Cree, but those who were invited were not welcomed by John Craig, the farm instructor. He gave orders that no more rations would be given out. In response, Poundmaker ordered two weirs to be built across the river so the congregating Cree could be fed with fish. The Cree were almost prepared for the dance, having completed their lodge, when the incident occurred.

Just before the dance was to start, some Cree men went to Craig's store and demanded food for a sick Native child. Since Craig spoke no Cree and the Natives no English, there was confusion. Craig ordered the men out of his store, and, as Jefferson later wrote, "Craig seems to have lost his head, since the controversy ended in his pushing the men out."[45] As he was pushing them out, one of the Natives, Lucky Man, grabbed an axe handle and whacked Craig across the arm with it. Jefferson, who saw Craig shortly after, observed, "Craig's arm was not injured, but his feelings were."[46] Craig was determined to charge the men for the blow he had suffered, but knew that with the large number of Cree gathered in the area, it would be difficult to apprehend Lucky Man at that time. He tried to follow and arrest him, but the chiefs gathered at the dance site to block his way and refused to give the man up.

Craig immediately rode to Battleford and reported the incident to NWMP

Superintendent Crozier. At 9:00 A.M. the next day Crozier, twenty-three men and two farm instructors rode into the midst of the Cree dance. As the participants were painted, it was not possible immediately to identify the perpetrators of the attack on Craig. In the meantime, supplies from Craig's store on Poundmaker's reserve were loaded onto wagons to be taken away to Little Pine Reserve. On numerous occasions, the police talked to the chiefs, demanding they give up the person responsible for striking Craig. Each time, the Cree refused and delayed. Finally, it was agreed that after the dancing was over, the police would be allowed to arrest Lucky Man, but, when the moment arrived, the Cree attempted to hide the sought-after offender with a show of strength. The younger warriors excitedly milled about, threatening the police while Lucky Man wielded a knife, defying arrest. Finally, with great coolness, Crozier walked among the men, then suddenly and boldly made the arrest. The tension that Jefferson witnessed was extreme, but the incident ended there:

> During that half hour, then, any little mishap would have started a row — a gun going off accidentally — a chance encounter — any roughness on the part of the police. Everything was ripe for our extermination; none would have escaped. However, it just was not to be.[47]

This was the end of the Craig Incident. It showed that the NWMP were still respected enough to be allowed to carry out their justice. They had developed a trust and had a reputation of acting fairly, but, in a short period of time, the Natives had reached their breaking point. The NWMP had foreseen the dire situation the Natives were driven to and tried to protest. Agent Rae of Battleford wrote to the commissioner: "If ... the department is bound to stick to these present orders then full preparations should be made to fight them as it will sooner or later come to this if more liberal treatment is not given." Crozier sent an angry letter to Ottawa:

> Considering what is at stake, it is poor, yes, false economy to cut down the expenditure so closely in connection with the feeding of the Indians that it would seem as if there was a wish to see upon how little a man can work and exist. ... My firm conviction is if some such policy as I have outlined is not carried out, then there is only one other and this is to fight them.[48]

The police were merely agents, there to enforce the laws and government Native policy that unfortunately, even as they had observed, were no longer in touch with the circumstances on the reserves. John Tootoosis described how the incident was remembered by the Cree of the area:

> What a bizarre affair it had been! If Craig had sensibly handed over the bit of food in the first place, all those lives would not have been placed in danger. The midnight run with the food supplies, (getting across the creek had been an ordeal) all the shouting and threats on both sides resolved simply by the final donations of rations to the Indians — Jefferson shook his head as he ruefully inspected his own garden. It had been trampled to the ground in all the excitement.
>
> He had just received another one of those orders easier given than obeyed: "You stay with the Indians until they quiet down to show them *we* are not intimidated." Fortunately, Jefferson had replaced the much disliked former farm instructor, was well liked by Poundmaker, was married to his half-sister, and was a diplomatic and tactful man. This made him almost unique among Indian Department employees in the North Saskatchewan.[49]

The incident was a harbinger of what was soon to happen among the Métis. Tootoosis stated that even that could have been averted:

If the government had planned to incite bloodshed it could not have done a better or more efficient job. Prime Minister Macdonald, preoccupied as he was with the affairs of the entire country (he was known as "Old Tomorrow" in the North-West) procrastinated on vital decisions until it was too late to avert disaster. Edgar Dewdney, Lieutenant-Governor as well as Indian Commissioner, seemed either unable to impress Macdonald, with the reality of the danger or he misjudged it himself. His Assistant Commissioner, Hayter Reed's, best known talent was that he could estimate exactly how much an oxen had to be fed to keep it working. He was not an expert in determining how much (or how little) Indians needed to eat in order to survive. The police filled their role as well as possible despite limited manpower and resources, but they were not the policy-makers.[50]

FOUR

The Social and Economic Life of Fort Battleford

The Mounted Police caught the imagination of the public because they were in terms of social class close to the popular image of what an ideal police force should be.

R.C. Macleod

With the waning of the fur trade and disappearance of the buffalo by the 1880s, many of the local economies were in decline. Most people looked favourably (some with heady anticipation) to the arrival of the Canadian railway and hoped to accommodate their enterprises to the National Policy. However, for many, the benefits had been exaggerated; for Native people, inclusion in the national and international economy had not been carefully planned at all.

That there was little concern shown to Native culture is not surprising after examining the ideology that determined the cultural attitudes of the times. The Canadian vision for the West was expressed in its most coherent form in the works of a group of men who gathered somewhat loosely under the umbrella of the "Canada First" movement. Prominent national members of this group included Charles Mair, William Foster, George Denison, Robert Haliburton and Henry Morgan. In western Canada, the group's vision was shared by John Christian Schultz and P.G. Laurie. Although professing to speak for all Canadians, the movement was pro-British and advanced the proposition that Canadians, because of their "Aryan" stock that enabled them to survive in harsh northern climates, were racially superior to other settlers of North America:

> Unlike the United States which had sprung from similar origins, the Canadians were sturdier for their having been nursed on "the icy bosom" of the frozen North. They, the "Northmen of the New World," were destined for greatness, a destiny which would be fully realized one day in a great "rattling war" with the then "weak and effeminate" Americans.[1]

The vision offered by the Canada First movement found sympathy in Ontario, where farmland was becoming scarce. Some promoters, like George Brown of Toronto's *Globe*, saw the possibility of a West dominated by Anglo-Canadians being able to tip the political scales in favour of Ontario. Thus the West would eventually provide the numbers to overwhelm French culture in the nation as a whole. It was clear from those Ontarians who arrived in the North-West after Confederation that the desire to see the English outnumber the French was perhaps as important, though covert, as the desire to own a half-section of farmland. In the case of P.G. Laurie, Battleford's first journalist in 1878, these sentiments were not suppressed, but given crude expression in tracts published in the *Herald*. It was a nationalist sentiment that sounded much like the writing of the Canada Firsters.

Canada First grew out of a cultural imperialism whose supporters were anxious to establish a new economy and legal system for western Canada. The new regime would include Canadian officials and entrepreneurs as well as the North

West Mounted Police who were to enforce its laws. Their vision was seen as having historical affinity with the United Empire Loyalists. The loyalists were firmly Tory in temperament. They had a determined belief in the evolution of a British imperial history, they believed in the importance of the community over the rights of the individual, they were true believers in religion as the mortar of society, they were suspicious of materialism and saw social growth as gradual and organic rather than revolutionary or cataclysmic. The sense of community as an organism would only be tolerated if it were British. This left little room to accommodate societies that existed in the North-West before the arrival of these British institutions and attitudes.[2]

The Toryism manifest in the thoughts and emotions of the Canada Firsters put them, by temperament, at odds with the republican characteristics of American society; so did the Victorian attitudes so willingly accepted in the young nation. Victorian society, embraced especially by Upper Canada, was defined by a loose amalgam of complex and contradictory concepts and beliefs. Far from being prudish, stuffy and hypocritical, the Victorian era was an age of transition in which the privileges that marked the world of the aristocracy were in decline while the commercial power of the bourgeoisie was ascending.[3]

It was an age where the image of pastoral agrarian life clashed with that of the rising modernity symbolized by the city and its mechanized factories. The middle classes flourished with the extraordinary developments in commerce, industry and politics, and writers mirrored these developments with great enthusiasm. It was in microcosm a time of optimism and moral earnestness. It was also an age of anxiety about the waning past and a fast advancing but uncertain future, and a literature that reflected a search for heroes. Progress and a sense of community preservation stood side by side in tension and contradiction. It was an age that was anti-intellectual, dogmatic and rigid.

This melting pot of ideas and feelings constituted the Victorian worldview. It found its way into the West through the Canada Firsters, who combined a particular version of Victorianism with their own brand of racial superiority and nationalism. Their ideas found expression in the North-West through the budding presses, in newspapers like William Coldwell and William Buckingham's *Nor'Wester*[4] and the *Manitoban* of Red River. In Battleford, the ideas of Canada First were disseminated in the first newspaper established west of Winnipeg — P.G. Laurie's *Saskatchewan Herald*. Through the formative years of the Canadian presence, these early newspapers were almost exclusively Conservative in their political leanings.

Laurie shared much with those moving into the area, especially the settlers who were inspired by the spirit of Macdonald's National Policy. He was perhaps Battleford's most significant journalist and had an important impact on the social and cultural thinking of his day. His worldview was one that the North West Mounted Police helped to entrench, both through laws that were established and by cultural activities to be shared by other newly arrived Ontarians. Laurie's vision of the West was promoted and disseminated very incisively in his columns in the *Herald*. His opinions and views were an important indicator of political and social attitudes of the white settlers in the Battleford region and it was primarily these people that the police had come to protect.

Patrick Gammie Laurie was born to the family of an Anglican minister in Pitsligo, Aberdeenshire, Scotland in April 1833. Three years later, after his mother's death, Laurie, along with his father and brother, made their first attempt to sail to Canada. Their ship was swept ashore during a storm and seized by striking dock workers at the port of Greenock. The family chose to remain there until 1842, when a second journey landed them in New York, en route to Toronto. In 1843 young Patrick entered grammar school in Cobourg, Ontario, but stayed only one year. After completing grade 5, he began his apprenticeship as a printer for the *Church*, an Anglican publication. In 1846 the *Church* moved its offices to Toronto and Laurie followed. Over the next ten years he lived in Brantford. Later, in Owen Sound, he worked on Richard Carney's *Advertiser* before returning to Toronto.

In 1855 at the age of 22, he returned to Owen Sound, married Mary Eliza Carney, and purchased the *Owen Sound Times*. He sold it in 1859 when John Christian Schultz persuaded him to establish a newspaper in the Red River area. Laurie only made it to Windsor before the news reached him that the *Nor'Wester* had already been established at Red River by Buckingham and Coldwell. For the next two years he commuted between Windsor and Detroit, working in both cities as a printer. In 1861 he bought the *Essex Record*, which he published until 1869.

In September of that year he arrived in Red River and began working for the *Nor'Wester*, but he was expelled from the settlement in December for refusing to print a proclamation for the Provisional Government. He returned to the East, only to journey back to Red River with his son William in September 1870. For the next eight years he worked in various capacities on a number of newspapers, including the *Manitoba Newsletter, Manitoba Liberal, Manitoban, Standard* and *Manitoba Free Press*.

On 11 August 1878 Laurie, then 45 years of age, moved to Battleford to establish the *Saskatchewan Herald*, the first newspaper in the North-West Territories. He made the 650-mile journey from Winnipeg in two months, walking beside an ox cart which carried his printing press. Two weeks after his arrival at the new territorial capital, Laurie published the first issue of the *Herald* and optimistically announced: "Today we present to the public of the Dominion the first number of the *Saskatchewan Herald* — the pioneer press of the Great North-West — the light that is destined to dispel the gloom that has long enveloped the Great Lone Land."[5]

Laurie had come to the North-West motivated by a missionary zeal to see a strong and independent society established north of the 49th parallel. But he was also an imperialist who saw Canada needing the guidance of the Mother Country. What Laurie most desired was to see the West as an extension of British Ontario. He hoped to control the make-up of society either through encouraging British and Anglo-Ontarian immigration or through assimilation.

Laurie's editorial policy, as outlined in the prospectus of the *Essex Record*, reflected the Victorian themes common to the time. In the conflict between the individual and the collectivist forces, Victorians preached that progress could be inspired only through the community, yet with leadership from the upper classes: "Reflecting their traditionalist orientation, they assumed a community was always endangered by the uncontrollable behaviour of individuals — especially those who constituted its lower classes."[6] Discovery, civilization and progress along with Christian morality provided the formula for a united and prosperous nation:

But while the publisher thus avows himself solicitous of attracting and arresting the favour and substantial patronage of a large public, he declines to use the same by putting forward a formal and pretentious catalogue of political theories, professions and pledges, by which he shall be henceforth circumscribed and governed. He says in a word, he hates all kinds of platforms, because both common sense and experience reject them as foolish and inappropriate, since they must necessarily eventuate in embarrassing and confusing their authors, and all others who adopt them. In a new country as this is, and in these days, when throughout the whole range of both physical and political sciences; such rapid and gigantic progress is taking place, and such new and unexpected developments are daily made, platform and systematic pledges are monstrous shams, or sheer impertinences...[7]

This common-sense view of politics had little patience with intellectual debate. The basis for the beliefs of conservatives like Laurie lay in the slogans of peace, order and good government, which to them were the most important of British traditions. The choice was either republicanism or monarchy, and Laurie clearly chose the latter:

He [Laurie writing in the third person] therefore, begs to give assurance that the *Essex Record* will, under no possible contingencies, "look to Washington" either for physical aid to remodel our political institutions, or the Halls of Congress for patterns to guide our own legislature. Whoever may hold the reins of government and whatever may be our temporary dilemmas, this journal will be conducted uniformly and persistently on true conservative and purely logical principles.[8]

Laurie believed in the great potential of Canada and pledged "to make the *Essex Record* all that a good country paper should be." With regard to general politics, there would be no recognition of a dividing line between what was called Upper and Lower Canada. It would "give sure and ready and zealous support to every act of the legislature, having for its object the greater prosperity and welfare of the united provinces..."[9]

Not only was Laurie an imperialist and ardent Canadian nationalist, he was also a vehement defender of western interests. It was not the environment, but ties with the Mother Country and the East that would mould the character of western Canada. Laurie continually attacked eastern newspapers for failing to understand the plight of those in the West and criticized their sensationalized reports depicting the prairies as a "Wild West" infested with uncontrollable "savages." This ignorance of public figures needed to be exposed, and eastern officials had to be made more aware of how important the West was to the whole county. In 1883 Laurie wrote:

It is time for the people of the East and especially those who occupy the position of legislators to recognize the fact that the prairies form an integral and most important part of the Dominion, that they no longer consist of an uninhabited tract of country lying somewhere beyond the great lakes, but having a population greater than some of the provinces, and in point of intelligence and enterprise equal to any.[10]

It was one of the avowed purposes of the *Herald* to dispel myths about the West. Laurie worked diligently to attack false reports by publishing lengthy articles on climate, soils, and the possibilities of mining and agriculture. He reported at length on the Peace River country and on scientific explorations such as those of John Macoun. Extensive coverage was also given to politics. The paper printed the complete text of debates from the House of Commons on matters relating to the West and the more important speeches of the Governor General. Extended reports also heralded the visits of dignitaries such as the Marquis of Lorne and various cabinet ministers.

For local consumption, the *Herald* included a section on local news, informing readers of comings and goings of members of the community, but, unlike other regional papers, this item was given front-page priority. Similarly featured was detailed coverage of the North West Mounted Police, as Laurie remained an unflagging supporter of the Mounties, trying to deflect criticism whenever possible. Frequently, "Victorian" stories appeared with their moralistic themes of muscular Christianity, self-help, self-education and self-denial.

Reports from Europe were provided when the mail allowed. Articles from eastern and European newspapers were reproduced, often in their entirety. He gave special coverage to events of significance to the empire such as the Fashoda Crisis, the Boxer Rebellion and the Boer War. Laurie's broader focus and imperial ideals prevented the *Herald* from becoming merely a local, parochial newspaper. He advocated support of the Conservative Party as the only reasonable choice open to Westerners. In 1887 he wrote: "we assume the favoured candidates will be of Conservative leanings. It was under Conservative rule that the country emerged from a state of painful solitude and barren unproductiveness."[11] The West could not be allowed to evolve without guidance; it would need responsible critics to direct its progress within a national and imperial framework. Laurie did little to speak for the majority of his community at the time — the Cree and Métis residents — but represented instead a smaller number of Anglo-Canadian "settlers" in the town that was protected by police. The West was an integral part of Canada and as the East provided the necessary British influence, the West provided a natural outlet for settlers from crowded areas of Ontario.[12]

Laurie's quest for social status arose out of his Anglican worldview rather than a desire for excessive wealth. He saw a strict but natural social structure in which the most civilized persons occupied the upper classes. Ironically but not necessarily inconsistently, Laurie lived in a rather humble house in Battleford without enough money to afford outside help, but he looked upon many in his community as "lower class" and considered the Natives as "lesser breeds." He saw himself as part of the governing elite.

Oddly, Laurie stayed in Battleford even after the transcontinental railroad was rerouted through the south in 1881 and the territorial capital was moved from Battleford to Regina in 1883. He remained convinced of the possibilities of the West and his optimism was further reflected in the *Herald*'s motto, "Progress":

> The word selected as our motto indicates most expressively the course laid down for the *Herald*. It will seek to promote the prosperity and further the march of progress of the whole North-West, by advocating all measures having this for its object, and by making known the vast resources now only waiting development and in keeping with the onward movement, the *Herald* will always be found in front.[13]

In Laurie's eyes, the police were the ideal enforcement mechanism for the North-West as well as representing the cultural institutions that Anglo-Ontarians hoped to establish on the prairies. The question of why the members of the eastern *petite bourgeoisie* found positions of influence in the West and why they so strongly supported the culture the Mounties were helping to establish has been discussed. Although organized hierarchically to reflect the class nature of their society, the NWMP were not from a broad spectrum of society. The members of the force, even those occupying the position of constable, were primarily from the upper and middle classes of Canadian society in the East. Careers and income considerations had been sacrificed for the status attached to being a member of the force. Many had left professional jobs to join the police and even though the members of the officer corps were not exclusively British: "[f]ew police officers would have been offended at being mistaken for a member of the English gentry."[14]

They arrived with a confidence common to those with a sense of election and imposed their sense of order when they arrived. The police literally walled themselves in and made themselves comfortable within their stockaded forts and kept out and away from the often-disturbing life outside the walls that surrounded them. Consistent with the Wacousta Syndrome and garrison mentality, they "did not celebrate the conditions of frontier life but spent most of their time trying to ensure that they disappeared as soon as possible."[15] They were able to do this through the material culture they carried with them and by social practices, such as retaining servants or "batmen" for officers and viewing criminal acts as "lower-class phenomena." These were dealt with by those higher up in the hierarchy who were "social superiors," able to exercise that moral discretion accessible only to those familiar with an upper station in society:

> They saw the Canadian West as having a definite upper class. This élite was most readily identifiable in the larger urban centres where such institutions as gentlemen's clubs existed to give concrete expression to ideas about social leadership.[16]

In microcosm, the police represented the values of middle-class Victorian Canada. Though carrying, protecting and disseminating middle-class values of property and material security on the exterior, many still looked with nostalgia to the age of aristocratic privilege. Identification with the style of the upper classes was still treasured through leisure activities the police enjoyed, both through their physical culture and in artistic expressions and entertainments. Yet most felt there was an inevitability to the ascendancy of the middle-class culture that the police so proudly represented and that Laurie promoted to the Anglo-Canadian elite of western Canadian society who read his paper. Confident promotion of middle-class Victorian culture resulted in the disregard of the Métis and Native cultures in the North-West. If the police seem benign, it is because overall their actions appear to have been those of "benevolent despots." The police sanctioned social behaviour through the culture they disseminated at their forts, virtually ignoring those already established forms of social control that had been developed by the Natives. Local culture was ignored. An exclusive social atmosphere was created at Battleford. It was a social life limited to those who shared their culture and worldview and one that excluded the larger community that had been present on the plains for thousands of years before the police arrived. The Mounties were in the West to assure that a new cultural template of social behaviour would replace the one they found.

North West Mounted Police band at Battleford, preparing to meet the refugees from Fort Pitt and parade them in, 1885 (Glenbow Archives, NWR 1.2-7).

Six-man band, 1900s (photo by C. West, Fort Battleford NHP Library).

North West Mounted Police gymnastic club, 1904. Left to right: Front row: Gavin Smith (from town), Charles Light, Ernest Letour, Ian Macdonnell, Sp. Const. Bill Williams; Middle row: Const. Darby Walker, Const. Thomas Dann, A.C. Macdonnell, Horace Rodgers (from town), George Meekings; Back row: Sgt. Major Arthur V. Richardson, Bob Colter (from town), Const. Shea, S./Sgt. W.C. Jackson, Const. Bob Hancock, Const. Archer, Sgt. A.H. Nicholson, piper (Glenbow Archives, NA-1034-4).

Cricket team, Battleford, winners over Winnipeg West End team, September 1892. Left to right: Front row: W. Gooch, W.A. Duffis, J.W. Cullin; Middle row: F. Nichols, J.B. Asby, A.C. Macdonnell (captain); Back row: H. Gregory, F.R. Godwin, S.C. Carter, R. Stevenson, J.F.D. Parken (photo by Steele and Wing, Winnipeg, National Archives of Canada, NA-299-13).

Interior of mess hall, 1900s (Fort Battleford NHP Library).

Interior of concert hall, 1910-20 (Fort Battleford NHP Library).

Interior of concert hall, 1897 (photo by P.G. Laurie, Fort Battleford NHP Library).

Interior of the concert hall where court was held, Judge Richardson is presiding. The North West Mounted Police had powers that allowed them not only to make arrests but also to serve as magistrates. Note the stove pipe. These buildings were heated by wrought iron stoves.

"Customers at Smart's Store, Battleford, August 30, 1891," by Sydney Hall, engraved by Edward Whymper (Glenbow Archives, NA-843-39). *Reserve residents were significant customers for Battleford merchants, especially following treaty payments.*

A Cree family and travois ready for a journey, ca. 1880s (Glenbow Archives, NA-4475-1).

Kahneepataytayo, Big Bear's head dancer (Saskatchewan Archives Board S-B387).

"Chief Beardy, who participated in the Duck Lake fight [sic], and afterwards surrendered to General Middleton," 1885 (Glenbow Archives, NA-1032-5).

Beardy (or "little moustache") was chief of the Willow band of the Plains Cree. Beardy refused to meet with Treaty Commissioner Alexander Morris because Morris would not respect the vision Beardy had of where the meeting was to take place. Beardy also expressed dissatisfaction with terms of the treaty. Like Big Bear and Treaty 7 chiefs, he demanded protection of the buffalo and management of the remaining herds. Beardy also protested when the assistance promised for agriculture was not forthcoming. Beardy remained neutral during the 1885 Resistance but in spite of this, treaty payments were suspended to his band after the fighting.

WANDERING SPIRIT.

Wandering Spirit (Saskatchewan Archives Board S-B6024).
Wandering Spirit was the war chief of a group of the Plains Cree in Big Bear's band. In one battle against the Blackfoot, Wandering Spirit was reputed to have killed thirteen warriors, more than any other of his fellow Cree. Wandering Spirit was one of the Cree who most resented the "work for rations" policy so rigidly enforced by the local Indian Agent, Thomas Quinn. At Frog Lake on 2 April, Wandering Spirit shot Quinn when Quinn refused his request for rations. He was a prominent leader during the remainder of the fighting. He was hanged at Fort Battleford softly chanting a love song to his wife.

Almighty Voice, Cree Indian, Duck Lake area, ca. 1892-94 (Glenbow Archives, NA-2310-1).
Almighty Voice was part Saulteaux and part Cree and a member of the Willow Cree of One Arrow's band. He was known as a superb runner and hunter. He resented the pass system and generally the restrictions of reserve life. In 1895 he was imprisoned for allegedly killing a government steer but escaped the same night. When threatened with arrest, Almighty Voice warned the police that he would shoot and he did, killing a Mountie. Three others were killed before Almighty Voice was bombarded by the NWMP in May of 1897. This incident marked the worsening relations between the NWMP and First Nations people.

"Old Mosquito, Chief of the Stonies. Sketches from life on the reserve," by William R. Rutherford, 30 May 1885 (Glenbow Archives, P-1390-49).
A number of Assiniboine or Stoney bands have reserves in the Battleford area, including the followers of Mosquito.

"The North-West Rebellion. A Cree Indian Thirst Dance," by William R. Rutherford, 22 July 1885 (Glenbow Archives, P-1390-9).
The Sun Dance held in the summer of 1885 was in defiance of the local authorities. The Cree bands continued to practice their traditional ceremonies in spite of the ban against these dances.

Indian Sun Dance near Battleford, June 1895 (National Archives of Canada, PA-28833).

Cree and government employees at Sweetgrass Indian Agency, Saskatchewan, ca. 1880s, photo by D. Cadzow (Glenbow Archives, NA-1223-4). The failure of the agricultural programs promised by the government was the cause of great discontent in the decade after Treaty 6 was signed. The problems with government programs included inadequately funded programs, failure to supply proper equipment, incompetent farm instructors, and harsh enforcement of "work for rations" policies and the pass system. Initial success of farming on some reserves was blunted by restrictions that did not allow the Cree to sell their own produce without permission of the Indian Agent. Frustrated Cree gave up and leased their land instead.

Cree Indians at Battleford, ca. 1896. Left: Calf Child; Right: Fine Day, photo by Mrs. G. Moodie (Glenbow Archives, NA-2306-6).

Fine Day was a warrior with Poundmaker's band when they were attacked by Colonel Otter. He was one of the main informants to David Mandelbaum, the anthropologist who compiled the major study entitled The Plains Cree. *Fine Day was interviewed by Mandelbaum just before his death in 1934, at which time he was over 80. Fine Day was a military leader of his tribe as well as a skilled hunter and trapper.*

Harry Nash and Thunderchild, Battleford, 1890, photo by D. Cadzow (Fort Battleford NHP Library).
As a young man Thunderchild was one of the followers of Big Bear who resisted signing Treaty 6 in 1876. Many of his fellow chiefs had signed initially but Thunderchild preferred to follow a more independant life on the plains until 1879. His band followed the buffalo into Montana but the diminishing herds led to starvation among his people. Thunderchild eventually chose a reserve for his people in the Battleford area. Thunderchild was an important source of Cree stories that were eventually published by Edward Ahenakew in Voices of the Plains Cree. *Much of the Thunderchild Reserve was lost in a fraudulent land surrender in the early twentieth century.*

Sweetgrass, or Abraham Wikaskokiseyin, head chief of the Cree, 1877 (Glenbow Archives, NA-47-26).
Sweetgrass was an important Cree chief present at the signing of Treaty 6. Sweetgrass had a large following up to the signing of the treaty but numbers were reduced following his death. Sweetgrass died shortly after signing the treaty and this was said to have been a bad omen. The leadership of the band eventually passed on to his son, the younger Sweetgrass.

Social Life at the Mounties' Barracks

Battleford's *Saskatchewan Herald* is a valuable documentary record of the social and cultural life of the mounted police. Laurie regularly covered and promoted the events and celebrations of the force, both for the police and the local white community. The very significance of the police as agents of culture and of the worldview advocated by "Canada First" is evident in the location of social events, which usually took place on police or government property. Their buildings were elaborate for the time and it was thought to be prestigious to attend an event hosted on police grounds. Usually the site of the events was a local barracks building, but after 1885 it was in the concert hall where the police staged a variety of activities, including dances, concerts and plays. The occasions celebrated were generally similar to the social life of Victorian Canada and served to disseminate this culture to the West. Rarely, if ever, were Native people present or invited. The events were primarily to be enjoyed by the townspeople and the police. These occasions were often grand and elaborate in contrast to the daily conditions that faced the police on what they saw as a desolate prairie frontier.

Concerts performed at the barracks were the most common and frequent forms of entertainment for the local white community. Usually the police played and orchestrated the music. As early as December 1878, a musical band had assembled:

> A minstrel troupe has been organized by the boys in the barracks. It is their intention to give several entertainments during the winter months, the first of which will come off Christmas Eve. As this will be the first performance of its kind given in this remote region, those who are getting it up should be greeted with a bumper house. Programs will be out in a few days.[17]

The concerts' content reflected the ethnicity of British culture and many of the humorous performances had racial overtones, often at the expense of black people. The very first performance of the police band was held in the council hall chambers of Government House with the Lieutenant Governor presiding. "The stage was neatly fitted up across one end of the room, and was tastefully decorated with flags."[18] According to coverage in the *Herald*, the band entertained with enthusiasm:

> The evening performance commenced with an opening chorus, "Stop dat knocking," which was well rendered, the voices of the performers harmonizing well. Warden's sentimental song, "Poor Old Slave," was well received, and Robert Wylie's comic song, "Green Corn" brought down the house. Those were followed by O'Neil, who sang, "So Early in the Morning." At the conclusion of Whitehouse's song, "Nigger on the Fence," the applause was deafening, and the first part of the program was brought to a close with the grand finale, "The Railroad," the locomotive whistle being supplied by Warden.[19]

Many of the events tended to be in the nature of variety shows, which usually included songs, humour, solo instrumental performances, and on occasion a patriotic speech or lecture. A typical evening would be similar to the one of 31 January 1881[20]:

First Part	
Overture	Orchestra
Opening Chorus	Company
Nigger on the Fence	R. Wyld
Old Cabin Home	J. Clisby
Old Black Joe	F.A. Smart
Foo-de-ad-de-doo-da-day	W. Parker
Poor Old Slave	S. Warden
A Little More Cider	W. Moulton
Do They Think of Me at Home?	J.H. Prize
Tapioca	R. Wyld
Why Didn't You Say So Before?	R.C. Macdonald
Pompey Show	W. Parker
Grand Finale — Off to Georgia	Company

Second Part	
Cornet Solo	P. Burke
Songs	Clisby, Smart, Parker, Warden
Address — Our Future	Professor Wyld
Guitar Solo	R.G. Macdonald
Song and Dance in Character	P. Burlee

The orchestra was central to these evenings and consisted of violin, piccolo, banjo, cornet, horn, piano and guitar. In 1883, a brass band had been organized and instruments were ordered. The change was welcomed as the New Year was ushered in with a new musical sound. By March 1884, the band had had enough time to practice. It performed in a crowded hall, and received a spirited review:

> One of the most enjoyable entertainments offered to the public was the concert and variety show given on the 25th... The hall was crowded to excess, there not being even standing room left. The programme was a long and varied one, and was carried out in a masterly manner, every piece being thoroughly well rendered, and many of them loudly encored. The local hits of Bones and Tambo were numerous and pungent and brought down the house every time. The band played several selections during the evening and showed remarkably good progress for the short time they had been practicing together, reflecting also the highest credit on Sgt. Bagley, their instructor... When the concert was over, the hall was cleared and dancing became the order of the night, and was kept up in a most enjoyable manner for some hours, the band furnishing much of the music.[21]

The music produced by the NWMP was an enjoyable form of cultural expression particularly appreciated by the white community, as it helped to reinforce their identity on the frontier. Certainly the police did their best to make their performances accessible; for the townspeople there was weekly exposure to their music if they could make the trip to the police fort. "The band practices twice a day, and gives an open air concert on the parade ground every Wednesday and Friday afternoon. It has made excellent progress since its organization and reflects much credit on its instructors, Corporals Bagley and Burke."[22] The band also performed for special benefits and in 1886 gave concerts in aid of those who died during the fighting in the spring of 1885:

The minstrel show and entertainment given on Friday evening by the Battleford Boys in aid of the memorial to those who lost their lives in the defense of Battleford, was without doubt the most successful affair of the kind ever held in this town. The acoustic properties of the hall and the seating arrangements were greatly improved, and the only thing left to be desired was more seats as a very large portion of the audience was compelled to stand. The songs were for the most part well rendered and the local hits numerous and fresh, the allusions to the "gophers" and the settlement of the claims especially bringing down the house.[23]

Later that year a benefit was also held to raise money for the building fund of St. George's Church.[24]

The "minstrel shows" of the Mounties served an important social function of establishing and categorizing "us" and "them." It would have taken little imagination for the white townspeople attending these entertainments to substitute Aboriginal or Métis for the blacks that they were ridiculing and marginalizing in their performances. The significance of blacks, or "coloured" people such as East Indians, would not have been lost on Victorian minds that had been inscribed with racist culture required for "othering" and marginalizing the many indigenous peoples while expanding the boundaries of the British Empire.

By the 1890s the nature of the entertainment had changed somewhat with new equipment and changes in the content and quality, if not the kind of cultural expression. The general tone of the musical discourse became more sophisticated, with less humour or "vaudeville," and more technically polished and serious musical performances and improved settings.[25]

One of the last reported concerts was a "smoking concert" given in 1911. The force's entertainment had evolved to reflect a more sober, serious content:

The officers and men at "C" division entertained the young men of town to a smoking concert on the evening of Coronation Day. Patriotic groups and times were the order of the evening in honor of the King and Queen and especially the one song which Mr. H.C. Adams rendered did the company cheer lustily at the mention of the king.[26]

Other popular social events were the dances, or "balls" as they were also called. They were hosted by the police and covered with flair and enthusiasm by the *Herald*. It seems these dances primarily brought out the local white community, who appeared to enjoy them thoroughly. The first reported ball was held in 1879:

It was well attended, the music excellent, and dancing was kept up with much vigor until the "wee sma' hours ayont the twal." A well got up supper was provided, and everything passed off pleasantly and well, the whole affair giving the utmost satisfaction to all present.[27]

Much effort was expended by the police and local citizens to make the dances enjoyable:

Among other "decorations" were specimens of the taxidermist's skills, from the gaunt and hungry wolf to the most graceful and gorgeously feathered denizens of the bush and brake. A pleasing effect was produced by a number of stately birds perched on the bough of evergreens with which the walls were covered. Opposite the main entrance was a crown supported by the legend "N.W.M.P." At midnight, just as the old year was passing away to the mournful strain of "Auld

Lang Syne" those well-known letters faded away and "1880" burst upon the view of the spectators. The supper table was supplied with "all the delicacies of the season" in the greatest profusion, and reflected much credit upon those who had management of it.[28]

The dances were invariably reported as huge successes and Laurie often added a touch of humour to his description and reporting of these events: "Our fashion reporter hasn't been around since the ball, so we have to go to press without a description of the toilets of the ladies; but as far as our own judgement goes they were seasonable and quite correct."[29] At some of the more grand balls up to two hundred people — that is, policemen and white settlers — attended, a testament to the popularity and degree of participation of the fledgling settler communities in such events as well as to their cohesiveness. After 1885, the police were able to display with pride trophies and mementos attesting to their role and participation in the events:

> The rooms were tastefully festooned with evergreen and bunting, while the walls were articulately ornamented with decorations made of flags, carbines, swords, revolvers and other military paraphernalia. Upon either side of the room was a shield bearing respectively the words "Battleford Rifles" and "Home Guards" while facing the entrance was a pair of clasped hands ... one wearing the sleeve of the policeman's tunic, while the other was an arm of a civilian.[30]

The glories of the empire were celebrated alongside the battles of the North-West campaign, both being exploited yearly with sentimentalized patriotism:

> The ball room was decorated with evergreens, pictures, mottoes expressing in words the welcome which beamed from the faces of the generous hosts, others showing that the memory of old friends and comrades has not dimmed with the lapse of time, and strange devices worked in weapons of almost every kind known in warfare. Flanking the bandstand were the two 7-pounder field pieces, now historic by their connection with Cut Knife Hill. The ball was brilliantly lighted and the glitter of light from the arms around the room served as a foil to the somewhat sombre background. Loyalty to the Queen and the profession of the force found vent in a magnificent picture of Her Majesty and copies of the well known military pictures "The Roll Call," "The Thin Red Line," "Scotland Forever," and "Balaclava."[31]

Not unlike the police balls and dances, the celebration of special occasions revealed the ideals and aspirations of Victorian and Christian society established at Battleford. For example, the birthdays of royalty were regularly celebrated:

> The Queen's Birthday passed off very quickly at this place. The Mounted Police fired a "feu de joie" at noon. In the afternoon, a picnic was given by the Rev. Thos Clarke to the children of the day school, at which there was good attendance. Singing and games were indulged in, a number of prizes being distributed among the youthful athletes.[32]

Weddings also provided the opportunity to affirm formal ceremonies that sanctioned certain social behaviour. Some of these occasions were also celebrated on police property. Once in a while religious ceremonies were held at the barracks. In 1883 a travelling preacher stopped at the fort and was provided with an audience:

> on Friday evening nearly all the men of the troop attended a short service, after which Canon Cooper delivered a short address on the points of similarity between good soldiers and good Christians.[33]

There was of course a great need for the Anglo-Canadians to celebrate their culture in an environment in which they felt alien. Their garrison mentality forced them together to commemorate their past and their hopes for the future. The annual dinner with the Mounties had become an institution greatly anticipated in the midst of long, cold winter nights. These sentiments were perhaps most eloquently expressed by Laurie after a New Year's Eve celebration in 1897:

> We, here, live on the verge of civilization, and our pleasures are few. The daily round is unvarying, not to say monotonous. So is the weekly round, and the monthly, and every break in the routine of existence in this circling round of sameness has a value unknown to those who live within reach of the varied distractions of more thickly peopled centres. We appreciate the brightness of a comet in proportion to the darkness of night, and our nights are Cimmerian. Displays of a more or less meteoric character are not unknown to us but comets are scarce, and when we are favoured with the sight of one we are apt to magnify the length of its tail.[34]

Beyond the ceremonial and social celebrations, the local white community could attend dramatic presentations staged by the NWMP and their fellow townspeople. Frequently the forum for these dramas was the concert hall that had been built with the necessary facilities. These performances were not part of the very early cultural life of the fort but began in the mid-1880s. The first performance of the NWMP Dramatic Association was reported on 15 February 1886:

> Owing doubtless to the attractive program promised, as much as to the fine evening, a large and appreciative audience was gathered together... The only fault we can find with Friday evening's entertainment is that there was so little to blame. There was none of those unfortunate stage "waits" which try the endurance of the audience and help to make the play fall flat and pointless. The programme consisted of a short comedy entitled "Chizelling" followed by a few songs, and recitations in character, and closing with a laughable Irish farce, in which Sergt. Major Lake, as Paddy Miles, put the "come thru" upon all the native wit at his command.[35]

Some performances were in the Mennipean tradition of theatre that emphasized the activities of royalty. Other plays that reflected the popular culture of the day were the comedy "Caste," "The Pied Piper of Hamelin," "The Irish Tutor" and "The Area Belle."

The sporting activities of the police at Battleford provide evidence of the kind of culture carried by the force onto the frontier. They introduced their own form of athletic competition into prairie society. The sports reinforced the need for the cult of "manliness," for accepting winners and losers as well as showing "good sportsmanship" before and after a contest. Sports helped serve as a mechanism to socialize citizens to their gender roles and to the ethics of daily life. It institutionalized and sanctioned leisure activities of those who held power and had occasion to organize and participate in these events.

What is clearly evident is that sporting events were very popular in the Battleford area and were held often. They were also given regular and extended coverage in the local paper. Needless to say, they were almost exclusively limited to the domain of the male townspeople and members of the NWMP. This was an opportunity for the Mounties to exhibit their manliness, reinforcing their military purpose. This message was implicit through a show of physical prowess inherent in the sporting competitions. The sporting activities that most reflected the competitive nature of Anglo-Canadian society were games such as cricket, soccer, baseball, hockey, rugby, broomball and curling. These team competitions were usually held between one side made up of policemen and another side made up of men from the town. They were most popular with the local white spectators and were the subject of long commentaries by Laurie. The police invariably showed superior strength and skill, thus proving their superiority in other events involving physical competition. Cricket usually received the most detailed coverage. The police victories were sometimes intimidating, as reported in an early cricket match:

> The townsmen proved themselves but indifferent hands at wielding the willow, the police winning easily by the score below. A return match was arranged for the 28th, and although the police had everything in readiness the townsmen failed to put in an appearance, a number of their players having gone out of town.[36]

There were also sports that featured individuals in competition with each other: track and field, horse racing and sharpshooting. Shooting competitions with pistols and rifles were very popular and winners in each category were usually prominently listed. Again, this exposure gave the police an opportunity to remind the local society of their competence in using firearms.

The Economy

The NWMP contributed substantially to the local economy of the Battleford area. Not only did the police purchase many of their supplies through local merchants, but the individual men also spent a considerable portion of their wages in local shops. Overall the arrival of the police was a welcome event for the fledging economy of the growing administrative and agricultural settlement. The local and regional economies of the Métis and Indians lacked vitality during these transition years as the fur-trade economy of the prairies declined. The barter and market economy of the plains Natives also suffered as their resource base, the buffalo, was depleted by American hide hunters by the end of the 1870s. Most goods were supplied either by the American companies of I.G. Baker and T.C. Powers, or the Canadian Hudson's Bay Company, while local merchants and farmers profited through the supply of fuel and fodder to the NWMP. The economy was not unlike that of an underdeveloped colony where manufactured goods and finished products were supplied by merchants in the larger metropolitan centres, and the locals produced the primary resource products.

The local people were able to sell significant amounts of livestock, wood and hay to the police through the tendering process. Amounts spent by the force grew significantly from approximately $200,000 in 1873-74 to $600,000 in 1884-85. Between 1873-85, roughly 30 percent of the NWMP budget went towards pay, 20 percent for food and clothing, 10 percent on fuel and shelter, 20 percent on horses and forage, and the remaining 10 percent was spent on a number of miscellaneous goods.[37] The majority of these contracts were won by the local townspeople, though sometimes with conflict. These tenders were regularly advertised in the *Saskatchewan Herald*. Some were specific one-time projects, as evident in a report of 1880: "The Finlayson brothers have obtained the contract for cutting posts for the stockade around the barracks. They expect to get the required number off the island in the Saskatchewan River opposite the barracks."[38]

There was, however, discontent noted over the number of contracts awarded to eastern and American merchants. Laurie exercised considerable pressure to help keep NWMP expenditures in the local community. Laurie levelled criticism at a tendering procedure that favoured eastern contractors. Western bidders, he argued, could be in a position to supply cattle, provisions and freighting if they had more notice of the contracts. Laurie defended western interests by saying that not only could the government save money by relying on contractors out West already, but that the supplies could be distributed to several posts, adding to the convenience of having local suppliers.[39]

The tenders that were advertised were usually for both the NWMP and the Indian Department, but there were problems over the ads. Ads appeared widely in eastern newspapers. For example, in 1880, they appeared in fifty or sixty papers at a cost of $2,000. The widespread advertising was said to be worthwhile since the competition resulted in savings on certain items. Western interests complained about a system that advertised everywhere but the place the supplies were needed, while local interests were simply not benefiting from the advertising system. The local contractors argued that "Oats, flour, hay and beef could all be supplied cheaper than they are now if the producers had a chance to bid for themselves, and direct encouragement would then be given to the settlers."[40] The contractors complained not only that they had no notice of the tenders, but that even if they had heard they would not have been able to submit their bids on time. The goods that were supplied locally tended to be hay, flour, beef, oats, potatoes, lime, straw, cordwood (dry and green), local charcoal and even local bricks, as indicated in 1883: "The manufacture of bricks on a large scale is to begin here next season, a powerful machine having been sent for by R.C. Macdonald."[41] The prices for these goods were frequently reported to show the advantage of purchasing local and regional goods. "Contracts have been made for the delivery here of good Prince Albert flour at $7.50 a sack. Winnipeg flour of the same brand is held at $10.00 to $12.50 a sack."[42] An indication of the kinds of prices at which local goods were sold to the police appeared in a report in 1883:

> The contract for mounted police supplies for this post for the year beginning July 1st, have been awarded as follows: Hay, Mr. Prince, $10.00 a ton; oats, Macfarlane Brothers, 90 cents a bushel; potatoes, the same, 57 cents a bushel; beef, Wyld & Bourke, 17 cents a pound; cordwood, Jos. Ducharme, $3.50 at 100 lbs. Beef and wood are higher, but all other articles are lower than in former years. No bids were made for the coal required.[43]

The majority of police business went to local white merchants, though on occasion contracts were awarded to local Native bands, usually for firewood and sometimes logs. For example, in the year of the uprising, it was reported: "The police contract for cutting and delivering green wood has been awarded to the Stony Indians at $3.25 a cord."[44] In some instances, it appeared that the contracts awarded to the local Natives were worth less than the local whites received:

> The contract for the extra two hundred tons of hay required for the mounted police here has been awarded as follows: Ronald Macdonald, one hundred tons at $25.00; Otton and Gospill, forty tons at $25.00; H. Hapur, twenty tons at $20.00; and the Stony Indians forty tons at $17.50. Offers were made for seventy tons more than were required.[45]

On other occasions, there were complaints from white businessmen that the Natives were bidding too low. One report complained that rumours in the street indicated that bids from Natives would be so low that there was no room for any profit for goods such as oats, wood and potatoes.[46]

In some instances, irregularities were reported in the awarding of contracts with veiled suggestions of favouritism and political patronage. Summarizing the complaints, Laurie wrote:

> Such are briefly the principal features in the several contracts awarded by the Commissioner. The exigencies of the public service have been disregarded and bona fide tenderers have been humbugged. In one case money was advanced to keep a favoured contractor going, while in the other the money earned is kept back for months and no explanation given.[47]

Aboriginal Women and the NWMP

The Anglo-Canadian vision of the culture and society it was thought ought to be established in the Battleford area and the whole North-West was narrow indeed. The vision as it was articulated by leaders such as P.G. Laurie paid little heed to the culture and society of those who had been there for hundreds of years before them. Overtly, through the enforcement of its laws, and covertly, through "entertainments" such as the minstrel shows, Aboriginal populations were marginalized and "othered" into categories that led to their exclusion from the mainstream culture in which Anglo-Canadians were being invited to share. Categorization of indigenous people as "disloyal," "savage," "criminal," and "uncivilized" helped to limit the roles they could play in the development of the Canadian North-West. Economically the underdevelopment of resources on the reserves served to give merchants a large and dependent population to supply with food as well as other items. But cultural marginalization of Aboriginal people by the NWMP could also be detected in the "marriages" between policemen and Native women. Treatment of Aboriginal women by the Mounties, as well as the laws that the Anglo-Canadian society brought with it, introduced notions of spatial and social segregation that kept Aboriginal women out of, and away from, white settlements. The either/or binary of the "Indian Princess" or the squalid, immoral "squaw" that Euro-Canadian culture applied to categorize Aboriginal women severely restricted social opportunities for them.

In spite of the negative stereotypes of Aboriginal women, many members of the NWMP took Aboriginal wives throughout the 1870s and 1880s. There were of course children from these marriages and in a number of cases policemen remained with their families for life. More often, however, the Mounties abandoned their Aboriginal wives and children when their term of service in the North-West ended. There were also periodic reports of abuse of Aboriginal women by both Mounties and government employees. Such was the case with James Payne, the farm instructor on the Mosquito Reserve near Battleford. Payne was reported to have beaten a young woman who came to visit his Aboriginal wife; the woman, a friend from the reserve, died shortly after the beating. Another farm instructor near Battleford, John Delaney, was involved in an abuse of authority when he had a man jailed by false accusations so that he was able to cohabit with his Aboriginal wife. There were frequent rumoured assaults of Aboriginal women but "on most of the occasions that Aboriginal women laid charges against policemen for assault or rape, their claims were hastily dismissed as defamation or blackmail."[48]

After the fighting in 1885 the Euro-Canadian settlers hysterically complained about the increased vulnerability of their women. Responding to this outcry the "government officials as well as the NWMP made strenuous efforts to keep people on their reserves."[49] The pass system was introduced that required any absences from the reserve be reported to their agent or farm instructor. For Aboriginal women especially, the pass system had the effect of limiting their access to towns where they had traditionally been able to sell their produce and handicrafts.

These restrictions imposed by the pass system had economic repercussions for Aboriginal women that had to be endured in addition to the mistreatment that many already experienced at the hands of those who viewed them as inferior. Also as Anglo-Canadian women arrived in greater numbers by the late 1880s, many white men abandoned their Aboriginal families. In a number of cases the courts failed to recognize the claims of the mixed progeny from these marriages to the sometimes substantial wealth that they stood to inherit: "Ideological constraints, combined with more formal mechanisms of control such as the pass system, succeeded in marginalizing Aboriginal women and limiting the alternatives and opportunities available to them."[50] Thus racial and economic obstacles combined with gender biases to work against the Aboriginal wives of the NWMP, preventing them from becoming welcome and full-fledged members of the western society that Anglo-Canadians toiled to entrench.

FIVE

Fort Battleford in 1885

From Macdonald's point of view, the more important aspects of the affair were showing the flag of British authority and proving that the railway had transformed Canada into a country capable of suppressing challenges to its sovereignty in the most remote sections of habitable territory.

Douglas Sprague

By the spring of 1885, the Plains Cree and Métis around Batoche and St. Laurent already had a long record of bringing forward grievances and communicating their dissatisfaction with the federal government. When their grievances went unresolved, a series of battles and skirmishes broke out. One hundred Canadians died in the fighting, leaving in place an establishment unwilling to rectify the problems of the Métis and Natives. These indigenous inhabitants of the prairies might have been able to force a negotiated settlement in their confrontation with the officials in Ottawa "had they not faced overwhelming formal discouragement from the acts of a colonial establishment created by the Government of Canada."[1] The fighting began with the Battle of Duck Lake on 26 March and was followed by the killings at Frog Lake on 2 April. After these two major events, Fort Battleford became mobilized for an attack as anticipated by the NWMP. To date, there have been different views of the events that occurred in the spring of 1885. George Stanley suggests there was an inevitability to the conflict; in a confrontation between European and indigenous societies, the latter would certainly, albeit tragically, lose.[2] This view lumped the Métis and Natives together as a people raging against the demise of their way of life and willing to die sacrificially for their traditions. A more recent interpretation put forward by John Tobias argues that there was nothing inevitable about the death of Native and Métis societies; instead, they were willing and even anxious to adapt to the new economic order.[3] This order was represented by the National Policy with its proposals for turning the western prairies into an agricultural region that was to supply grain to markets throughout the world. Tobias suggests that the government was not serious in helping the Aboriginal people adapt to an agrarian way of life once they were on their reserves. As well, Douglas Sprague has recently argued that the Métis may have been provoked into fighting by a clever prime minister willing to crush a Métis rebellion to justify the completion of the Canadian Pacific Railway.[4]

When Métis and Native dissatisfaction with federal policies threatened to become violent, the government reacted first with tactics of delay and later with repressive measures and coercion. The answer that eventually came was a military one. An army was sent instead of the promised resources which were necessary to help the Native people acquire a land base and establish an agricultural economy. Any hope the Métis and Natives had for a peaceful, negotiated transition to a new way of life was dealt a severe setback. For the Métis, there had been mounting uncertainty regarding land claims, coupled with an altered social landscape: "Informal discouragements included intimidation of the original population by hundreds, then thousands of ultra-Protestants from Ontario who intended to establish new homes for themselves and to become a new majority transforming the Quebec of the West into a new Ontario. Newcomers appropriated Métis land and made the old settlers feel like strangers in a new land."[5]

Tobias also argues that the Métis and Natives must be seen as acting separately throughout the spring of 1885. Along with Blair Stonechild,[6] Tobias states that, in spite of the appearance of coordinated action, the Métis and Natives never had any intentions of rising together in violence. The Cree resistance was already a decade old, having begun with the "treaty rights" movement that demanded the government make good the treaty promises. Tobias documents Lieutenant Governor Dewdney's willingness to exploit the appearance of a general uprising in order to subjugate the Cree and eliminate their leaders. This approach was largely successful as the major Cree leaders — Big Bear and Poundmaker — were imprisoned and Piapot, Little Pine and Thunderchild were put under strict surveillance. The apparent rebellion became the excuse Dewdney needed to use the military and NWMP to complete his policy of breaking the concerted efforts of the Cree in bringing forward their grievances with a unified and strong voice.

Dewdney had long advocated a policy of rewards and punishments to gain control over the Natives. Those who did not agree to take reserves where they were allocated, or those who were unwilling to farm as the government dictated, would be dealt with by force. This policy of denying to the Natives what they were entitled to had been pursued by Dewdney in the early 1880s. He saw the chance to exploit the unrelated circumstance of 1885 to achieve his policy of disrupting a united Aboriginal front.

There were both political and cultural reasons why the government wanted to lump the Métis and Natives together as rebels, and then to use this situation to silence their leadership through imprisonment and by dispersing concentrated pockets of political discontent. Economically and politically, the government was bankrupt and unwilling to spend money in an area where there were few votes, even though it had offered much in the treaties to convince the Natives to take reserves. Once Natives were on the reserves, government officials seemed conveniently to forget their commitments.

Life at Fort Battleford

The year 1885 was most eventful for the Mounties at Fort Battleford. The otherwise daily routine they followed was now disrupted by threats to the town and the newly arrived settlers and government officials. The fort became a beehive of activity during and after the outbreak of violence at Duck Lake. Prior to March 1885, the recorded events in the diaries of the men focussed on the mundane: weather, announcements of mail arriving, or the reporting of maintenance fatigues. Occasionally, some incident broke the usual quiet at the fort, such as the report of 4 March: "Const. Worthington returned to duty and fined $10.00 and 10 days CB for being drunk in Barracks on 3rd inst."[7] Or the report of 7 March: "Instructor Applegarth laid information against an Indian 'Jean Baptiste' whom he charged with breaking into storehouse at Red Pheasant's reserve and stealing therefrom Flour and Bacon."[8] But ordinarily the routine was undramatic. An average day as recorded in the police diary would begin with a report on the weather: "Freezing very Hard," "Thaw set in last night — Temp. rose 25 deg.," "Weather Frosty." The morning might be taken up with the following:

Reveille	6:30 A.M.
Stables	7 to 8
Breakfast	8:15
Office	10:00
Parade	10:30
Stables	11:30 to 12:30

Afternoons included various drills and fatigues. Among these would be carbine-revolver drill, barracks inspection, riding school, shingling stables and buildings, as well as other repair fatigues. An average afternoon would be divided up as follows:

Guard Mounting	1:45 P.M.
Parade	2:00
Tea	4:30
Stables	4:45 to 5:30
Retreat	4:45
Picquet-Mounting	5:30
Night Guard	6:30
First Post	9:30
Last Post	10:00
Lights Out	10:15

The reporting of duties often was interrupted by the excitement caused by the arrival of mail or reports from one of the local reserves: "Staff Segt. Mackay was sent out this afternoon to Red Pheasant's Reserve to examine an Indian boy who was reported as having been badly beaten by the Schoolmaster."[9] Often the evening activities were recorded: "Concert this evening in Council Chambers in aid of English Church."[10]

The plain diet of the men may have contributed to their boredom. The following list of items is from the recommended diet established by NWMP regulations in the 1880s:

	Pounds	Ounces
Beef or Bacon or Pemmican or Dried Meat	1	8
Flour	1	4
or Bread	1	8
or Biscuit	1	4
Potatoes	1	4
or Beans		2
or Dried Apples		2
Tea		1/2
Coffee		1/2
Sugar		3
Salt		1/2
Pepper		1/36
Rice		1

The yearly routine changed near the end of March. Until then, the most commonly accepted interpretation of Native participation in the 1885 Rebellion had been that Poundmaker and Big Bear's men were ready to destroy the fort and its inhabitants. This view is well expressed in a popular history of the Battlefords:

> some six hundred frightened, miserable people sought refuge from Indian war parties within the palisades of Fort Battleford in 1885. ... [It was a time when] many slept on the ground or in large hastily-erected tents; cooking facilities and meals were vexatious; babies were born; the frail sickened and died; and young men were killed in skirmishes beyond the stockade. ... a time when fear, lack of privacy, material losses and crises were compounded by an isolation from the outside world so complete as to terrify.[11]

This version of the siege at Fort Battleford is basically grounded in the reminiscences of white participants and those in the stockade. It uncritically accepts the narrative descriptions of the siege with a few passing observations concerning the conditions faced by the Cree, and dwells primarily on the suffering of those inside the stockade. Little sympathy is shown for the Natives.

The townspeople expected some trouble from the Native population through rumours heard from a number of Native women of surrounding reserves. The women reported that large groups of Natives were gathering and the whites feared this could mean violence. Rumour became more concrete with the events at Duck Lake. The effect of this fight reinforced the fear that an uprising was impending. Less than a week later, reports of the killings at Frog Lake supported the opinion of those who thought that the Métis and Cree were acting in concert.

On the day before the Duck Lake battle was fought, fifty Battleford townsmen who made up the local Home Guard were sworn in and supplied with arms. They drilled regularly in Barracks 4. On 27 March, twenty-four men left for Carlton and returned with reports that the fort was endangered. During these early days, men were dispatched each day to work on the bastions to prepare them for defence.

The boredom with the daily routine, as noted in the diary entries, changed drastically after the Duck Lake episode on 26 March 1885. The tone describing the daily activities became more urgent as the situation grew more dangerous. On 26 March, "No news from Carlton: great anxiety prevails." By 27 March, the fort was crowded with a frightened white population: "Militia and volunteers attached to police here and living in Barrack rooms and working together under police rules and regulations." Fears increased each day: "All hands busy fortifying and removing all buildings that may prove a shelter to the enemy. All whites in district within the Fort now..."[12]

The population felt threatened by the local Cree and many were terrified by early rumours:

> Stockade strengthened. Indians collecting on bank of Battle River around Gov't House and Indian office & have sent some of their instructors to treat for them... Barney Tremont reported to have been killed by Indians: Applegarth and Payne and Cunningham also said to be killed. Stoney Indians reported on War path. Indians burning and plundering in Eagle Hills hid up [sic] Battle River. Indians had entered all the stores and houses on the south side during the night and taken away all stores and clothing and destroyed what they could not carry away.[13]

On Sunday, 29 March, it was reported that Poundmaker was expected to attack Battleford the next day. In preparation for this attack, men were detailed to strengthen the walls of the stockade and reinforce the bastions. All women and children were brought into the barracks and the telegraph was moved to the orderly room. Some farm homes, not in the vicinity of Battleford but located some miles away, were reported to have been looted by Cree. Cattle and horses also were taken. Many families, including the Pambruns, Finlaysons and Macfarlanes, came to seek refuge within the fort. Others such as Judge Rouleau, Indian Agent Kane and A.T. Berthiaume left for Swift Current.

Effie Storer remembered life inside the stockade. Her parents, the Lauries, lived in the town on the flats. She accompanied them on 29 March 1885 as they crossed the Battle River, which was slowly thawing, to seek refuge in the stockade.[14] Families were distributed throughout the fort, some occupying the commissioner's residence while others took shelter in the stables. The Lauries and numerous others were put up in the NWMP barracks. Each family marked out its territory with blankets in the long barrack rooms heated by a black stove which stood along the wall of this building. By Monday, 30 March, most of the settlers had taken refuge within the stockaded walls of the fort. Earlier on, any fears that might have been felt by these refugees were given credence when two men were reported killed. Barney Tremont, a local farmer who was the Stoney farm instructor, was reported to have been shot by the Natives. Communication with the other major centres at Prince Albert and Swift Current was curtailed when telegraph lines were cut. The only connection with these two towns came through those daring enough to carry messages by horse.

With almost all of the local community inside, the men were put on repair detail, reinforcing the somewhat flimsy stockade with sand-filled sacks. The younger men were organized into units responsible for patrolling the four sides of the fort, though not all of them were armed. Some 200 men out of the 500 refugees were organized and dubbed the "Home Guards and Rifles," and a number of them would later follow Colonel Otter to Cut Knife Hill. The men were directed by the twenty-five Mounties still at the fort and had one 9-pounder gun at their disposal.

Men were separated from women during the siege. Supplies had been piled around the central flagpole in case a breakthrough occurred, and the women and children could gather in the centre of the fort close to supplies. The whole fort population adhered to a strict discipline: they began in the morning with reveille, busied themselves during the day with various tasks, and ended with the last post. Food consisted of coffee, rice, bacon, dried apples, salt, pepper, sugar and on special occasions some flour, currants and raisins. For those with money there was condensed milk, anchovy sauce and canned cocoa. Bread was baked and rationed daily. The rare eggs brought in from patrols were given to the sick children. Obtaining water became a problem. A guard was needed morning and evening as water could not be hauled up the steep banks of the South Saskatchewan River, but had to be transported under escort from the more distant Battle River. The heating system was a major concern as those closest to the stove sweltered in order to provide enough heat for those at the far end of the room. The close quarters resulted in a number of inconveniences due to what Effie Storer referred to as "rude suitors" who kept others awake at night. There were more pleasant moments when on Sundays the weekly hymn singing was led by the Anglican minister. Considerate sympathies also went to the soldiers out in the cold on patrol. On these occasions, the older girls would brew up a pot of coffee to take out to the suffering sentries.

Overall, fright and apprehension pervaded the atmosphere among the refugees. Reports from Frog Lake and Fort Pitt as well as news of the women prisoners with Big Bear made life anxious. It must have reminded them of the many stories told of the 1857 Sepoy Mutiny in India. Reports of burned homes and businesses were also brought by the continual arrival of messengers. Tragedy struck within the stockade when the baby of a Bresaylor couple died after a brief illness. Later, while on patrol, trader Frank Smart was found shot in the back, though no one knew for certain who perpetrated the deed.

On Monday, 30 March, the men again were dispatched to reinforce the stockade. The Cree from the surrounding reserves were seen across the river in south Battleford. Estimates put the numbers from 120 to "over 200." It appears from a policeman's report that they were headed towards the Indian office in town. At this time Rae, the Indian agent, and William McKay of the Hudson's Bay Company attempted to cross the river to talk to the Natives, but were fired upon and subsequently returned to the fort. It was reported that local storekeepers did send over some food to the Natives who were now occupying the industrial school. They were apparently peace offerings. Later that evening, considerable activity was reported around the school and some shots were fired. This resulted in a general alarm being sounded with all men responding to the call. Nothing ensued.

More activity from the Cree was reported on 31 March. They were seen entering the stores in town, including the businesses of the Hudson's Bay Company and Mahaffey and Clinskill. They were also reported to be taking belongings from the homes now deserted by the townspeople. It was further rumoured that the Stonies from the Eagle Hills were coming to join Poundmaker for the purpose of war.

From outlying areas there came more disturbing news. James Payne, farm instructor on the Mosquito Reserve, was killed; Barney Tremont was also shot dead. George Applegarth was apparently spared when a friendly Cree warned him to escape. The homesteads of Tremont, Harry Nash, A.J. Prongua, George Gospill, Joseph Price and Harry Philips were raided. Some Natives halted George Gospill with his baby and Thomas Hodson, but they were left unharmed after turning over their horses and wagon to the Natives. Joseph Price and his family were stopped as well, but were left alone when they also gave up their horse and wagon. These events served to heighten tensions within the fort and increase the population inside the stockade as more settlers arrived. Anxiety over the possibility of collaboration of Métis with the Cree also increased when local resident Godwin Marchand was arrested on the suspicion of providing arms and ammunition to the Natives.

Wednesday, 1 April, brought attempts from the Home Guard and NWMP to drive the Cree out of the townsite on the opposite bank. The 9-pounder gun was taken outside the stockade and fired at the Cree on the other side of the Battle River. People continued to arrive at the stockade. Some of the half-breed families from the Bresaylor area were torn as to what they should do — join Riel or seek the protection of the NWMP. There was apprehension among those who feared arrest for sympathizing with the Métis of Batoche. Two men, Bird and Ballantine, were sent to Swift Current with messages to Superintendent Herchmer which said, no doubt, to hurry.

The morning found Bird and Ballantine back at the fort, with Ballantine unwilling to make the trip. His place was taken by Constable Storer who departed with Bird at 10:00 A.M. These messengers were necessary as dispatches could not be sent due to the telegraph lines being cut down. A Mountie's diary recorded that the stockade reinforcements were continuing.[15]

On 3 April, a number of patrols were sent out from the fort. Two men, Thomas Hodson and Louis Flamond, went to search for the body of Tremont. Sergeant Major M.J. Kirk and guide Joseph Nolin set out with twelve men to check on the state of a group of Métis camped a few miles away in a ravine. These Métis were brought in and resettled "in and around Constable Macdermott's house at the corner of the barrack square."[16] One other report came as the result of a foray made by John Wright who, while on the north side of the Saskatchewan River, found that the sawmill of J.G. Oliver had been plundered. Wright said the plundering was done by the Natives of Chief Nepabase. Another group that went to the townsite found the house of James Clinskill ransacked:

> A large round-topped trunk, which had contained his wife's clothing was smashed in and emptied. Most of the dishes in his living room were broken, all the cups were gone (although the saucers were left), and the silver cupboard was empty. The mirrors in the bureau were broken, and a fine writing desk was hammered open. In the garden he found a clock and a fine work box of inlaid ivory, brought from China by his wife's uncle.[17]

The stores had been emptied of groceries. The records and files in the Indian Department office were torn and scattered about. Within the stockade there were also difficulties and discomfort. Food and water were scarce and living conditions cramped. Diet was monotonous. Unease heightened that evening as the refugees watched the store of Mahaffey and Clinskill burning. The next day, the stables of the Indian industrial school were aflame. Fears of attack were increasing.

The Frog Lake Killings

On 5 April 1885, news arrived at the fort of the Frog Lake "massacre," and some days later came the news that a large number of Natives were encamped with Poundmaker. Details of the Frog Lake encounter sent paroxysms of fear throughout the Battleford area.

The Frog Lake episode traditionally has been viewed as an act of unprovoked violence by the young warriors of Big Bear's band against the innocent and unsuspecting local townspeople. This interpretation was vividly laid out in some of the reminiscences penned by survivors and those who were held captive by the Cree throughout the spring of 1885. The usual image of the Cree would suggest that they were on the warpath and out of control. More recently, an account from the Native perspective was published which presents a very different interpretation of the actions of the Cree at Frog Lake.[18] While indeed a tragic story, it is usually the killings that have been emphasized, not the events which provoked the Cree to violence.

As the Cree account indicates, one must go back to the signing of Treaty 6 and analyze the subsequent events in order to appreciate the position the Natives found themselves in by the spring of 1885. The treaty was to be a partnership in which both sides would forthrightly live up to their promises, or so the Natives thought. When the treaties were followed by the appearance of a cumbersome, unsympathetic bureaucracy which was to administer Aboriginal affairs, the Cree were disappointed. The use of the Indian Act to control their activity was a sign to many Natives that the whites and government representatives had not bargained in good faith. The system of Indian agents and farm instructors so regulated and restricted Cree movement that many had reached a breaking point. As John Tootoosis has written, it might be compared to "a ticking time bomb."[19] One of the methods used by the government to bring the Cree into conformity with their programs was to starve them into submission. This led to numerous confrontations between the Cree and their farm instructors. These government agents had been told that "demonstrated work" was the only way food would be distributed to the Cree. Of course, this did not prevent the more diplomatic farm instructors from distributing food when the need was clearly evident.[20]

The background to the Frog Lake incident was linked to the restricting government programs. The situation was exacerbated at Frog Lake by an intransigent, foolish Indian agent, Thomas Quinn. Quinn is remembered as being "contemptuous of Indians and enjoyed demonstrating his authority over them,"[21] and was notorious for hoarding supplies in the face of starving Cree. Quinn had provoked the Cree in the fall of 1884 when he refused to supply meat to Big Bear's band. The Cree had hoped to use that meat for the feast which traditionally preceded the annual payment of treaty money. The failure to provide the food frustrated the Cree, especially the younger members. They also explained to Quinn that the buffalo were gone and they rarely had the opportunity to eat fresh meat. It made no difference to the agent. In the wake of this refusal, a number of Natives, including Big Bear, Little Pine and Miserable Man, threatened Quinn. To defuse and perhaps save this moment, the Hudson's Bay Company trader, William McLean, ordered one of his steers to be slaughtered and donated it as a gift to pacify the Cree.

Other members of Big Bear's band had also been humiliated by imprisonment for actions they believed were justifiable. Wandering Spirit, for example, had been imprisoned for three months when he stole horses from a group of Métis, as he thought the horses were invading his territory. Wandering Spirit carried this injustice with him to Frog Lake in the spring of 1885.

There were other resentments the Cree felt, as suggested in Native accounts, including the humiliation of simple and crippled Cree and the implication of local white men in seducing young Cree girls. These factors, though only alluded to, may not have been crucial to the outbreak of violence at Frog Lake, but they certainly contributed to the aggravation felt at that time.

Throughout March, Quinn closely monitored the rationing of food to Big Bear's band. During this time, the Cree were required to work at Gowanlock's sawmill, piling logs before any food was dispensed. While the weather was mild they were able to work, but when conditions deteriorated, they could not continue. On these occasions, no rations were forthcoming. When the farm instructor, John Delaney, gave out supplies to the desperate Cree, Quinn reported him to Dewdney, and Delaney was subsequently reprimanded. The news of Duck Lake reached the settlement a few days later and the Cree of the area withdrew into silence. They were preparing to confront Quinn, who was now being referred to as the Dog Agent, again on the issue of food rationing. The situation at Frog Lake was becoming more and more desperate when the priest, Father Fafard, who was not particularly well liked by the local people, proposed a plan that would have taken the townspeople to the protection of Fort Pitt. The events of the next few days followed the same pattern: requests for food by the cold, hungry Cree on behalf of their families were rejected by Quinn, against the advice of others around him, including Inspector Dickens of the NWMP. One of the last reasonable requests for food was made by Big Bear's son, Imasees:

> Brother, let me tell you one thing. The way I think everything will work out for the best. My father, Big Bear, is poor and old. He went north to try and hunt for food. Whatever he kills, he gives to the people. He puts on a feast and feeds everybody. Maybe you should give him food from your supplies so that he could invite all the people and feed them.[22]

The offer to distribute the food in the well-stocked house was again refused, and the situation worsened. Ironically, on 1 April, Corporal Sleigh left Frog Lake with a supply of ammunition thought to have been targeted by the Cree.

Big Bear made a number of last-minute attempts to defuse the worsening situation diplomatically, but the uncompromising Quinn rendered any negotiations futile. On the night of 1 April, the frustrated and furious younger Cree took the Wood Cree chief, Isidore Mondion, captive, as they were afraid he would warn the townspeople of the danger they posed. Shortly after this, Imasees and another man broke into Quinn's house, but they left after Lone Man and Sitting Horse reminded them that Quinn's wife was a Cree and one of them. Respite for Quinn was short-lived, however, for at dawn Wandering Spirit broke into the agent's house, seizing all the guns and informing Quinn that he was a prisoner. A number of other houses were also invaded, including that of John Delaney. There was one more attempt by the Cree to ask for meat from Quinn peacefully, but it again failed. Then Wandering Spirit ordered all the townspeople to a new camp about one mile from town. Quinn told the townspeople to refuse, though most of them disobeyed him. Quinn was now confronted by Wandering Spirit who thrice more asked him to move to the new camp. When Quinn refused, a witness remembers Wandering Spirit saying, "I don't know what kind of a head you have that you do not seem to understand. I may as well kill you."[23] At this point Wandering Spirit raised his rifle and fired at Quinn, killing him. A number of the townspeople fled for safety, but Charles Gouin, George Dill and William Gilchrist, who were closest to Quinn, did not make it. Then John Williscraft, John Delaney, John Gowanlock and two priests, Fathers Fafard and Marchand, were gunned down. The priests' bodies then were taken into the church and the building set on fire.

The Natives were still looking for William Cameron, the young clerk from the Hudson's Bay store. However, he was protected by some Cree women who covered him with a blanket and refused to give him up. The remainder of the townspeople were taken captive, including the two widows, Theresa Gowanlock and Mrs. Delaney. The following day Big Bear came to the camp where the prisoners were held and expressed his sympathy to the two widows. He had lost control of his younger men who were now headed for Fort Pitt. In an effort to curtail further disaster, Big Bear dictated the following note:

> I want you (the police) all out without any bloodshed. We had a talk, I and my

72

men, before we left camp at Frog Lake, and thought … to let you off if you would go. Try and get away before the afternoon, as the young men are all wild and hard to keep in hand.[24]

One more Mountie was to die near Fort Pitt from the bullets of the young Cree. Fortunately for the rest of the fort, it was ordered evacuated by Inspector Dickens. Twenty-eight civilians were turned over to Natives encamped close to the fort and the twenty-three policemen boarded a scow which went upriver to Fort Battleford. They were not pursued. There was not the degree of hostility toward the mounted police as there was to the government officials who were allowing the Cree to starve.

Frog Lake and its aftermath shows that the young Cree did not indiscriminately kill any white who crossed their path. Rather, they were selective. Those killed were Indian agents, farm instructors, priests and one Mountie. Many were spared or protected by other Cree. The killings occurred in spite of the restraints urged by Big Bear and other older Cree leaders. They could no longer control the frustrated, humiliated and once-proud young Cree who would not sit idly by and watch their people starve. While the action of the Cree at Frog Lake may have been triggered by the battle of Duck Lake, they were not acting in concert with Riel and the Métis. The Cree were frustrated too, but for other reasons, and acted under a different set of circumstances.

Waiting for Colonel Otter

All this, of course, was not evident to the refugees at Fort Battleford. The only report that reached them was that ten people had been massacred. Scouts were dispatched to determine the fate of Fort Pitt. On Monday, 6 April, a snowstorm was recorded in a Mountie's diary.[25] On 8 April, some shots were fired across the river at those Natives loading supplies from Government House onto wagons. The same day, Joseph Alexander returned from Fort Pitt and reported that he had been stopped by a group of Stoney Natives who took his arms, ammunition, saddle and food supplies. The 9-pounder was used to fire on these Natives and a brief encounter took place in which the Mounties recorded one Native being killed.

By 9 April, the telegraph lines had been repaired and communications from Middleton were received. Other reports from Fort Pitt reported that relations between the Cree and the fort's inhabitants were tense. News from Prince Albert indicated that cattle were being driven out of farms by the Natives and Métis. Two days later, the ice on the Saskatchewan River broke as the cold weather gave way to a warming sun, and two scouts were dispatched to discover Poundmaker's whereabouts. On 12 April, news reached Battleford that Otter and his column were on their way, having left Swift Current two days earlier. Apprehension was further heightened that evening: "The northern horizon is fearsomely red with fires which stretch more than twenty miles across."[26]

There was continued reconnaissance of the area around Battleford on 13 April, during which the Prince brothers' house was inspected and reported ransacked. Scouts surveyed the vicinity for Cree but found none — they were rumoured to be at Poundmaker's reserve. The search for and fear of the Natives was constantly on the white people's minds, and the stockade of the fort was continually being reinforced. Some Stoney Natives gave credence to these fears when they told a group of scouts on 14 April that Poundmaker was planning to cross the Battle River to attack.

This triggered a flurry of activity around Battleford, including a detail to dig trenches around the entire stockade and move supplies to the centre of the square.

On the evening of 14 April, the Cree were again seen in the town across the Battle River. Yet the police could still write, "Think it likely that Indians will not attack Barracks."[27] The next day, however, information gathered by Constable Storer and guide James Bird indicated that the Cree from six reserves were preparing to cross the Battle River and attack the fort.

Thursday, 16 April, was reported as very cold and was accompanied by a snowstorm. Patrols continued to move to and from the fort. On 18 April the barracks were scrubbed and the atmosphere was calmer. "Everything quiet no news of any kind."[28] One scout who had travelled fifty miles up the Battle River found no sign of any Natives and reported that the Cree had not left Poundmaker's reserve. On 19 April, Fort Pitt was abandoned by Dickens and the remainder of the Mounties boarded another scow and headed down river to Battleford.

Tensions were lessening by the next day and teams of horses were travelling to the old town and hauling goods back from the Hudson's Bay store and the industrial school, but the calm was short-lived as the two scouts, Bird and Pambrun, returned from Fort Pitt to report that it had been abandoned by the Mounties. Furthermore, they stated that two policemen had been killed in an encounter with some Natives.

On 20 April, the scow with the men from Fort Pitt was seen forty-five miles from Fort Battleford up the Saskatchewan River. On 22 April, the constables from Fort Pitt arrived. On board the scow were Inspector Dickens, Sergeant Martin, Staff Sergeant Rolph and Corporal Sleigh, armed with a considerable supply of guns and ammunition. The story of the evacuation of Fort Pitt was then related. The inhabitants had heard of the presence of a large group of Cree camped near the fort shortly after the Frog Lake massacre. Attempts had been made to bolster the fort's defences, but supplies were low, and even though civilians had been sworn in to increase the force's fighting capacity, the risk was obviously not worth it. After negotiations with the Cree and having a number of patrol police killed or wounded, Dickens decided to abandon the fort. The civilians gave themselves up to the Cree and the police quietly left by river. It was an arduous trip:

> The first day they were up at 4:30 after a wretched night. There was snow and wind. Several men were frost bitten, and their clothing froze to their backs. On April 17 they had some narrow escapes in ice jams.[29]

But the police were not pursued any further by the Natives, and in spite of fears expressed by Big Bear about his young warriors, the Mounties were not attacked. This restraint towards them reflects the respect that the Natives had for the police, and the apparent goodwill that had built up between them in the years since the treaty of 1876. Had they wanted to, the Cree could have attacked and destroyed Fort Pitt. It is not known what, specifically, restrained them. But what seems certain is that there was far less animosity towards the NWMP than there was towards Indian agents and other government officials administering its policies under the treaties.

During the night of 22 April, a number of buildings were burnt, including Judge Rouleau's house. It was a selective burning, as the Natives no doubt were aware of the approaching column of Colonel Otter. On the same evening one other death occurred around Fort Battleford. Frank Smart was on patrol with Constable White when they were fired on by what was reported to be a group of Natives. Thirty-five policemen were sent out and found Smart's body some three miles from the barracks. Tension in the fort was again mounting as Smart's death was followed that evening by a fire that burned the Hudson's Bay store in Battleford. A general alarm was sounded and the men remained on guard around the stockade until four that morning.

Otter Arrives

Fear of Native attacks decreased with reports that Otter and his men were now close to the fort. "The women all cried and embraced each other! At last the suspense was almost over."[30] But the relief was coupled with the thought that the Cree would attack at night since the fort would still be vulnerable as Otter was camped some miles away for the night:

> Nothing is worse than waiting, especially when it's dark. This evening our bugler, Paddy Burke, climbed up to the top of the stockade to play Last Post. The reply from Otter's camp some three miles away was reassuring.[31]

Rumours ran rampant through the fort, and as the long night hours passed, it was believed forty Cree had crept up the river and were crossing it on the scow. By morning, however, the scow was found undisturbed.

On 24 April, there was some relief for the refugees: Otter's column arrived, including forty NWMP under Inspector Neale who was accompanied by Superintendent Herchmer. Otter's group comprised 250 men of the Queen's Own Rifles, forty-eight of the Toronto School of Infantry, fifty with the Ottawa Foot Guard and another fifty with the Battery contingent. However, that same day, a report reached Battleford of the fight at Fish Creek. An expedition into town by Otter's men led to the discovery of two dead Natives near the Indian office and the body of Payne in a stable. It was during this time that Otter, unknown to General Middleton, forged his plan to move against Poundmaker's Cree.

The column set up camp in town in front of the Lieutenant Governor's house, close to the industrial school. It was given the name Fort Otter. The scene was described in some detail by Lieutenant Cassels:

> Battleford is very beautifully situated. The "Old Town" as before stated is on the South Bank of the Battle River; and the New Town and Fort lie on the grassy plain sloping south, and between the Saskatchewan and Battle River, about a mile and a half from the junction of the two. The ground rises sharply from each River and numerous groves of trees lend to the scene a beauty to which we have for some time been unaccustomed.[32]

Shortly after looking around the fort and listening to the terrified refugees Otter began to assess the situation:

> After the tents are pitched we are able to go about and take observations, and then the extent of the ravages committed becomes apparent. On this side of the River there were originally some dozen houses and two or three stores forming what is called the "Old Town." Four or five of these houses have been burned, the others dismantled and pillaged, and the stores completely gutted. Scarcely anything has escaped: what could not be taken has been destroyed. About us we see scattered in dismal confusion feathers, photos, books, tins, furniture and desolation reigns supreme. The Indians have, we hear, been holding high

carnival here for some weeks: they were out of rifle shot from the Fort and shells were too precious to be often sent at them. Each night an attack was expected but beyond firing at the men drawing water from the Battle River (the source of the supply) they molested the garrison but little.[33]

The police reports from Fort Battleford were of routine matters for the next few days, and the inhabitants now felt more secure. There was less alarm over a Native attack in NWMP reports, though Colonel Otter seemed concerned about a confrontation with the combined forces of Big Bear and Poundmaker. For the troops at Fort Otter the experience was not as placid:

Last night I had the pleasure of being out on picquet [guard duty] and cold and anxious work it is. The prospect of being potted any minute from one of the numerous clumps of bushes that one's duty obliges one to pass is not pleasant, but that is comparatively nothing to the misery one suffers from the cold.[34]

Though the troops were suffering hardships, those inside the Battleford stockade were in an even more desperate state. On visiting the fort for the first time, Lieutenant Cassels was astonished at what he found:

I was quite overcome when I visited the Fort and saw the miseries the poor people there have been enduring. A small enclosure two hundred yards square with one or two log houses or barracks and store houses, and inside this enclosure were pent up for more than a month five hundred and thirty people of whom over three hundred were women and children. Dozens and dozens had to huddle together in one tent. In the Commandant's house, a two storey frame cottage, seventy-two persons were quartered. Food was scarce and water to be produced only at the risk of death. No wonder these poor creatures were glad to see us.[35]

Having secured the immediate area of the townsite to his satisfaction, on 29 April Otter ordered the people back to their houses. Many, especially from the old town of Battleford, were reluctant to comply as they had little to return to. Slowly, though, they began to return.

As the settlers started returning to what was left of their homes, Colonel Otter was mulling over his choices. His biographer, Desmond Morton, suggests that Otter's objective was never much in doubt,[36] as he was determined to attack the Cree at Poundmaker's reserve at any cost. There appear to be a number of possibilities for Otter's decision to go after them. One was the destitute state of the refugees. Another was his anger at the looting and burning of Judge Rouleau's home and the Hudson's Bay store on the evening of 23 April, which was done while his force was just a few miles away from the town. He may have wanted to teach the Cree a lesson, and perhaps also felt embarrassed that the Natives' attack against the old town occurred while he was in the immediate vicinity, yet was unable to respond at the time. Such action was interpreted by Otter as arrogant defiance of government authority, and it was probably important for him to establish his authority over the Cree for the sake of his own men and the townspeople. His own troops were especially surprised when their colonel took no action on the evening of 23 April:

Instead of attacking the relieving troops, the Indians used their last night of freedom to burn Judge Rouleau's house and blow up the Hudson's Bay Company store. From their camp the troops could see flames and sparks rising and they wondered, with rising anger, why they were not unleashed to destroy the marauders.[37]

While the men did not understand Otter's restraint, it may have been because

"Their commander ... was all the more determined that no Indian ruse would tempt him into a cunningly planned ambush."[38] On the other hand, those refugees enclosed within the stockade for many days had a great desire for revenge. Their desperate conditions were recorded in some detail by the troops and they encouraged Otter to take action.

Released from their prolonged confinement in the fort, most of Battleford's settlers were furious for revenge. Otter's arrival dissolved their early terrors and the sight of their ransacked homes made them merciless. Battleford was strewn with shredded clothing, shattered furniture, china and all the homely keepsakes which the settlers had abandoned in their panic. Their anger was easily communicated to the militiamen, few of whom had ever seen such devastation. In any case, they had not endured the hardships and fatigues of the long journey from Toronto merely to keep company with the people of Battleford; they had come to punish Natives.[39]

One other pressure on Otter to pursue the Cree was that a successful attack would provide him with an opportunity to bask in glory. The eastern newspapers were anxious for a Canadian hero to write about and Otter was aware of such possibilities for personal glory and future promotion. All of these were reasons for attack; the reasons against an offensive soon would become evident. Certainly, it appears that some understanding of the Cree motives gave Otter little reason for moving against them. His column had proceeded unprovoked from Swift Current — a distance of 180 miles — and there was no reason to believe that he could not keep going.

Almost immediately upon arrival, there were rumours of preparation for a move on Poundmaker. On 27 April, Cassels' diary contained the following entry: "I hear today that an expedition of some kind is going out to see what Indians are doing..."[40] On 29 April, Lieutenant-Colonel Hamlyn Todd wrote: "a flying column would be sent tomorrow to Poundmaker's reserve, Cut Knife, to see if he was there, and to know that he had not joined with the Batoche force."[41] It appears that Otter was not intimidated by the possibility of a battle with the Cree.

At any rate, Otter was prepared to attack the Natives: "Their commander needed little persuasion."[42] Middleton's communications with Otter always carried a tone of wariness. It may have been his experience at Fish Creek which led him to hesitate and motivated this sense of caution in his advice to Otter. Middleton had told Otter to use his own judgement in the defence of Battleford, and Otter used this order as an opportunity to map out an offensive plan to keep Fort Battleford safe. By moving out against the Cree, Battleford would certainly be safe. Otter had telegraphed Dewdney, telling him he would take part of his force to punish Poundmaker in light of the great depredations committed. Dewdney responded eagerly: "Think you cannot act too energetically or Indians will collect in large numbers."[43] In the meantime, Middleton had warned Otter to exercise greater caution, apparently not wanting another of his columns involved in a battle that might turn out unfavourably: "You had better remain at Battleford until you ascertain more about Poundmaker's force and the kind of country he is in."[44] By this time, Otter had already carried out his reconnaissance and was prepared to move at any time. On 30 April, Otter impatiently wired Middleton, asking whether he could march on Poundmaker. It was the beginning of an exchange of telegrams that was somewhat confusing. Middleton was sure his telegraph to Otter on 1 May had relayed a note of caution:

Fighting these men entails heavy responsibility. Six men judiciously placed would shoot down half your force. Had better for the present content yourself with holding Battleford and patrolling about the country.[45]

By this point, it appears that Otter could not be restrained. On the same day, he sent back a message to Middleton: "Poundmaker hesitating between peace and war — am going to-day to try and settle matters with him."[46] Middleton, obviously frustrated that Otter had not appreciated his warnings, responded immediately:

Don't understand your telegram about Poundmaker. Hope you have not gone with small force, he must be punished, not treated with. You had better confine yourself to reconnoitring for the present.[47]

It was too late.

The Battle of Cut Knife Hill

On 1 May, Colonel Otter issued orders for the advance on Poundmaker's camp. At 3:00 P.M., part of his column moved to Cut Knife Hill. There were eight scouts, sixty Mounties under Inspector Neale, eighty men with Major Short of "B" Battery, forty-five men with "C" Company under Lieutenant Wadmore, fifty-five men of the Queen's Own Rifles under Captain Brown, forty Battleford Rifles with Captain Nash, twenty Guards with Lieutenant Gray and ten men with the ambulance corps of the Queen's Own Rifles. It was clear as the column advanced that they would not catch the Cree by surprise, as fires from their camp on Cut Knife Hill could be seen. The men rested briefly for approximately four hours when it was darkest, but began to move again when the moon had risen around midnight.

In the early dawn the column reached Poundmaker's reserve, which had been vacated. It moved on and came to the Cree campsite. At this point, the layout of the land could be discerned. The column was on a slight hill which looked down at Cut Knife Creek and rose steeply to Cut Knife Hill. The top of this hill was bald, but around its summit were thickly treed woods. It was decided to cross the creek, eat breakfast there and allow the horses to rest. The descent to the creek was rough and the men had considerable difficulty in crossing. The steep ascent through the dense vegetation was even more arduous. The hill was terraced with a number of ravines running off to each side.

Just as those men leading the column reached the top of the first level, a shower of bullets came from all sides. "C" Company was ordered to advance towards the bushes on the right while those with the Queen's Own Rifles moved to the left flank. The NWMP and "B" Battery were in the advance guard straight ahead while the Battleford Rifles protected the rear. This first contact is estimated to have been around 5:15 A.M. There was heavy fire for approximately thirty minutes and after this time the positions on the right and left front had been silenced.

"C" Company under Wadmore was then ordered forward, while a base camp was formed part way up the hill. The wagons were pulled into a square inside which the wounded men were cared for. Close by, the horses were corralled. The heaviest fire from the Cree was now coming from the left. At this point the men were ordered to fire at what was believed to be the centre of the Cree position. This, however, proved difficult. The guns were almost useless as they were too light and had to be tied down with ropes to be effective.

At about 11:00 A.M. Otter decided to pull back momentarily to assess the situation, as there was very little fire from the Cree during this time. The land ahead was rough and any advance would be difficult. It was here that Otter decided to move the wagons back across the creek in retreat. "C" Company along with the Gatling gun would provide cover during the withdrawal. The men suffered during the retreat:

> We drive for about an hour and then stop and water the horses and have some-thing to eat, and not before we need it. We have had nothing since last night and are almost exhausted now that the excitement is over. After a short rest we press on and reach Battleford about 11 p.m. The journey is very trying to the poor fel-lows who have been hit; they are made as comfortable as possible with blankets but the jolting over the rough road causes them agony. At Fort Otter they receive some much needed attention.[48]

Otter's move against the Cree caused much hardship. It was ill-advised, poorly planned and proceeded against the wishes of Middleton, but the loss of life was less than it might have been since the Cree allowed Otter an unencum-bered withdrawal from the battle site. The Cree left untouched those Canadian militia who had intruded on their territory and were now tired and in retreat. Eight men of the Canadian force had been killed and eighteen were wounded in this needless battle; seven Cree were also killed. Otter had gone all the way to Cut Knife Hill to find that Poundmaker was indeed hostile.[49]

The column returned to its base and was then besieged a second time. How-ever, it was in all probability a siege of fear more than a real attack. The fear of "savage reprisals" was partially stimulated by an increased number of Cree seen around the town. From the Natives' perspective, they were worried about what these soldiers would do next. From the perspective of the Canadian militia, an at-tack by the Cree again seemed imminent and loomed large in their minds. Reports were received of supply trains that had been captured by the Cree:

> Gloom among the troops was all the greater when it was wrongly supposed that the waggon train had consisted largely of comforts contributed by the ladies of Toronto. The thought of Indians feasting on jams, jellies and canned fruit while they forced down dry biscuit and corned beef was almost too much for them. At Swift Current, teamsters, understandably, refused to move without arms or a strong escort, protection which Middleton's standing orders explicitly forbade.[50]

These stories added greatly to their fears.

There was little action between 2 and 24 May when Middleton's troops ar-rived. On 26 May Poundmaker — the cause of so much anxiety — came to the fort and was arrested. The events that are commonly referred to as the North-West "Rebellion" would now culminate in the arrest of Big Bear and his men — those deemed responsible for the so-called massacre at Frog Lake. The episodic portrayal of these events has always focussed on the battles and killings, not on the long-term factors of starvation and the sense of frustration felt by the Cree. Now their leadership would also be undermined at the subsequent trials with the sentencing and eventual hanging of eight Cree.

Aboriginal Trials

Fort Battleford returned to a more normal routine as the settlers went back to their houses. After the fighting ended, police work focussed on the many prison-ers in the fort. The work was often found to be arduous:

June 20 Prisoners becoming too numerous for guard room to hold them, the new stable has been transformed into a prison and prisoners transferred to it. Number of prisoners on this date is 34.[51]

Natives and Métis continued to be arrested throughout July as police were sent out to reserves with warrants. The principal leaders — Poundmaker, Big Bear, Breaking-Through-the-Ice, Yellow Mud Blanket, and Lean Man — were shipped to Regina for trial. The others stood trial in Battleford. In spite of considerable evidence to the contrary, both Big Bear and Poundmaker were found guilty. It was especially surprising that Big Bear was convicted, considering that evidence given by one of the prisoners showed that he not only tried to restrain his men, but also had prevented more killing from occurring, especially at Fort Pitt. The trials showed that the judges and lawyers involved did everything in their power to get convictions. They also demonstrated their lack of knowledge of Native decision making and made little effort to understand their culture. Even allowing for Native guilt, it was surprising how little compassion was shown toward them when so few had participated in the violence.

Big Bear spoke eloquently, not only for himself, but for his people. He talked primarily of starvation, something few seemed to appreciate at the time, but after his conviction, Big Bear spoke for himself:

> I think I should have *something* to say about the occurrences which brought me here in *chains*.
>
> I knew little of the killing at Frog Lake beyond hearing the shots fired. When any wrong was brewing I did my best to stop it in the beginning. The turbulent ones of the band got beyond my control and shed the blood of those I would have protected. I was away from Frog Lake a part of the winter, hunting and fishing, and the rebellion had commenced before I got back. When white men were few in the country I gave them the hand of brotherhood. I am sorry so few are here who can witness for my friendly acts.
>
> Can anyone stand out and say that I ordered the death of a priest or an agent? You think I encouraged my people to take part in the trouble. I did not. I advised them against it. I felt sorry when they killed those men at Frog Lake, but the truth is when news of the fight at Duck Lake reached us my band ignored my authority and despised me because I did not side with the half-breeds. I did not so much as take a white man's horse. I always believed that by being the friend of the white man, I and my people would be helped by those of them who had wealth. I always thought it paid to do all the good I could. Now my heart is on the ground.
>
> I look around me in this room and see it crowded with handsome faces — faces far handsomer than my own (laughter). I have ruled my country for a long time. Now I am in chains and will be sent to prison, but I have no doubt the handsome faces I admire about me will be competent to govern the land (laughter). At present I am dead to my people. Many of my band are hiding in the woods, paralyzed with terror. Cannot this court send them a pardon? My own children! — perhaps they are starving and outcast, too, afraid to appear in the light of day. If the government does not come to them with help before the winter sets in, my band will surely perish.
>
> But I have too much confidence in the Great Grandmother to fear that starvation will be allowed to overtake my people. The time will come when the Indians of the North-West will be of much service to the Great Grandmother. I plead again, (he cried, stretching forth his hands) to you, the chiefs of the white men's laws, for pity and help to the outcasts of my band.

I have only a few words more to say. Sometimes in the past I have spoken stiffly to the Indian agents, but when I did it was only in order to obtain my rights. The North-West belonged to me, but I perhaps will not live to see it again. I ask the court to publish my speech and to scatter it among the white people. It is my defence.

I am old and ugly, but I have tried to do good. Pity the children of my tribe! Pity the old and helpless of my people! I speak with a single tongue; and because Big Bear has always been the friend of the white man, send out a pardon and give them help!

How! Aquisanee — I have spoken![52]

The less eloquent who were tried at Battleford had little to say. Many charges had been laid, including arson, high treason and assault. Eleven were convicted of murder and sentenced to death; three of those had their sentences commuted. Most of those convicted remained unrepentant. Only Wandering Spirit showed remorse:

Tell the Crees from me never to do again as they did this spring — never to do as I did. Tell my daughter I died in the white man's religion; I want her and her cousins to have that religion, too. I am not thinking much about what is going to happen tomorrow. I am thinking about what the priest says to me.[53]

The others sang their Native chants. The dramatic hanging was held on Friday, 27 November, and described at length by an eyewitness:

At half-past seven, I strolled down to the barracks. The scaffold stood in the barrack-square, the platform, twenty feet long by eight broad, ten feet above the ground, with a railing enclosing the trap in the centre, reached by a stair.

As I entered the square the death chant of the condemned red men, a weird, melancholy strain, came to me from the guardroom. A group of Cree and Assiniboine Indians sat with their backs against the blacksmith shop in the open space before the scaffold. The authorities, hoping it would have a salutary effect, had allowed a limited number to view the executions. Small knots of civilians conversed in low tones inside the high stockade about the fort; everywhere was that sense of repression always freighting the atmosphere of tragedy. The curtain was about to rise on the final act in the shocking drama which opened eight months before at Frog Lake.

Suddenly the singing ceased and a hush fell upon the men gathered about the square. A squad of mounted police marched up, black military cloaks over their shoulders, their rifles at the support, and formed a cordon about the foot of the scaffold. Major Crozier, the commandant, paced restlessly up and down on the left, talking with Wm. McKay, of the Hudson's Bay Company, who acted as interpreter.

Sheriff Forget appeared, dressed in black and carrying in his hand the warrants of execution. A Roman Catholic priest and a clergyman of the Church of England followed. Next came the prisoners, eight in all, their hands bound behind their backs. They marched in single file, a policeman before, another following, and one on either side each of the doomed men. They stepped almost jauntily, dressed in their new suits of brown duck. The weights had been removed from their ankles. Round their shaven scalps were the black caps ready to be drawn over their faces. Immediately in front of them walked Hodson. Intense silence had fallen upon the square, the only sound the measured tramp of the sombre procession.

At the foot of the stair leading to the scaffold the police escort stepped aside and the sheriff, missionaries, interpreter and hangman ascended to the platform. Miserable Man, Manichoos, Walking the Sky followed in the order named. Wandering Spirit came next. He paused at the foot of the stair, gazing up at the structure of death looming dismally above him; then mounted after the others with a firm step. Napaise and Apischiskoos followed him. Bringing up the rear were two Assiniboine Indians, the murderers of James Payne and Bernard [T]remont, settlers of Battleford.

The Indians passed through a gate in the little railing enclosing the trap and were lined up, facing outward, in the order in which they had ascended the stair. The gate was closed, and while Hodson went round behind them and strapped the ankles of each man together they were told they would be given ten minutes in which to speak, should they feel disposed. All, I think, except Wandering Spirit, availed themselves of the privilege.

The elder of the Assiniboines — Payne's murderer — spoke defiantly. So did Little Bear. He told the Indian onlookers to remember how the whites had treated him — to make no peace with them. The old Assiniboine turned and harangued his companions, urging them to show their contempt for the punishment the government was about to inflict on them. All but Wandering Spirit smiled, sang and shouted short, sharp war-cries.[54]

A policeman also described the scene.

Morning opened dull, dark & cloudy threatening snow. General parade at 7.30 to form guard during execution of the eight Indians condemned to death. Police formed three sides of hollow square around scaffold, other side, stockade & Q.M. Store. Many settlers present; about 30 Indians, principally "Moosomin," admitted to witness execution. Mounted men patrolling around Fort. Very cold, waiting for prisoners to be bro't from Guard House. At last they appeared about 8.15 am, with escort of police, prisoners' hands tied behind their backs and wearing black capes with veils to cover the face. They seemed calm and resigned to their fate, others crazy & excited, most of them assumed a false, bravado, don't care-a-damn sort of air. Miserable Man tried to get up a War song & dance on way to scaffold but it proved a failure.

All ascended the scaffold with comparatively firm step, some silent — while nooses were being adjusted, others singing war songs, Peres Cochin and Bigonesse on scaffold with them to the last. Nooses fixed, lever pulled and all were in eternity in a second. They died without a struggle and were cut down 10 minutes later, coffined, and buried within half an hour. Indian prisoners silent during day. Moosomin Indians seemed awe inspired. So ended the actors in the Frog Lake massacre and Battleford murders. Snow during forenoon. Patrols & Guard same as usual during night.[55]

Punished by the combined power of the Canadian militia and the NWMP, the Natives began a long period of withdrawal onto the reserves. There they initiated strategies of resistance and collaboration. These were the same strategies indigenous peoples in other parts of the British Empire had to adopt when faced with a military presence that was impossible to fight openly. At Battleford, the fears of the newly arrived whites justified in their own minds the largest mass hanging in Canadian history.

In the official history of Battleford, the scene of the Aboriginal graves is described:

After the hanging, the bodies were placed in rough wooden boxes and buried in a common grave on the hillside below the police barracks. So dark were the recollections of those terrible March days that for years Battleford people put them out of mind, and the grave was all but forgotten. More recently, however, it has been covered with a concrete slab encircled by chain railing. Only a rough trail leads down the hillside to the spot, but it is located in a beautiful sheltered gully overlooking the Saskatchewan River.[56]

With the dead of both sides buried, life at the fort returned to the normality it had known before the spring. The Cree of the area were, however, watched more closely than before. The monitoring of their movements began almost immediately after the surrender of Poundmaker.

On 20 August, the NWMP diary contained the following report:

> Two men mounted patrol duty to see that no Indians are in town without passes — Orders — to send squaws away from behind Mr. Rae's house to reserve, and to bring any Indian found without a pass into Barracks.[57]

There were reports of defiance among the Cree. A number of farm instructors were uneasy working on the reserves and a few warned of the possibility of another outbreak of violence. One major problem and a cause of tension was the difficulty in getting the Cree to work, but those methods that were used previously were employed once more to gain compliance. Food was rationed only to those who would work, and eventually hunger became the best friend of the local farm instructors. Besides the combined effort of trying to keep the Cree on reserves and working, there was an increased emphasis on education. The children of those who had defied the government were to be educated in the industrial school at Battleford, which was run by Canon Matheson of the Church of England.

The View of a Local Farm Instructor

In attempting to interpret the events around Battleford in 1885, it is useful to keep in mind the experiences of the farm instructor on Poundmaker's reserve. While the traditional story suggests a concerted effort of collaboration between the Métis and Natives against the whites, it goes against the observations of Robert Jefferson. This traditional view of the Cree being committed to rebellion can be found in texts published as late as 1980.[58] After the Craig Incident, Jefferson found that the Cree on his reserve were willing to work:

> The members of the band were mostly young and, with the limited means placed at their disposal by the department, made a respectable showing. They really wished to try out the white man's means of livelihood. This is speaking generally. There were a few to whose confidence I never could find entrance.[59]

Their spirits were not disheartened even by drought and crop failure in 1885. Furthermore, Jefferson thought that, in the period between the winter of 1884 and spring of 1885, there were concerns to have the government spend more money in the area and redress grievances felt by the Métis in relation to their scrip:

> The idea of bringing this about by force of arms, though talked about, was never entertained seriously by those who started and helped forward the agitation. There was no question of the Indians being in any way interested.[60]

There was a careful distinction made in Jefferson's account of the situation that existed in the settled areas along the Saskatchewan River. Those around Prince Albert and Duck Lake were poor and in great need of assistance, while the settlers around Battleford and Bresaylor were not. There was a sense of uneasiness between those wealthier persons who did not join in the fighting and the poorer residents from Duck Lake and Prince Albert who did. A "class" distinction developed between those who would join and those that remained passive, but there was a general grievance that united the Métis and Natives:

> They had owned the country; they had lived well and easily; now both their country and their means of existence were gone. The white man had deprived them without giving adequate return.[61]

Even after the battle at Duck Lake it was not clear if the Natives were committed to any violence. There is no doubt that they did gather together, making the three farm instructors — McKay of Sweet Grass, Craig of Little Pine and Jefferson — concerned about further violence. McKay had spoken to Sweet Grass after an initial meeting with all the Cree in the area. Sweet Grass had informed him that the Cree were merely going to Battleford to speak to the agent there, thinking that going in a large force would give greater weight to their demands. "He did not anticipate any trouble. They did not seek it."[62] The fear felt by the farm instructors was enough to send McKay to Battleford for shelter. Jefferson stayed at the reserve, though with some trepidation. His fear was based on what he had experienced while working with the Cree, and he recognized the bitterness felt by these Natives:

> They had accepted the statement of the white man that a living — independence — could be obtained by tilling the ground. This hope of eventual escape from dire poverty, alone had kept their inexpert hands at work; had restrained their chafing openly at the assumption of superiority and domination of men, nearly as ignorant, and not more intelligent than themselves. In this hope they had borne hunger, disease and want for several years and they were no nearer their goal. It looked as though they might die off before they had reached it — that is, if it existed.[63]

Jefferson was aware of the discouraged state of the Cree and of Assistant Indian Commissioner Hayter Reed's assumption that they were lazy and unreliable. Through his own tightfisted policy and as punishment for what he saw as slothfulness, Reed limited their rations to a bare minimum so that they were in a constant state of hunger. He also limited the amount of equipment and animals with which the Cree were allowed to work their land, so those who were eager to farm felt a great futility. Though terrified and conscious that he might be part of a cynical program that could not help the Natives, Jefferson was able to document a number of instances to show that the Cree were not responsible for any indiscriminate killing of whites. When they did kill, as the Stonies did farm instructors Payne and Tremont, it was a kind of revenge against those who had mistreated them. One eyewitness remembered the circumstances surrounding these deaths:

> The Stonies had killed, at that time, at least two white men in the district, Barney Tremont, a rancher [sic] and Payne, a farm instructor, and the settlers from the districts in which these murders took place, took refuge in Battleford. It is thought, however, that the Stonies killed these men more as a result of private revenge than in the course of a regular uprising.

> He [Payne] had a common-law Indian wife and several children. Returning one night from Battleford under the influence of liquor, he drove his wife and children out of doors into a snow storm. Before they succeeded in reaching an Indian shelter, the poor woman, who had used her own garments to protect the children from the biting frost, had both her breasts frozen and never quite recovered from the effects of that dreadful night. When the rebellion broke out, her Indian relatives sought revenge against the farm instructor and shot him to death.

Barney Tremont had an undying hatred of Indians. On one occasion, a young Indian had lost his way in a blizzard, when he saw the light in Tremont's house. He knocked at the door and sought shelter. When Tremont saw that he was an Indian, he shut the door in his face and the Indian had his feet frozen. There is little doubt that the friends and relatives of this unfortunate young man also took advantage of the turmoil to avenge themselves upon the rancher. He was shot down while greasing his wagon preparatory to making his way to Battleford.[64]

Not all farm instructors, however, were to be disposed of in this way. Frightened for his life, Craig was able to peacefully pass through a group of Cree and continue on unmolested to the safety of the stockade. McKay, also on his way to the barracks, came across the same Stonies who had killed the farm instructors and was helped by them across the Battle River.

On 30 March, the Cree under Poundmaker proceeded to the fort and found the town deserted. They approached the barracks and asked to speak to Indian Agent Rae. From Jefferson's account, it was obvious these Natives were pressuring for more food supplies, but Rae refused to come out to talk with them, seeing them as a monolithic force. Apparently, it was only at this time that Poundmaker heard that the Stonies had killed the two farm instructors and a settler. Here Jefferson suggests that all the unrest of the time might have been avoided had the two farm instructors not been killed, a fact that kept Rae from meeting with the Natives. If he had given them additional supplies, all might have been settled without further incident. Subsequent to their failure to meet the farm instructor, the Natives moved down to the old town along the flats where the houses and stores had been deserted. The only resident of the town not to go to the fort had been the cook at Government House and he was left unmolested. Around this time the judge's house was found aflame, but little is known of who or what was responsible for this. The Natives were involved in some looting but "the principal looting was the work of the white man. As soon as the coast was clear in the morning they came over in detachments and finished what the Indians had begun. They made a clean sweep."[65] Throughout his account, Jefferson does not deny the looting done by the Natives or their threats to other inhabitants of the area, but states this was perpetrated by a small fraction of the total number of Natives. Indeed, his own life was protected by the Cree of Poundmaker's reserve who gave him a haven. Poundmaker had personally assured him that he would be protected, even though the chief told him the Natives would rise again to be led by the light of Crowfoot to the south. Poundmaker still had a dream to return to the old god of the Cree. He was quoted by Jefferson as saying:

> Of old, the Indian trusted in his God and his faith was not in vain. He was fed, clothed and free from sickness. Along came the white man and persuaded the Indian that this God was not able to keep up the care. The Indian took the white man's word and deserted to the new God. Hunger followed and disease and death. Now we have returned to the God we know; the buffalo will come back, and the Indian will live the life that God intended him to live.[66]

Jefferson makes important distinctions in the make-up of those who were gathering at Battleford around Poundmaker. The wealthier Métis from Bresaylor were reluctant to join and preferred to protect their land, property and cattle. This was unacceptable to the Cree who did not want some people standing by while they were taking risks that would later benefit everyone else. When the Cree confiscated their cattle, these Métis reluctantly joined them. The Wood Cree of the Moosomin and Kahpitikkoo bands were also less aggressive and rarely engaged in conflict. Unlike the Plains Cree buffalo hunters, the Wood Cree were a more sedentary population and it was easier for missionaries to live among them and convert more individuals to Christianity.[67] Poundmaker thus could not form an alliance with Moosomin. But while Poundmaker did gather a large force, he was not involved in any looting at Battleford. In fact, the only things taken were the food supplies and other goods from the vacated stores on their reserves: "His dignity prevented him from engaging in scrimmages for loot, and his position as head man could not be taken advantage of to acquire even necessaries."[68] Jefferson's account, which was written as he moved with Poundmaker's camp, also throws an interesting light on the fate of Frank Smart. Jefferson indicates that the killing was an isolated incident by two Natives who, while scouting, fired at two men they came upon. These Cree did not have the approval of Poundmaker nor were they acting on any plans the chief might have had. Instead, it appears they were rather embarrassed by what had happened:

> The Indians did not venture up to inspect the fallen man but came home the shortest way, rather awed by their successful audacity. The event was not paraded at all, owing, I believe to fear of the consequences when the accounting should be made. After things had quietened down, the man who did the killing ran off across the Line, disbelieving that the white man would call this killing different from ordinary murder.[69]

Jefferson was also present when Riel's emissaries asked Poundmaker to help the Métis of Batoche, who were anticipating defeat should the Natives not assist them. Though Poundmaker listened politely, he took no action. He heard of the plan to cut off the railway lines, to attack the NWMP, and to move towards Prince Albert taking all the posts along the way. This, Poundmaker was told, would be accompanied by the rising of the Blackfoot led by Crowfoot to the south. Poundmaker was unimpressed. He sharply gave instructions to his Natives to undertake frequent scouting missions, to watch the roads and not waste ammunition. On a number of occasions these Natives came under fire. One Cree and one Nez Percé were killed by snipers. The threat to those who thought they were besieged was indeed imagined. The Natives had as much to fear as the whites:

> During the whole of the outbreak, there was no organised attempt at besieging the barracks; indeed there were not enough Indians to do it. Such men as thought fit prowled round the town at night, but at a safe distance. In the daytime when they would appear on the hills on the south side of the river, they were saluted with bullets from watchers on the other side and at night they were too few to do any harm. Great consternation prevailed in the white camp but it arose altogether from the preconceived idea of Indian warfare and the barbarities that accompanied it. The Indians were not sufficiently worked up to attempt offensive measures, especially against a force as great if not greater than their own. They did not expect to have any fighting of any account to do: Riel and his Halfbreeds had undertaken that part of the business — theirs but to create a diversion. Just as little did they anticipate an attack.[70]

But an attack is what they got as they camped at Cut Knife Hill. From Jefferson's perspective, the Cree were vulnerable. They were fortunate to have had some warning of Otter's attack. Jefferson thought that Otter might have overwhelmed Poundmaker in spite of the warning had he pushed his first initiative further. As it was, the Cree, Stonies and two Nez Percé were able to occupy the strategic positions around the hill and stall Otter's column. As the battle wore on

Minnie Laurie
(Mrs. Gauvreau)

Effie Laurie
(Mrs. Storer)

The daughters of P.G. Laurie, publisher of the Saskatchewan Herald. *Both were in the stockaded fort during the fighting. Effie Storer wrote a book-length manuscript about her life, with one chapter describing her life at the fort during the "siege"* (Fort Battleford NHP Library).

Hayter Reed, 1894 (Notman Photographic Archives, no. 106454-BII, McCord Museum of McGill University, Montreal).

Hayter Reed was an Indian Agent in the Battleford area from 1881-1884. He was made Assistant Indian Commissioner in 1884 and was Commissioner of Indian Affairs from 1893-1897. He was also an appointed member of the North-West Territorial Council. Reed was known to the Cree, Saulteaux and Assiniboine of the Battleford area as "Iron Heart." Read advocated that the pass system remain in effect after 1885 and also advocated extremely repressive measures be implemented in the aftermath of 1885, even though very few Battleford reserve residents participated in the fighting. He demanded strict adherence to the rules, refusing to entertain evidence of starvation on the reserves. He called the First Nations People of the Battleford area "the scum of the plains."

P.G. Laurie (Fort Battleford NHP Library).

Patrick Gammie Laurie was anxious to attract white settlers to the Battleford area and asked that the strictest punishment be meted out to the local Cree to ensure that the West would be safe for the kind of settlers he wanted to encourage. Laurie promoted the settlement of white, Protestant, English-speaking people and held the local Cree in disdain.

P.G. Laurie and the *Saskatchewan Herald* office in 1878 (Fort Battleford NHP Library).
Laurie promoted middle-class Victorian values even though he lived in very humble circumstances himself.

Robert Jefferson (Fort Battleford NHP Library).

Robert Jefferson, the farm instructor on the Poundmaker Reserve, was an important eyewitness to Cree actions during the events of 1885. He documented the reluctance of the Cree to participate in the fighting. In spite of his evidence, the Cree leadership was removed by imprisonment while eight others were hanged. Jefferson, who was liked by the Cree, did not feel threatened by them; the Cree did kill a number of farm instructors who mistreated them.

Colonel William M. Herchmer, NWMP, reclining in chair, Battleford, 1885, photo by Lieutenant Wadmore of the Infantry School Corps (Glenbow Archives, NA-1353-18).

Superintendent William Herchmer was commanding officer at Battleford during the crucial years 1880-84 at which time the main purpose of the police was keeping the Cree in the Battleford area under surveillance and control. The sketch here depicts him as a Victorian gentleman enjoying his leisure time. It was a matter of great prestige to be a member of the force and some men gave up professional jobs to enlist, even though the pay and working conditions were poor.

Inspector James Walker, 1876-80 (Fort Battleford NHP Library).
James Walker was the first commanding officer at Battleford. He oversaw the building of the fort in 1876 and in the same year he assisted Commissioner Alexander Morris at the signing of Treaty 6 at Forts Pitt and Carlton. Like other policemen from eastern Canada, he settled in the West following his service. Walker was involved in ranching and established a successful sawmill and lumber company in Calgary. He became the first civilian justice in the North-West Territories.

General Frederick D. Middleton (National Archives of Canada, PA-12197).
Sir Frederick Middleton in 1886 in the full dress uniform of a major general of the British Army. He is wearing the insignia of the Order of Saint Michael and Saint George, with the Order of Bath and the Knighthood he was awarded for his services during 1885 in the Canadian North-West, as well as campaign medals for New Zealand, the Great Mutiny in India, and the newly issued North-West Canada medal. After the fall of Batoche, Middleton moved to Battleford, which was his base for the pursuit of Big Bear.

W.D. Otter (National Archives of Canada, C-14533).
Colonel William Otter was one of the only Canadian officers serving under Major General Middleton (who preferred British officers). Otter advanced against Poundmaker's Cree contrary to the wishes of Middleton. His column of 358 men was soundly defeated in the battle and he was fortunate the Cree did not pursue him or he would have suffered heavy losses.

North-West Territories Legislative Assembly, 1886 (Manitoba Archives, 237). 1. Edgar Dewdney, 2. Judge Rouleau, 3. Judge Richardson, 4. John G. Turiff, 5. Hayter Reed, 6. H.S. Cayley, 7. Robert Crawford, 8. James Ross, 9. David F. Jelly, 10. Major Irvine, 11. J.C. Secord, 12. J.D. Lauder, 13. Senator Perley, 14. Charles Marshallsay, 15. Owen E. Hughes, 16. Sam Cunningham, 17. A.E. Forget, 19. Jimmie McAra, X. Lord Boyle.

David Laird (Manitoba Archives, N10451).
David Laird was appointed Lieutenant Governor of the North-West Territories in 1876. He served as Minister of the Interior from 1873-76 and was a Treaty Commissioner for Treaty 7. The First Nations of Treaty 7 claimed shortly after they negotiated the treaty that Laird did not include all of their demands in the written treaty. They also charged that he had no intention of living up to the promises made to them.

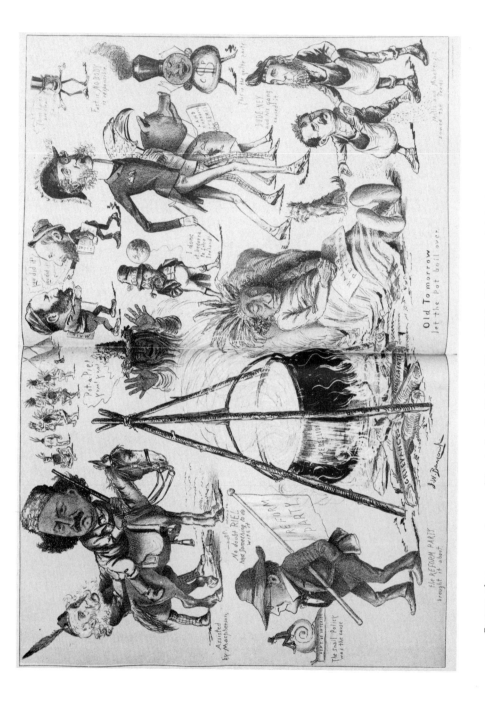

Cartoon of government personalities during the Riel Rebellion, 1885, by J.W. Bengough (Glenbow Archives, NA-1480-22).

Cartoon of the indecision of Prime Minister Macdonald concerning Riel's fate, 31 October 1885, by J.W. Bengough (Glenbow Archives, NA-3012-13).

JUSTICE STILL UNSATISFIED.

Cartoon after Riel's death, 21 November 1885, by J.W. Bengough (Glenbow Archives, NA-3012-15). Captioned: "*Sir John* - Well, madam, Riel is gone; I hope you are quite satisfied. *Justice* - Not quite; you have hanged the EFFECT of the Rebellion; now I want to find and punish the CAUSE."

EN ROUTE.

[With Apologies to the Artist of the War News.

Cartoon depicting load of public debt of Dominion of Canada, 4 July 1885, by J.W. Bengough (Glenbow Archives, NA-3012-6).

A comparison of Indian policies of the United States and Canada, by Henri Julien, 22 July 1876 (Glenbow Archives, NA-1406-165).

Canadians have always congratulated themselves on having a more humane policy than that of the Americans and certainly they did not hunt down the tribes that did not move onto reserves. But less honourable was the failure to live up to the promises so solemnly made at the treaty negotiations.

in this territory familiar to them, they almost succeeded in encircling Otter's men. The field force retreated in time to avoid this. There might have been a huge disaster, even a massacre, had these tired soldiers in retreat been followed as they withdrew. Some Natives were anxious to pursue them but,

> There was no pursuit. A number of Indians had mounted and were about to start after the retreating soldiers, but Poundmaker would not permit it. He said that to defend themselves and their wives and children was good, but that he did not approve of taking the offensive. They had beaten their enemy off; let that content them. So there was no pursuit. Poundmaker had no hope of the Rebellion succeeding.[71]

The Natives had been severely frightened by the attack and they moved their camp frequently in the intervening days, constantly on the alert. They asked Jefferson what they might expect when all the fighting was over, as they were afraid they would all be massacred. But Jefferson tried to reassure them that this would not happen:

> I said that those who had committed the murders would be hanged and the heads of the movement put in prison, but that the mass of the people would be sent back on to their Reserves and things go on as before.[72]

This was indeed to be the case.

Jefferson was then sent by Poundmaker to Middleton to find out how peace could be restored. Middleton demanded an unconditional surrender. The Natives' response was cautious as this answer did not state how they would be treated. From recent experience they had found they could not trust the whites. Eventually they came to realize there was no choice and reluctantly they rode to Battleford. Middleton and Poundmaker met:

> Poundmaker rose and came forward to accost the General, holding out his hand but Middleton waved aside the proffered salute saying that he did not shake hands with rebels. The Indian gathered his blanket around him and resumed his seat, while Middleton proceeded to reprimand him for taking up arms and murdering innocent settlers. The chief replied that he had murdered nobody; that he had defended himself when attacked, which he thought he was entitled to do; but they now came to give themselves up; the General had them in his hands and could work his will on them. All that the Indians asked was that the women and children might go unharmed. When the chief got through, the two Stoney murderers came forward one by one and confessed their guilt, making some sort of excuses for themselves. The General ordered these into custody, along with Poundmaker and a few others and told the rest to go back to their Reserves.[73]

On the reserves their movements were restricted; they could not leave without passes issued by the government. The Cree had lost almost everything, but the department responsible did little to alleviate their situation. Without horses and wagons and restricted by the pass system, they were unable to sell wood in town, which they had done for so many years. Treaty money was also suspended for a number of years. The Indian Department took the view that the Natives had broken the treaty and would have to pay a heavy price for this defiance.

A Necessary Revision

In an article by John Tobias, "Canada's Subjugation of the Plains Cree," a case is made for a systematic policy engineered by Lieutenant Governor Dewdney to control the Cree. Tobias traces the determined refusal by Dewdney and the

Department of Indian Affairs to deal with the Natives openly and equally as signatories of the treaties. Instead, they aimed to undermine the agreements and Cree leaders whenever possible. In their weakened position, the Natives would not pose a threat to settlement and could no longer agitate from a strong position for government fulfillment of its treaty obligations. Tobias also suggests that Dewdney saw the events of 1885 as an opportunity to take action against the Cree. Dewdney chose to interpret the acts of the Natives as rebellion despite strong evidence to the contrary. It was Dewdney, not Middleton, who was most anxious that Otter march against the Cree encamped at Cut Knife Hill:

> The Cree acts of violence in March 1885 were the excuse Dewdney needed to justify the use of troops against them. He maintained that Battleford, Fort Pitt, and Duck Lake Cree were part of the Riel Rebellion. Privately, Dewdney reported to Ottawa that he saw the events at Battleford and Frog Lake as the acts of a desperate, starving people and unrelated to what the Metis were doing. In fact, Dewdney had sought in late March to open negotiations with the Battleford Cree, but Rae refused to meet the Cree leaders.[74]

Dewdney was now able to neutralize the strongest of the Cree leaders. Red Pheasant and Little Pine had died during the spring of 1885, Piapot had been intimidated into remaining on his reserve, and the two most powerful remaining leaders of the Cree were in prison. In this weakened state, the Cree were no longer a threat. Dewdney would have had the unwavering support of Laurie for his action:

> Dewdney had deprived the Cree of their principal leaders and of their autonomy. He used the military to disarm and impoverish the Cree by confiscating their horses and carts; he increased the size of the Mounted Police force, and used the police to arrest Cree leaders who protested against his policies; he broke up Cree bands, deposed Cree leaders, and forbade any Indian to be off his reserve without permission from the Indian Agent.[75]

The traditional view that the Métis and Cree were acting together must be reconsidered. Those historians who put forward this view have relied too heavily on government sources and explanations. They chose to use those reminiscences that supported their view and rejected the ones that did not. There is no doubt that facts arranged in a certain way support the belief that the Natives were on the warpath. Special sympathy must be extended to those who felt besieged within the stockade. With only a few exceptions, the killings perpetrated by the Cree were selective. Their targets were those they felt had done them injustice. The example of Robert Jefferson is interesting in this regard. While other farm instructors who withheld supplies from the Natives were shot, Jefferson, who dealt more equitably with the Cree, was spared.

SIX

Years of Waiting: 1885-1897

We planted potatoes, cut fence poles, put up hay and kept bothering the Instructor for food. Then wheat and barley was given to us to sow. The potatoes and wheat froze the first time. Then the potatoes were taken to the Instructor's cellar for winter.

Fine Day

Controlling the Natives

According to the standard histories, little appears to have changed in the Fort Battleford area after the conflict of 1885. One official police history mentioned that in 1886 "tranquility had prevailed on all Native lands throughout the summer, although about 60 Indians left Poundmaker's reserve and moved to the vicinity of Lake Manitou, some distance to the west."[1] There was no doubt that the police in their military capacity were in control, but beneath this official calm there were concerns about the Natives, and there was a definite move towards asserting new control over them. A redistribution of the forces in the West showed that the police still feared potential violence from the Native population. Division "C" was sent to Battleford in 1885 to bolster the strength of the fort already occupied by Division "K". There was strict surveillance of the Cree, though on record the police were careful not to convey any indication that they could not handle the situation; such an impression would, it was thought, damage settlement potential. There were specific measures taken to prevent the development of any circumstances that might erupt into violence. What was especially significant was the increased assistance of the police for those working with government programs. Their presence was a constant reminder to the Natives that they were there to ensure the success of the government's Native policy:

> Every month, sometimes under most trying and severe weather conditions, patrols visited the surrounding Indian reserves, making careful enquiries as to the general state of the Indians, the nature of their employment, and manifesting to them that they were under the continual watchfulness of the Force. Every possible assistance was given to the Indian Department in this respect, including the establishment of an outpost at Onion Lake 12 miles north-west of Fort Pitt, and another at the settlement of Bresaylor between the Saskatchewan and Battle Rivers, about 24 miles west of Battleford.[2]

Concern for the problems of the plains tribes was evident in the correspondence and reports of the NWMP and government officials up to the mid-1880s. Even if some of the government programs were poorly conceived and informed by an ideology that portrayed the Aboriginal as inferior, there was nevertheless a discernible note of solicitude in the handling of "Indian Affairs" by most government agents. This changed after 1885. By that time, much of the good will that had been built up, especially by the NWMP with the Native populations on the plains, was spent. Added to this was the fact that much of the vocal Aboriginal leadership was gone. Policies that lay dormant or unenforced while Aboriginal leaders protested could now be raised again by government officials to allow them to work more forcefully to remove the "Indian problem." The industrial schools for Native children were used to "aggressively assimilate" the Natives, and the implementation and enforcement of policies related to reserve life and certain provisions of the Indian Act kept their movement and activity under strict control. Even the agricultural policies the Natives had asked for were not developed in a manner compatible with their culture. When Natives asked for changes they were not listened to.

These policies and their enforcement were issues that were increasingly the cause of conflict. The Mounties, now more often than before, had to enforce laws and regulations that were unpopular among the Native population. Along with the politicians administering the policies, the NWMP were less concerned about protecting and assisting the Natives, and seemed to grow more insensitive to their circumstances.

To date, scholars have assumed that the problems of Native administration vanished after the treaties put them on reserves. Much remains to be written about the late 1880s and 1890s.[3] Indeed, the era of 1885-1914 may be a most revealing one for the history of the Canadian Native. Originally the colonizers of the Canadian West envisioned an evolution of Native policy from protection of the Native population, to "civilization" and ultimately to assimilation. Unfortunately, and somewhat paradoxically, the aims and practices were not synchronized and often could not be reconciled. What happened worked against the ideals that lay behind this policy.[4]

The government, hoping to "civilize" Canadian Natives, decided to ban various forms of Native cultural celebration, including the Potlatch, Sun Dance and similar ceremonies. Legislators believed these practices encouraged pagan beliefs that were incompatible with the civilizing process, as well as being contrary to individual initiative and to the value of private property that Euro-Canadians were so actively promoting. To make agriculturalists out of the Natives was the ultimate aim, and many of the regulations of the 1876 Indian Act reflected this. But government officials also wanted to control them. They were prohibited from travelling to sell their produce, discouraged from hunting and fishing by game laws enacted throughout the West, and restricted by pass laws that prevented their free movement. Furthermore, Aboriginal children were encouraged to forsake their parents' way of life. Though these regulations and programs were begun before 1885, they were accelerated afterwards to speed up the process of civilization.

Thus, while economic change received lip service, the government also promoted cultural changes that were to be implemented in Native communities. One of these was the introduction of industrial schools in the mid-1880s. As the result of an 1879 report prepared by Nicholas Flood Davin, MP for Assiniboia West, three industrial schools were established in 1883. The Natives in the numbered treaties had asked for schools, and a number of day schools connected to missions had been set up. The industrial schools recommended in Davin's report represented a new initiative called "aggressive civilization." The report was comprehensive, including not only aspects of education but land subdivision, cultural issues and assimilation as well.

The industrial schools were to be administered by the churches. Children were to be separated from their parents. The philosophy behind the program was based on the 1869 American model outlined in the preamble of the report. Davin cited American examples where the program had been considered successful. Some Natives were apparently more suited for education because they had physical similarities to Europeans. Such was the case for the Cherokees, Chickasaws, Choctaws, Creeks and Seminoles.[5] There were also examples of Natives who were, in Davin's estimation, as yet "undeveloped":

> The Indian character, about which some persons find such a mystery, is not difficult to understand. The Indian is sometimes spoken of as a child, but he is very far from being a child. The race is in its childhood... The Indian is a man with traditions of his own, which make civilization a puzzle of despair. He has the suspicion, distrust, fault-finding tendency, the insincerity and flattery, produced in all subject races. He is crafty, but conscious how weak his craft is when opposed to the superior cunning of the white man. Not to speak of him — even some of the half-breeds of high intelligence are incapable of embracing the idea of a nation — of a national type of man — in which it should be their ambition to be merged and lost. Yet he realizes he must disappear, and realizing this, and unable to associate himself with the larger and nobler idea, the motive power which inspired a Pontiac and a Tecumseh, is absent. The Indian's stolidity is in part assumed, in part a stupor produced by external novel and distasteful conditions, and in both respects has been manifested in white races at periods of helplessness and ignorance, of subjection to, and daily contact with, the power and superior skill and refinement of more advanced races, or even more advanced branches of the same race.[6]

In Davin's eyes, hope for the Natives of the future was with their children. Since the influence of the chief was so strong on the reserve, Davin suggested that education in white settlements away from their parents and the chief be made available to Native children. He then listed thirteen recommendations. In one of these items, Davin included not only the positive elements of the program, but also what was to be criticized and exorcized from Aboriginal culture:

> The importance of denominational schools at the outset for the Indians must be obvious. One of the earliest things an attempt to civilize them does, is to take away their simple Indian mythology, the central idea of which, to wit, a perfect spirit, can hardly be improved on. The Indians have their own ideas of right and wrong, of "good" Indians and "bad" Indians, and to disturb this faith, without supplying a better, would be a curious process to enlist the sanction of civilized races whose whole civilization, like all civilizations with which we are acquainted, is based on religion. A civilized sceptic, breathing, though he does, an atmosphere charged with Christian ideas, and getting strength unconsciously therefrom, is nevertheless, unless in instances of rare intellectual vigour, apt to be a man without ethical backbone. But a savage sceptic would be open to civilizing influences and moral control only through desires, which, in the midst of enlightenment, constantly break out into the worst features of barbarism.[7]

The ultimate goal of Davin's report was to establish three industrial schools in western Canada. This area had the greatest urgency since it was to be settled by immigrants from eastern Canada, Europe and the United States. The education of Aboriginal children would specifically attempt to achieve the broader moral philosophy as delineated by Davin:

> in addition to the elements of an English education, the boys are instructed in cattle-raising and agriculture, the girls in sewing, bread making, and other employments suitable for a farmer's wife. In the case of the boys, agriculture is principally aimed at cattleraising requiring but few hands.[8]

The attempt to civilize and assimilate Natives by concentrating on educating their children ended in failure. This policy had been another attempt to destroy their tribal system and replace it with one based on individual initiative and private property. There were great fears among Native parents over what was happening to their children in the schools, especially when epidemics swept through and claimed many young lives. Eventually, as with other government programs that professed to assist the Native population, industrial schools were viewed by the Natives as a destructive force. The parents grew suspicious of them and agitated to have them discontinued. Eventually they disappeared:

> The government reports demonstrate most emphatically that the Cree did not want to have their children apprenticed in "civilization." Indian parents complained that although they may have wanted their children to learn to read and write, they did not want them to work as cheap or forced labour for the school administrators under the guise of "instruction in trades." Cree men probably considered instruction in or employment at year-round, individual, free-enterprise farming as tedious, womanish, and selfish — even though they did seem to enjoy those aspects of industrial-school training which were not too much at variance with traditional Indian patterns of life, such as plentiful housework for girls, and musical instruments and fancy uniforms for boys in the brass band.[9]

What happened after 1885 was to speed up the process of "civilization," with emphasis on "educating" Native children. The events of 1885 were a watershed that brought more all-encompassing and stringent regulations. Had the government been able to find fault with the policies that had produced such disastrous results in agriculture or realized that the Cree around Battleford were not involved with Riel and the Métis, it might have been able to pursue new directions in working with the Natives to solve problems on the frontier. In this regard it could have followed the advice of the concerned farm instructors and listened to the Natives themselves, who had already shown a willingness to move to an economic livelihood more accommodating to the European settlers, but instead the government seemed intent on continuing to attack and undermine Native culture and organization, encouraging the disintegration of tribal and band life rather than concentrating on agricultural development. While the government's motives were allegedly economic revitalization, the preferred result appeared to be the hope that a whole way of life would simply disappear as an obstacle to settlement. The economic basis of Native society was to be agriculture, but as with other programs proposed by government, the main goal was undermined by other actions.

What was particularly difficult and discouraging for the Natives, especially of the Battleford area, was that they knew what their Indian agent was like. In 1881, Hayter Reed, then working as a land guide, took the job of agent for the Battleford area. He soon developed a reputation as an inflexible and authoritarian man. He accepted his new job with distasteful zeal. He had at one time described the Natives as "the scum of the plains," and his "vision" of their future in the West was myopic and without sympathy for their point of view. Reed had little aptitude for the job and the skills he brought to the position "were those of a military man — of the drill instructor and the officer; he was a man accustomed to giving commands and having them obeyed without question."[10] He was without qualities of tolerance and compromise, had no patience for those who questioned the system, and would not listen to any alternatives to rules he laid down. Reed even went so far as to prohibit Natives from presenting their views at the annual treaty payment, which previously had been the custom.[11] Even some of the local farm instructors were critical of his rigid attitude and the consequences of his dogmatism. His own position was paternalistic in the extreme. As he wrote:

> As well might the Christian or civilized parent allow his children to follow uncurbed the dictates of their blind promptings of their own unregenerate human nature and grow up outcasts of society, as leave an ignorant savage to determine his own course for himself.[12]

Reed was of the opinion that Native poverty on the reserves was not the result of broken treaty promises or shortages of supplies, implements and oxen. He was convinced that the Natives' problems grew out of their propensity to avoid work at all costs. Reed's severe program and inflexible beliefs earned him the nickname "Iron Heart" from those forced to work for him.

It was unfortunate that by the mid-1880s conditions were ripe for a man like Reed to assume his position and disseminate with impunity the beliefs he held. There were few to criticize the manner in which he exercised power. Certainly Lieutenant Governor Dewdney and others approved of his actions, though they might have found fault with the exuberance and zeal he used to pursue his goals. They may even have been pleased that someone other than themselves would take the approach that Reed was taking. What was most unfortunate was that Reed had such influence. For the Natives, he was in the wrong place at the wrong time:

> Reed advocated extremely repressive measures in the aftermath of 1885. His memorandum relative to the future management of the Indians ... revealed a wrathful, vengeful anger and Dewdney found parts of it intemperate. The memo nonetheless defined the basic lines along which Reed would guide Indian policy as he acquired power and influence in the late 1880s and the 1890s. Certain measures that were presented in 1885 as punitive, temporary, and for selected bands only became permanent and universal.[13]

Reed's approach did not go without criticism. Malcolm Colin Cameron, MP for Huron West, launched a scathing attack on the government for its Native policy. Besides problems of corrupt administration, he claimed that the government's commitments with the Natives had been "shamefully, openly, persistently and systematically broken by this Government."[14] Unfortunately, Cameron was an opposition backbencher and his criticism was categorically denied; indeed, the government took great pains to counter his claims. In this atmosphere there was little chance for anyone to entertain alternative solutions and methods for problems on the western Canadian reserves. The Battleford newspaperman, P.G. Laurie, would have agreed with the stringent measures advocated and implemented by Hayter Reed. Though he may not have had any impact on the actual definition of the policies and their enforcement, he was certain not to criticize them. If Laurie can be seen as a spokesman for the attitude of the local white community, it is fair to assume that it mattered little to him what happened to the Natives after 1885. Laurie's editorials were clear and vengeful. Punishment, not education in agricultural practices, became his remedy.

Laurie's attitude toward the defeated Cree and Métis was harsh and vindictive. The winter of 1885 had been a hard one and even Laurie admitted before the outbreak of violence that provisions for the Natives had been inadequate. Many Cree had not survived the winter because of lack of food and poor shelter, and some were barely able to subsist on what they had. Though it appears that punishment of the "rebels" was the sentiment of the majority of the population in the territories, Laurie became excessively vengeful, especially when compared to the more balanced analysis of Nicholas Flood Davin, now editor of the *Regina Leader*. Davin, like Laurie, favoured the hanging of Riel and spoke out against French Canadians who demanded amnesty:

> That he had some French blood in his veins [Davin asked]. Is this an excuse? Has it come to this in Canada that any criminal has only to prove himself French and tables of law are to be broken at the bidding of thoughtlessness and justice to be flung prone on the street? But what have the French Canadians to do with Riel any more than the Irish or the Swedes? One should think it is the half-breeds and the whites in the North-West who are most concerned. Do we hear the half-breeds discontented with his sentence? No indeed, they understand Louis Riel too well.[15]

But though he agreed with Laurie on the sentence for Riel, Davin's condemnation was less severe. They also disagreed over the punishment to be handed out to the other "rebels." For example, their reactions to the early release of Poundmaker differed considerably. Davin, an admirer of Poundmaker — "The Great Chief" — was pleased that he was released early from prison for good conduct, while Laurie denounced it as unjustifiable because of the suffering Poundmaker had wrought. Laurie also sarcastically commented on Big Bear's sentencing even though his guilt in the rebellion was at least questionable: "Big Bear was found guilty with a recommendation for mercy. He gets three years board at Stony Mountain, unless his admirers can induce the government in the meantime to transfer him to a first class hotel in Winnipeg."[16]

Laurie's uncompromising position towards the "rebels" must be understood in relation to the events of the rebellion at Fort Battleford while it was "besieged" by the Natives. His greatest concern still was to woo settlers to Battleford, while Davin, a resident of the capital, was less concerned with the consequences of leniency towards the Natives. Davin wanted Riel executed for two reasons: as a western lawyer, he did not want to see a western decision overturned by an eastern court; as a Conservative, he was bound to stand up for and defend the Conservative cause. Laurie, closer to the fighting during the rebellion, had more practical, existential reasons for demanding stiff sentencing. Justice had to be done for the protection of the residents and to ensure that settlement could resume. In the Battleford area the measures imposed by Reed on the Native population would be fully and officially sanctioned.

Monitoring Measures

Agriculture as an alternative economic base for Aboriginal society was not only suggested by a government anxious to sign treaties with the Natives, but was a means of survival that the Natives were eager and willing to adopt. Agriculture as practiced by the Europeans was an integral part of their way of life, one which they wanted the Natives to adopt. Prior to settlement and the treaties, there was also pressure from Christian missionaries urging the Natives to take up sedentary farming practices. It was seen as one way to stop the Natives from searching for food and "roaming" — which made it difficult for the missionaries to know their whereabouts — and it was also hoped that a more sedentary existence would give them a better appreciation for private property. This in turn would promote economic individualism, thrift, industry and punctuality. The

missionaries supported policies based on these ideas and were anxious to introduce measures to speed up the advancement of civilization, especially if it meant
reaching the assimilation phase.

The Department of Indian Affairs had not embarked upon any major initiatives since the doomed model farm experiment of 1879, but after 1885 programs
under the direction of Hayter Reed were introduced to control the distribution of
produce, not to improve the farming practices of the Natives. The general goal
was to undermine and destroy the Natives' band and tribal systems. This was
achieved by discouraging their religious, educational and traditional social activities, dismantling communal ceremonies like the Sun Dance, disposing of the Aboriginal leaders, and making the people take separate farm lands.

What changed in particular was the introduction of rigid supervision of all
Native movement. In response to fears that another uprising might occur, the
number of agencies and personnel was increased in order to supervise the so-
called agricultural projects. The pass system was introduced to keep the Natives
on their reserves during seasons when agricultural activity was highest. In fact, it
managed to control all Natives whether they were agriculturalists or not. They
were not allowed off the reserves without a pass signed by their Indian agent,
which had to state the reason for their departure and length of absence.

Complementing the pass system was the enforcement of a permit system, included in the Indian Act of 1876, for selling agricultural produce on reserves. It
forbade Natives to sell, barter, exchange or give away their crops or livestock
without first having secured a permit from their agent. As demonstrated among
the Dakota on the Oak River Reserve, the system discouraged their profit motive
in agriculture.[17] Instead of being able to sell their own produce and be directly re-
warded for their labours, they were obliged to obtain a permit for selling purposes. And when their goods were sold, the money was not paid directly to the
producer, but rather to the Indian Department. Again, the government's desire to
establish a sense of private initiative among the Dakota was sabotaged by its own
contradictory policy. Any debt owed by the Dakota selling the produce was settled immediately by the Indian agent without consulting the seller, with the remainder then given to the Natives. Therefore, they could not take out loans to
obtain machinery or expand operations by this system. Buyers who broke these
regulations were subject to fines, so bypassing the system was impossible. There
were many complaints and signed petitions from Dakota protesting these systems of control, but all were to no avail. Increasingly, the Dakota saw little reason
to farm their own land due to these frustrating restrictions. It eventually became
less bothersome and more profitable not to farm, but rather to lease the land to
others; then the income from these leases went directly to the Dakota.

By the late 1880s, the government initiated yet another policy to break the
tribal traditions of the Natives and to further direct them into the concept of individual initiative. This was the policy of allotting lands on reserves in severalty. It
was designed to give each family forty acres and provide it with certain rights for
that specific piece of land. It was hoped this would break up the practice of
working the land communally and sharing the profits collectively, as well as
facilitating assimilation between the races and eventually allowing intermingling
through settlement of Natives and whites side-by-side. By the 1900s, this policy
of severalty began to achieve its goals as subdivision surveys of the land resulted
in the surrender of reserve property.

The peasant farm policy of the 1880s and 1890s had important effects on Native agriculture as well. It was based on the belief that the Native would not need to be involved in agriculture beyond a subsistence level for himself and his family. Two acres was considered enough to supply all the food that one family would need each year. No provision was made for those who wanted to be involved in the market economy, even though that was precisely what the Natives desired in the early years. Instead, the Department of Indian Affairs insisted that the Natives work with the most labour-intensive tools: the cradle, sickle, flail, hoe and rake. The department seemed more concerned with keeping the Natives under control than with assisting them fully to develop their skills as agriculturalists. It is clear from the most recent research and evidence contained in primary documents that the Natives were anxious to work for inclusion in the market economy. Those early successes in agriculture unfortunately were left unnurtured, as most government policies seemed to exist to snuff out Aboriginal participation in the western Canadian "Eden." Indeed, as the acres broken in the period up to 1896 shows, there was decline rather than progress in the Battleford agency.

Government Policy

Among the more well-known complaints against government policy of the time towards the Natives was a speech made in the House of Commons in 1885 by Malcolm Colin Cameron. It took the form of a comprehensive attack on the past practices of the Indian Department and it apparently hit a nerve for, in 1886, the government published a response entitled, "The Facts Respecting Indian Administration in the North-West."[18] Cameron began his critique by referring to those who felt the Natives had no reason for rebelling against the government. He claimed that no statement "could be more at variance with the report of the Department of Indian Affairs."[19] He alleged treaty promises were broken, dishonesty and corruption existed, and that those men who were unfit and unsuitable to work with Natives were given precisely such positions. Of Commissioner Dewdney, Cameron said, "He has been charged, and correctly charged, with being domineering, arrogant, tyrannical, unfair, untruthful in his dealings with the Natives."[20] Cameron quoted local papers in support of his contention. One of these excerpts was from Lawrence Clarke, a member of the North-West Council:

> Brutal ruffians were appointed as farm instructors over the Indians, who maltreated the poor people in the most brutal manner, answering them with kicks and blows, accompanied by showers of profanity and disgusting epithets; of the farm instructors killed by the Indians two were universally known to be brutal wretches such as I have mentioned, and the priests lost their lives in attempting to save them from the pent-up wrath of the savages.[21]

According to clergymen who had lived in the North-West, the problem was with the officials in charge of Aboriginal farming:

> At the Presbytery meeting at Brandon, Manitoba, Rev. Mr. Cameron, who spent many years among the Indians about Battleford, contended that Indian uprising was in great measure due to the character of the instructors and agents appointed by the Government. If the Government officials had been the right kind of men the uprising would never have taken place. In many cases their treatment of the Indians was calculated to have the most injurious effect — some of them treating the Indians like dogs — never speaking to them without an oath, and paying no regard whatever to their word.[22]

Among specific complaints presented by Cameron were unfulfilled treaty promises. One of these was from Poundmaker: "We entreat Your Honor to send him the grist mill with the horse-power you kindly presented him at Cypress. We expected it last summer, but in vain."[23] The litany of incompetence in the North-West was so pronounced that the process of distribution had become chaotic: "In other words, our agents in the North-West, in charge of the Indian Department were so indolent, so lazy, so indifferent and so careless that they delivered to some bands of Indians far more of one class of tool than they required."[24]

Seeds and rations were sometimes sent in a half-rotten state. Instead of fresh meat, rancid meat was frequently supplied. Cameron blamed the continued sickness among the Natives on this supply of poor food: "In other words we fed the Indians on salt pork until they became sick unto death, and then we fed them on fresh beef to restore them to health again."[25] From Battleford, Poundmaker reported that "[t]he flour was inferior and of light weight."[26]

The response from the government attempted to answer comprehensively each of the accusations levelled by Cameron. It countered every charge of corruption and mismanagement with its own statements to the contrary, citing local newspapers, settlers and Indian agents. It then attacked Cameron's motives and suggested he was attempting to incite the Natives to further fighting. There was absolutely no admission of any complicity on the government's part.

Changing Attitudes of the NWMP and the Canadian Government

Why did the unique and relatively harmonious relationship between the NWMP and the Natives change around 1885? The NWMP's earliest dealings with the Natives had been tolerable.[27] By eradicating the whiskey traders such as those involved in the Cypress Hills Massacre, the police had been able to show the Natives they would protect them. They were helpful in establishing the government in the territory and assisting with the making of the treaties. They were also sensitive to the problems on the reserves in the early years as they tried to protect the Natives from dishonest traders and known offenders. The police acted as protectors, not persecutors. This was true of the rank and file as well as the officers. Under Colonel Macleod's tutelage (1876-80), "[t]he Indians were given time to understand white laws ... his enlightened and humane outlook was in sharp contrast to the police and Indian officials' attitudes of insufferable superiority which began to surface after the 1885 Rebellion."[28]

This tradition of fair dealing and tolerance for Native culture was significant for the police, especially since their beliefs and lifestyle were so different from that of the Natives. Though paternalistic, the police showed admiration for the Natives' hunting and survival skills and the way they could live off the land. The NWMP were, in the tradition of the "Tory fragment," to preserve class distinctions yet respect differences:

> The Police officers were determined that the Canadian plains would not have a classless society such as that which they thought existed in the American West. There were many disparaging remarks in their reports about the lack of discipline and social order South of the border; they were determined that it would be different in their jurisdiction.[29]

This Toryism viewed society as a growing organism with functionally related parts that needed to be protected and nourished, not something having differences to be removed. Such had been the American experience that the NWMP resisted, but perhaps more importantly, the cultural baggage the police carried with them onto the plains included preconceived images of the Natives without the experience of living with them. Thus they were free from the negative stereotypes of Native peoples that were common throughout the West: "The Police soon gained a reputation for incorruptibility, partly because they were totally removed from the influence of local prejudice and manipulation."[30]

Slowly, this tolerance and understanding began to erode. As government policies failed, the Natives came into conflict with the law more frequently. The coming of the railway and the early trickle of white settlers were harbingers of the significant change that was to follow. During the era of contact up to 1890, with the exception of 1886 and the arrests made in connection with the resistance, the rate of Native arrests for some years was as low as 3 percent and never higher than 32 percent. The high arrests for Natives in 1879-80 occurred during the years of the worst starvation on reserves.[31] What did increase significantly were the arrests for whites. Overall there were more arrests in the West as railway workers and settlers ran afoul of the law and came into conflict with the Natives. The West became a territory of increased instability as the white population grew. These settlers and workers also brought with them heightened anti-Native sentiments:

> The sad fact is that Western Canada's much lauded history of peaceful and enlightened Indian relations did not rest on the tolerance and understanding of early settlers... If it had not been for the influence of the Mounted Police it is hard to avoid the conclusion that Indian wars would have broken out in the Canadian West.[32]

Reserve life changed both the Natives and the NWMP. Pressures grew on both groups as government policies proved unsuccessful in providing a new economic base for the Natives. Inevitably, as the Natives grew dissatisfied, they presented the police with a potentially volatile situation, and hence the NWMP had to watch them more closely. The police appeared on the reserves more often to arrest offenders. By the mid-1880s the relationship between the Mounties and Natives had changed: "[t]he Policeman was now someone more to fear than to welcome."[33]

The Mounties' perception of the Natives changed as well. At first they still saw some evidence of their image of the "noble savage." Some Natives were still able to live off the buffalo and carry on their life in nature, which was envied by those romantics of Victorian society who had joined the force to see precisely this. The free movement of the Native was something these men had heard about in boyhood stories but, when the Native lost his freedom as he went on the reserve, there was a gradual loss of respect by the police for this once noble savage. Destitute, starving Natives dependent on government assistance no longer fit the image the Mounties had read about. It became harder for these Victorian policemen to respect a people who had virtually become a welfare society:

> No longer is there the breathless sense of adventure that is so striking in the first reports and biographies of the early Police. Gone, too, is the tone of respect for a proud warrior people. The Police after 1885, in most cases were still scrupulously fair in their dealings with the Indians, but their early emphasis on understanding began to be replaced by one of coercion.[34]

The NWMP treatment of the Natives thus became less respectful and more callous. Where their attitude had once been different from that of the government, the two perspectives now became almost indistinguishable. The police gradually became little more than agents of ineffective government policy. This began with harsher sentencing in the mid-1880s and escalated into a more frequent use of force against the Natives toward the end of the century. While ranchers and police wanted contented, well-fed Natives, government policy resulted in dissatisfied, starving Natives whose movements were restricted as their grinding poverty continued unalleviated. In an attempt to get them to work, the government was keeping them in a state of starvation. By the use of the pass system, the government had clearly shown a flagrant disregard for the liberty of the Native:

> [the pass law] … had no validity in law and ran directly counter to the promise made to the Indians that they would still be free to roam the Plains. It came dangerously close to a policy of apartheid.[35]

As 1885 approached, what had once been a relatively harmonious situation had already shown signs of deterioration. The Natives, through the treaties, thought they had negotiated government assistance for a new economic base, but what resulted were greater restrictions in all facets of their life and in areas that had no apparent relation to the agricultural society towards which they were ready to work:

> They were compelled by the Police to stay away from cattle ranges; they were compelled by agents, through the threat of loss of their rations, to work at the occupation of farming for which both they and the land were not suited [sic]; they were compelled to send their children to schools which they did not like; they were compelled to remain on their reserves unless given a pass by the agent. This was the price of harmony in the Canadian West.[36]

The Aboriginal participation in the events of 1885 was not solely responsible for the severe deterioration of NWMP-Native relations; instead, government policies that were massive failures promoted distrust. What seems apparent, however, is that white authorities thought the Natives actually deserved tougher and more callous treatment. The situation may not have been so bad had the Natives been viewed as a force separate from Riel and the Métis, but leaders like Dewdney were able to misrepresent the nature of Native participation in 1885. The rest was history: "The golden era of harmony with the Indians was at an end."[37] As the police lost respect for the Natives, they were also no longer their protectors or as sympathetic to the Native cause.

By the 1890s, government officials were convinced that Aboriginal behaviour justified their policies. They believed the Natives' cultural traditions were to blame, and economic programs were of secondary concern to those determined to change that culture. The agricultural policies were geared not to establishing a vibrant economy on the reserve, but towards breaking up the collectivism of tribal life and replacing it with individualism. The pass system effectively succeeded in making all Natives act according to restrictions usually reserved for the undesirables of society or its criminals. Resistance to the pass laws was nearly impossible since the already starving Natives could be cut off from any rations at all. Assimilation was the goal usually mentioned to justify policies, but what in fact resulted was an accentuation of differences between white and Native. In the eyes of older Natives, industrial schools had attempted to make their own children despise the life and beliefs of their parents. Also, traditional Native authority was further undermined by the humiliation of chiefs who were unable to exercise authority over the more restless and dissatisfied young persons. Yet, there were many official complaints directed to Indian agents and government officials who, heeding the warnings of Hayter Reed, remained unresponsive.

By the 1890s, there was little compassion from the Indian Department for the plight of the plains Natives. White settlement was proceeding rapidly at exactly the same time that the failures of the reserve system became most evident. The irony of assimilation stood starkly against the new facts that were there for all in the North-West to see:

> The sad fact is that by the 1890s there was reason, certainly from the Police perspective, for enforcing a separation between races. By the 1890s the Indians had the choice of capitulating to reservation life or of shirking agricultural duties and living like scavengers off the reserve, finding occasional game and dead cattle, or begging, stealing and killing cattle. The Indian off the reserve had become an automatic threat to the settlers. The Indians in the towns often encountered the worst element of white society and some appeared eager to pick up their habits. Certainly the Indian Department, because of this, thought that its moral responsibility to segregate Indians transcended treaty obligations.[38]

The decade of the 1880s saw "the human rights of the Indians, as well as the treaty promises, sacrificed in deference to the success of the National Policy."[39] Yet, from 1885-95, there was little violence from reserve Natives who had resigned themselves to the tragedy that had evolved. When that peace was broken, the violence came with full force against the Natives rather than from them.

The Almighty Voice Incident

The deteriorating relations between the Natives, the government and the NWMP culminated in an incident in 1897 that involved a Cree by the name of Almighty Voice.

The incident began when Almighty Voice killed a cow, for Natives were not allowed to sell or kill cattle without the permission of their agents. For this act, he was arrested by the NWMP and held in jail at Duck Lake. He subsequently escaped when, as the story goes, he was told he would hang for the offense. Over the next two years he killed five policemen as he tried to elude arrest. He had vowed he would never give himself up and would rather die than fall into the hands of the Mounties. Almighty Voice was pursued by 200 policemen who, having located him, bombarded his hideout with 9-pound guns until he was killed.

There are a number of reports describing this incident contained in NWMP and government records. Newspapers of the time reported the journalistic facts but, as with other situations concerning Native history, the fuller portrait is not widely known. Most of these histories focus primarily on the facts that begin with the killing of the cow. Thus the apparent criminal act is the main point and the aftermath justifies the actions of the police. In this sense the story is dramatic and ends with the Mounties getting their man: a story of resolution. The story, however, becomes more realistic, if less dramatic, if it takes its starting point further back in time. Then it is placed in perspective against the problems facing not only Almighty Voice, but also many other Natives. What makes the incident stand out is the way the police handled the situation. It also shows how the Natives' behaviour toward the police had changed. They no longer had the same regard for the NWMP and were much more willing to shoot in anger at these law enforcers.

Almighty Voice was unlucky from the start. He was the grandson of One

Arrow, the Cree who had participated alongside Riel during the Battle of Batoche on 9-12 May 1885. As a result of their alleged participation in the rebellion, One Arrow and his band were seen by the police as troublemakers, to be watched closely. Government officials and the NWMP were determined to make an example of the Cree on One Arrow Reserve.[40]

The Indian agent responsible for the One Arrow Reserve was unsympathetic toward these Natives and their claims that they fought with Riel because their cattle had been taken and that without them they would have starved. As punishment for their part in the rebellion, the government proposed that the Cree of One Arrow's band be moved and amalgamated with the Beardy Reserve. This was rejected by the band, but the government, through Indian Agent Rae, persisted in efforts to achieve this end. The Cree were enticed by promises that their chief would be released from prison if they agreed to the move and that if they did not comply, rations would be refused. Yet, even with these threats, the Cree remained adamant in their refusal.

There were other tensions on the One Arrow Reserve. Rae was rumoured to have been sleeping with a number of Native women, and in the early 1890s the agents had been instructed not to distribute rations unless the Natives appeared at the store in a clean state. There were also problems with the schools on the reserve and lack of attendance was a complaint of the local clergy. Cree on the One Arrow Reserve were seen as troublemakers. It was against this backdrop that the story of Almighty Voice must be understood. He was from a band which had been labelled as dangerous by government agents. His acts and those of his pursuers should not be looked at in isolation.

On 22 October 1895, Almighty Voice and a companion, Flying Cloud, were arrested for stealing a cow from a nearby settler and were imprisoned at Duck Lake. A week later, Almighty Voice escaped from jail, because he was told that he would be sentenced to death for his actions. While this may have been possible, it was highly improbable. What is more likely is that Almighty Voice, like many Natives, had a great fear of imprisonment, as it was a terrible punishment for a people who knew no such banishment. It was also a place associated with death and disease.

The NWMP immediately began their pursuit of the escaped Native. He was considered dangerous by the police and it was known he was likely to resist until killed. Almighty Voice was followed to the One Arrow Reserve by Sergeant Colebrook and interpreter François Dumont. They located Almighty Voice and the sergeant moved in to arrest him, even though the Native warned that he would shoot if the Mountie advanced any further. The warning was not heeded; Colebrook was shot through the neck and died instantly.

The NWMP began a massive hunt for Almighty Voice, offering a reward of $250. On past occasions the Natives were assured they would be dealt with fairly if they cooperated with the Mounties, but in this instance it was clear the police would get no such assistance; in fact, the Natives were keeping them away from Almighty Voice. Indeed, the police felt the Natives of the area had grown defiant and more independent as the manhunt wore on. Though extensive surveillance of the reserve was undertaken and efforts to follow all leads were pursued, no clues or traces of the offender were found. One policeman suggested giving up the hunt.

Finally the police were informed of suspicious behaviour on the One Arrow Reserve. On 28 May 1897, the police closed in on the area and saw Almighty Voice flee after he had fired on the police, wounding their interpreter, Napoleon Venne. The Mounties followed three Natives to a poplar copse situated in an open field, which they then surrounded. It was towards evening and the police were ordered to open fire on the bush and move in slowly. A small army stood around the poplar bluff with a 7-pound and a 9-pound gun. On one of many charges on the bush, two more men were killed: Constable Kerr and the volunteer postmaster, Ernest Grundy. As the police prepared to move in, the haunting chant of Almighty Voice's mother could be heard from a nearby hill, reminding her son of the tradition of bravery among the Cree people. She was joined for a time in her chants by her son. At 6:00 A.M. Constable Smith ordered the surrounding rifles and cannon to open fire. When the smoke cleared the police moved in to discover three dead Natives. Two of them had been dead for some time, apparently killed by cannon shell fragments; the third, found further away, had also been dead for some time. They were "blown up on May 30, 1897."[41]

This event was representative of a new and uncaring pattern of police behaviour towards the Natives. Since 1885, this attitude had grown from the circumstances that accompanied the settlement of the West and the government policy that determined the way the NWMP would treat the Natives. It was an event that showed how the Natives had lost faith in the NWMP — men they had once trusted and a force that had once protected them:

> Almighty Voice, in his last moments, does become symbol for his people, a symbol of a once proud race hurling futile defiance at the Government's attempts to recycle them into wards of the state. It is hard to endow Almighty Voice with nobility, but he did, at the end, epitomize the Indian protest against the inevitability of the new era, against the coercion of the Police and the Indian Department, against the systematic destruction of Indian culture.[42]

The years 1885-97 were a time when the Natives waited to see how they would be included in the society that was moving westward, but they were years of waiting for the fulfillment of promises that would never come.

Captain Howard with the Gatling gun used at Batoche (National Archives of Canada, C-1882).
Captain Howard shown here was with the United States army and was in the Canadian West during 1885 promoting the rapid-fire Gatling gun that was very effectively used at the Battle of Batoche. The Gatling gun was also brought by Colonel Otter to the Battle of Cut Knife Hill, though it did little good there, as his men were driven from the battlefield by the Cree.

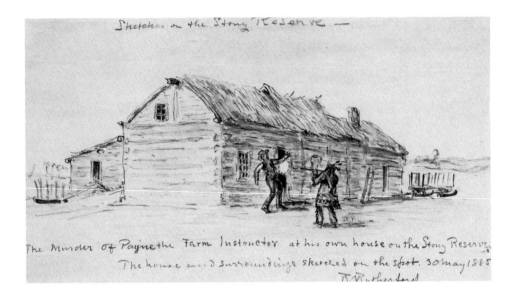

"The murder of Payne, the farm instructor, at his own house on the Stony Reserve," by William R. Rutherford. "The house and surroundings sketched on the spot, 30 May 1885" (Glenbow Archives, P-1390-33).
William Rutherford, the artist, was with the North-West Field Force, and could not have witnessed many of the scenes he portrayed, although he passed through some of the areas after the events that he sketched.

"Struggle between Payne and his murderer for the possession of a rifle in his house prior to his being shot," by William R. Rutherford. "The building sketched on the spot 30 May 1885" (Glenbow Archives, P-1390-34).

"Barney Tremont's ranch, 7 miles from Battleford where he was murdered by 5 Stonies while greasing the axle of his wagon," by William R. Rutherford. "Sketched on the spot 30 May 1885" (Glenbow Archives, P-1390-40).

"Escape of Applegarth the farm instructor, and his wife from the Red Pheasant Reserve. Red Pheasant and Brave helping him to get off from the Stony Indians who pursued him," by William R. Rutherford. "Sketched on the spot 29.8.85, from details given by Red Pheasant" (Glenbow Archives, P-1390-41).

"Full cry on the war path," by William R. Rutherford, ca. 1885 (Glenbow Archives, P-1390-37).
The Cree were often portrayed at eye level as sinister and threatening, as enemies that needed to be dealt with severely. Photographs of the time rarely show them to be so threatening.

"Sketches on the Red Pheasant Reserve. Searching the camp for firearms and stolen goods after the surrender of Poundmaker and his forces," by William R. Rutherford, 29 May 1885 (Glenbow Archives, P-1390-46).

Robert Jefferson, the farm instructor on the Poundmaker Reserve who was an eyewitness to much of the action during 1885, said that Otter's troops did at least as much looting as did the local Cree. Subsequent histories rarely mention this fact.

Miserable Man surrendering at Battleford, 1885, photo by Captain James Peters (Glenbow Archives, NA-363-78).
Miserable Man, in the centre, was one of the eight Cree hanged at Fort Battleford. It was the largest mass hanging in Canada since Confederation.

Chief Poundmaker with his fourth wife, ca. 1884 (National Archives of Canada, PA-66596).
Poundmaker was the leader of a tribe of Cree who settled on a reserve in the Battleford area. When the fighting in 1885 broke out, many local Métis and Cree people came to his camp for protection as they feared an American-style campaign against them. Ironically it was Poundmaker who was attacked by Colonel Otter, even though he tried to stay away from the fighting and to keep his men peaceful. In spite of the evidence to this effect supplied by the local farm instructor, Robert Jefferson, he was imprisoned by Canadian authorities, as were other Cree leaders even though evidence against them was flimsy.

Group photographed during trial of Riel Rebellion, July-August 1885, photo by O.B. Buell. Left to right: Front row: Horse Child (youngest son of Big Bear), Big Bear, Alex D. Stewart (Chief of Police, Hamilton), Poundmaker. Back row: Louis Napoleon Blache, Rev. Father Louis Cochin, Supt. R. Burton Deane, Rev. Father Alexis André, Christopher Robinson, Q.C. (Glenbow Archives, NA-3305-11).

Big Bear, taken in Stony Mountain Penitentiary, Manitoba, 1886, photo by Hall and Lowe (Manitoba Archives, NA 1315-17).
Shorn of his shoulder-length hair to humiliate him, Big Bear was imprisoned at Stony Mountain Penitentiary even though there was considerable evidence to suggest that he protected lives and tried to prevent violence.

"Sketch of the engagement between General Strange's column and Big Bear's band at Little Red Deer River, 15 miles from Fort Pitt on 29 May 1885," by William R. Rutherford (Glenbow Archives, P-1390-4).

The "battle" of Frenchman's Butte was indecisive as the Cree were well-entrenched on the hill across the valley. Strange fired his 9-pound guns at Big Bear's encampment but did not risk an advance through the swampy valley bottom. Among those in Big Bear's camp were Theresa Delaney and Theresa Gowanlock who were survivors of the Frog Lake killings. Only one Cree, He Who Speaks Our Language, was hit and died the following day.

View of the battle of Cut Knife Creek, 1885 (Glenbow Archives, NA-1353-14).

The dramatic portrayal of battles during the 1885 Resistance were often painted much later and had little to do with what actually happened in the battles. The painting here shows a Cree being hit by gunfire even though the Field Force hardly even saw the Cree, as the Cree fired from well-concealed positions around the edge of the hill and suffered no deaths. The Field Force was never able to occupy an orderly position of control and strength as depicted here. In fact they hardly were able to move out onto the hill and were forced into a motley retreat. Poundmaker forbade his men to pursue Otter's retreating column.

Theresa Delaney and Theresa Gowanlock, whose husbands were among the nine men killed at Frog Lake early in April 1885, were taken hostage by the Plains Cree of Big Bear's band for two months. Rumours that circulated about their "fate worse than death" during this time served to galvanize weary, footsore soldiers. The two women and a large party of Métis and Aboriginal hostages parted company with the moving Cree camp under cover of fog one morning and travelled for three days until NWMP scouts stumbled upon them. Although the women announced immediately that they had met with little suffering and coped well, this was not the overall impression left in their published account of later that year, which stressed their suffering and privation (Glenbow Archives, NA-1480-31).

The looting of the town of Battleford, *Illustrated War News*, 4 July 1885 (Saskatchewan Archives Board R-D290). *This ridiculous caricature of the Cree looting, drinking and lazing under umbrellas, succeeds in underlining prevailing attitudes of settlers, many of whom shared Victorian racial prejudices and thought of the Cree as "savages set on the warpath." The Cree in fact did no more looting than did Otter's soldiers and even tried to approach the "besieged" fort for food.*

Poundmaker (second from right) and Lt. Col. Van Straubenzie (second from left) inside the stockade after soldiers had relieved the post and Poundmaker had surrendered, 1885, photo by Captain James Peters (Fort Battleford NHP Library).

Miserable Man and Poundmaker speaking to Colonel Van Straubenzie, who was one of the British officers serving under Major General Frederick Middleton. Van Straubenzie was responsible for engineering the final charge which led to the fall of Batoche. After the surrender of the Cree at Battleford, many of them were put on trial. Poundmaker received a jail sentence and Miserable Man was hanged, along with seven others.

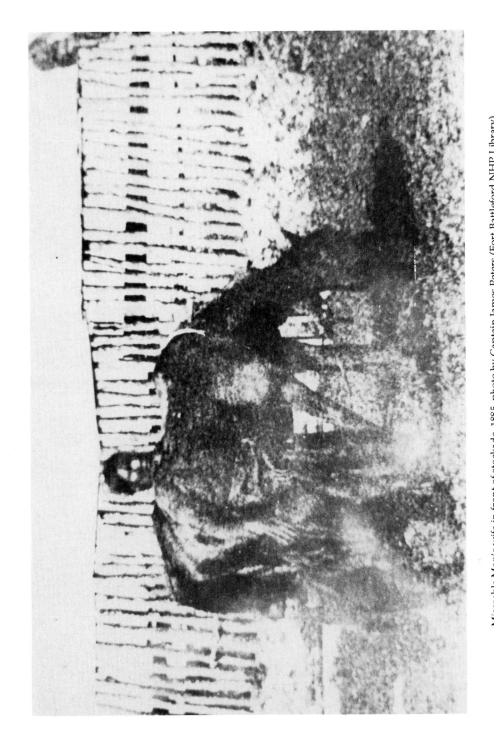

Miserable Man's wife in front of stockade, 1885, photo by Captain James Peters (Fort Battleford NHP Library).

Poundmaker and his men in front of stockade, 1885, photo by Captain James Peters (Fort Battleford NHP Library).

SEVEN

Fort Battleford as an Historic Site

Myth deprives the object of which it speaks of all History. In it history evaporates. It is a kind of ideal servant; it prepares all things, brings them, lays them out, the master arrives, it silently disappears: all that is left for one to do is to enjoy the beautiful object without wondering where it comes from.

Roland Barthes

It is not uncommon to have history and mythology in competition as we interpret the past at our historic sites. Images of the past are constantly in the process of change as each generation finds something new to tell or forgets a part of what was there. Not surprisingly, when interpreting the history of sites like Fort Battleford and Batoche, there are tensions among various ideologies as well as between regional and central Canadian perspectives. Today, we increasingly find the Native peoples' point of view challenging the established versions of Canadian history. One of the problems has been many of our national historic parks have become sacred sites and serve, ideologically, to commemorate the past as the conquerors see it. The many military sites in our system underline the emphasis on history as the chronical of winners and losers. Thus, in the wide range of potential nationalisms that our historic sites present, some have been valorized and made available for public consumption, while others have been ignored. The same symbol can of course have many meanings depending on who is looking at it. History at our sites ought to draw attention to the wide range of interpretations and the visitor can choose to consider various meanings depending on his or her perspective and experience. A member of the NWMP, for example, who may have been within the stockade at Battleford during the fighting in 1885, is likely to see a dramatically different significance in the fort than might a local Cree who witnessed the hanging of eight members of his tribe on the gallows within the stockade. Gradually there seems to be a recognition of the importance of encouraging many meanings, drawing attention to complex and multivocal histories rather than staying with older monological histories that invoke closure on meaning.

Up until the 1970s, the metropolitan thesis of Canadian history dominated the narrative form, providing the framework for those anxious to relate how exploitation of fish, furs, lumber and wheat produced a wealthy and prosperous Canada. The consequences associated with development rarely appeared in the pages. The predominant paradigm was national: what was best for the nation was best for everyone. Local and regional attitudes were hardly ever considered.

Emerging regional perspectives during the 1970s began to challenge the one-sided version of Canadian history produced by the metropolitanists, and the cost of progress, not only to Natives, but to settlers as well began to be assessed. In the early years of the decade, the story of the history of the Métis at Batoche changed as more was discovered about the social and economic life of these pre-Confederation westerners. No longer was the emphasis at the site on the military theme alone, nor was Batoche simply presented as the place where the Métis were defeated. Indeed, the events of the so-called 1885 Rebellion took their place alongside the social and economic history of the Métis. New research challenged the dominant national myths held so dear that depicted these people as carefree, hard-living, unpatriotic buffalo hunters. Moreover, the history as it related to the public at the site no longer ended in 1885 with the Battle of Batoche, but extended well beyond this watershed favoured by those who saw the Métis as an impediment to the development of the West.

At Fort Battleford myth and history clashed for ideological reasons and because only one side of the story was emphasized in the established histories. The history of Native people and especially their role in the events of 1885 altered the way in which the official history of Fort Battleford was told. The myth of the Mounties riding triumphantly into a "savage" and "wild" West for the sake of a "civilized" nation had to be deflated and reconsidered. Instead of being represented only as heroes of law and order, it seemed more sensible and balanced to also show them as agents of John A. Macdonald's National Policy, which aimed at developing the western hinterland for the national good. Historians studying Native people also became more interested in examining not only how Natives changed as a result of contact with the NWMP, but also how the Mounties and the society they represented changed in their attitudes towards Natives. Gradually, as the Native point of view was better appreciated, a new history began to replace myth, a history that presented many points of view rather than one. For years the history at Fort Battleford was related to the public as though the Mounties had come into a void, the context of their arrival and the reasons for their large numbers in the Battleford area being only vaguely understood. This is not to suggest that outsiders alone are responsible for the one-sided history that existed for so many years. Anglo-Canadians who held positions of power and influence in the West were no more interested in Métis and Aboriginal history than were central Canadians who wrote most of the mainstream histories. Most Anglo-Canadian westerners internalized the biases of national history and reproduced them in schools and churches established during the settlement era.

There were some exceptions, such as teacher and historian Campbell Innes, who tried to have the Native point of view put forward in the interpretive program at Fort Battleford. Though Innes was a member of the Historic Sites and Monument Board from 1951-54, it appears his efforts remained largely unsuccessful. He supported the move towards interpreting fur trade and Native history, but there were many others who opposed his approach and favoured using Fort Battleford solely to valorize the role of the NWMP. It proved difficult to challenge the myth of the force and to place its role in a more balanced perspective. The myth of the Mounties served the vision of the colonizers well, and while historical research might have helped to demystify their image somewhat, there were few to write the new history and still fewer who were receptive to it.

The conflict between myth and history stood most starkly during the early years when Fort Battleford was first recognized as a national historic site. In the early 1950s, the Director of the Canadian Parks Service advised his Deputy Minister that Fort Battleford should be considered a site of national significance. The focus was to be on the establishment of the fort and its construction. His memo outlined a brief chronology of the fort, beginning with its founding by Walker and Frechette in 1876 with a troop of fourteen men and six horses. The fort expanded and sub-posts were established at Carlton, Duck Lake and Prince Albert in the next year, when the telegraph line reached Battleford. By 1878, the year in which Battleford became the territorial capital of the North-West, the fort had grown to contain a force of thirty-four men and forty-one horses. The director mentioned in passing that the first stockade constructed in 1878 was built with the assistance of Natives from Big Bear's band. By the 1880s, greater energies were expended on improving the stockade and buildings. As well, the fort was honoured with a visit by the Marquis of Lorne and Princess Louise in 1883. The seat of government was then moved to Regina as a result of the rerouting of the CPR. Following the move the government buildings became the home of the first Native industrial school, and in 1885 Battleford

> became a very important centre and police from this point [the fort] went to Fort Carlton and took part in the Battle of Duck Lake and settlers in the Battleford district congregated at the police fort for protection. Battleford was besieged by the Indians; relieved by General Middleton later in the early summer. Captain Nash formed a Home Guard. Inspector Dickens, son of the novelist, Charles Dickens, was stationed at Battleford and subsequently engaged the Indians at the Battle of Cut Knife Hill not far from Battleford. Battleford was used as a base for the attack on Big Bear at Loon Lake. Poundmaker made his offer to surrender. General Middleton arrived to dictate terms to Poundmaker. Eight Indians guilty of murder were tried at Battleford and hanged.[1]

This thumbnail sketch of Battleford's significance concluded with mention of the 1886 arrival of "C" Division under Superintendent John Cotton. Then, in 1886, the stockade was removed. Until sometime between 1914 and 1916 the police post continued to operate, though with gradually declining importance. From 1914-16 to 1924 the post was supervised by a caretaker, "but as time went on, they [the buildings] became a stomping ground for relic hunters."[2] The property was used for a variety of purposes until 1936, when it was transferred from the federal government to the province of Saskatchewan. During this period the fort fell into disrepair. In the mid-1940s, Campbell Innes initiated a drive to save the remaining buildings with the purpose of using them to interpret the history of the area. In 1945, the fort opened as a Native museum and police memorial, and in 1948 the site was officially opened by Governor General Lord Alexander.

The memo reflects the metropolitan perspective. Highlighted are events initiated by agents of the Canadian government, and the focus is on describing the establishment of Canadian authority through the NWMP and the territorial capital, putting down western rebellion, building an industrial school, and narrating visits of royalty into the empty North-West. It was history from a central Canadian perspective — the West made safe for white settlement. The Canadian government had chosen to commemorate the "civilization" of the West.

This was not, however, the way in which the history of Battleford was presented by Innes and those who began the move to have Battleford recognized as nationally important. The initial project was to establish a Native museum along with a "memorial" to the NWMP. Thus, the story was to be broader, and was to include the history of those who were in the North-West before the Canadian government arrived. In the promotional literature the history of the early occupants was told:

This locality is the home of the Cree Indian. In the early days they successfully held back the Blackfoot. There are also tribes of Saulteaux, Assiniboine and Sioux, with their long history and cultural development. The Indian Agency office is still located here.[3]

Also mentioned in the prospectus of the museum was the significance of the fur trade to the area:

Such early explorers as McGillivary, Pink, Cocking, Frobisher, Pond, Henry, Pangman, Umfreville, Thompson and Harman passed up the North Saskatchewan and crossed to the Beaver River and Isle a la Crosse to Churchill. Their fur post sites are still to be seen. It has been a pleasure to search for these and have Professor A.S. Morton come up from Saskatoon and check them over. These posts should be rebuilt or remarked, and the thrilling story of early days retold: Manchester House, Pine Island Post, Eagle Hills Post, Turtle Post, Buckingham House. The rich fur and pemmican trade of the Hudson's Bay and North-West Company was centred in this part of the Saskatchewan River and of Green Lake, Isle a la Crosse, Prince Albert and Edmonton.[4]

There was a real (if paternalistic) hope held by members of the Battleford Historical Society that presenting the history of Native people would assist them in regaining pride in their traditions. The post-World War II consciousness evident in the promotional literature clearly saw education as a way not only to avoid catastrophes of war, but also to raise the Natives from the spiritual and material depression it was thought many suffered:

In order to fit the cultural needs of the Indians it is felt here this program should be enlarged. Our increasing number of visitors is evidence that the sphere of research be enlarged. There are frequent students of Indian lore visiting here. Indian handicrafts need developing in our schools. This museum may become a central place for exhibitions and sale of their work. All this will tend to make their racial consciousness share in our Canadian Unity. Creative art and Indian folklore will always have an important place here. At present there is an urgent need to assist in saving valued individual collections. As you are aware collectors from across the borders do carry away so much which has its place in western Canada.[5]

Thus it was the need for a Native museum that prompted these early preservationists, not only the need to establish a North West Mounted Police site. This was expressed many times by Innes, but particularly so in a 1949 letter to Dr. Keenleyside, Chairman of the Historic Sites and Monuments Board (HSMB) of Canada:

Today so many citizens are anxious to forward collections and various articles interpretive of Indian life. Its scholars are assisting in various ways. It is so necessary that such material may be studied and properly classified in the next three months before the rush of visitors. Besides there is the general furnishing of the Indian Museum Building. You will note that the Administration has an Indian Committee or Division. Your Department is free to make additions or changes and to initiate your own policy. Your Department may take the control or the members of the Division may carry on any policy you so initiate to advance this phase of National life.[6]

Motivated by a desire to present a comprehensive picture of the history of the North-West, the Battleford Historical Society pressed on with great energy and initiative towards the establishment of an historic site at the fort. In the early years it did not always have a firm financial commitment from the government, but eventually the society was able to operate with funds from local subscribers, the provincial government and eventually the federal government.

The work of Innes was remarkable. In the period from 1945 to 1951, when the site was taken over by the federal government, he wrote scores of letters to politicians and bureaucrats for amounts of money to assist in stabilizing, furnishing, acquiring, and preserving the buildings and their contents.

In the early years immediately after the war, assistance to preserve buildings came from the newly elected Co-operative Commonwealth Federation government of Tommy Douglas. This happened after numerous requests to the federal government failed. After considerable lobbying, the HSMB still thought the fort was of local interest only, stating in 1948: "It is suggested that there should be sufficient local interest in Saskatchewan to take care of [the] Police Memorial and Indian Museum of Battleford."[7] Then Innes, as spokesperson for the local historical society, applied to have funding awarded to Battleford on the basis of its status as a museum. In a memo written to Keenleyside, he stated that the museum had raised $8,000 in 1949, made up of $600 from local subscriptions as well as a $5,000 grant from the Saskatchewan government. Innes asked the board for an additional $2,000, half of which was to go to pay an "Indian curator or keen student of Indian lore."[8]

In 1949, in response to the persistence of Innes, the HSMB adopted the following resolution at its annual meeting:

> That this Board recommends to the Department that through the National Museum and the cooperation of the Indian Affairs Branch and the National Parks Service, they consider the establishment over the years of a series of local or branch Indian museums at what seems to be the strategic points, of which the Committee appointed by this board suggested that Battleford should be one.[9]

After long negotiations between J.H. Brockelbank, Saskatchewan's Minister of Natural Resources, and Robert Winters, the federal government's Minister of Natural Resources and Development, the site was plaqued and the land transferred from the provincial government to the federal Department of Indian Affairs. The plaque read:

> On May 24, 1948, this memorial to the North West Mounted Police was officially opened by His Excellency Field Marshall the Right Honourable, Viscount Alexander of Tunis, K.S. Governor General of Canada. The work of restoring this historic fort established in 1876 as district headquarters by Sub-Inspector James Walker NWMP was begun in 1945 by the Government of Saskatchewan under the direction of the Honourable J.L. Phelps, Minister of Natural Resources.

> On July 1, 1951 this monument was transferred to the government of Canada to be maintained as a national historic park.[10]

Yet, in spite of all the work done by the local community to write its own history, there was no mention of Native people in this first commemoration.

Several brochures and pamphlets produced for the site still tried to present a broader contextual framework for the history interpreted at the fort, but gradually the emphasis shifted towards the history of the police themselves as highlighted by the first plaque. Directions from Ottawa continued to be unresponsive to the broader history of the area as a whole. The emphasis on the NWMP, entrenched in the 1950s, continued through the 1960s and 1970s. It was not until the

1980s that the original intention of including Native history at Battleford again emerged and was integrated into the storyline. Generally the evolution of the interpretation and commemoration at Fort Battleford reinforces the trends noted by C.J. Taylor's "National Historic Parks and Sites, 1880-1951: The Biography of a Federal Cultural Program." A distinctly centralist bias in the recommendations of the HSMB emerged over the years, one that seemed unable to decentre itself enough to recognize the regional nature of Canada's varied cultural traditions. As a result, those areas underrepresented by the board were ignored — regions such as Quebec, the Atlantic provinces and the West. Controversy in the 1920s over whether or not to commemorate sites of the 1885 North-West campaign had a lasting effect even two decades later. The problems persisted and regional preservationists had to lobby vigorously to be heard. On some occasions, such as the commemoration of the 1885 Rebellion, the board was able to offend more than one region:

> A controversy ... arose over the commemoration of a series of sites connected with the Northwest Rebellion of 1885. The interpretation of these sites exhibited a distinct English Canadian bias and was rooted in an Ontarian based nationalism which saw the rebellions as an obstacle to the material evolution of Canada. This ran counter to the views of Quebec nationalists who viewed Louis Riel as a French Canadian martyr and to native Canadians whose legitimate grievances were ignored.[11]

A dismissal of the regional perspective in explaining the causes for the fighting in 1885 was evident in the emphasis given to the interpretation of other sites in the West. The tendency to overlook the role of the Natives (which even the whites in the West were anxious to understand) was a general problem. The composition of the board was primarily responsible for its inability to include other points of view. This helped explain the difficulties faced by people like Innes:

> Given the inherent bias of the members to emphasize the history of their own neighbourhoods, it is not surprising that the prairie provinces received only a small proportion of national historic sites in the years leading up to the Second World War. Moreover, the sites that were designated were likely to be interpreted from perspectives alien to regional/historical traditions. This is just what happened in the case of the Northwest Rebellion sites in Saskatchewan which embroiled the board in some of its most virulent controversies. It was a difficult episode for the board for not only did it result in unfavourable publicity, but it forced the members to face the possible conflict between the historical and ideological significance of a site. Usually the historical events associated with a potential site involved the board in a discourse of subjective interpretation. In the case of Cut Knife Hill and Batoche commemorations, discussions became polemics.[12]

By the 1950s, the Massey Commission began to analyze the state of heritage preservation in Canada. It drafted recommendations intended to make historical commemoration more representative of all regions of Canada, but especially of Quebec and the West. Unfortunately, the final report of the board, whose overall perspective remained predominantly centralist, was vague and indecisive regarding how best to achieve better representation for regional interests. The criticisms of a centralist focus had been made known in hearings held across Canada:

> The presentations at regional hearings, on the other hand tended to note the inability of the Historic Sites and Monuments Board to represent regional peculiarities. They also dwelt on the presentation aspect of the program which was of little interest to the custodians of culture on the Massey Commission.[13]

But the points made to the commission, while heard and apparently appreciated, were not dealt with:

> The resulting report on the historic sites programs, which passed along criticisms gathered at regional hearings as well as including the commissioner's own analysis, made little effort to reconcile these two perspectives with the result that it presented a confusing array of opinions and recommendations.[14]

The commissioners saw themselves as "custodians of culture" and were attempting to foster a unified national outlook in their recommendations. It never occurred to them that greater regional expression might lead to a strengthened sense of community within the larger national framework.

In the 1980s, the move was towards a more contextual approach to the interpretation of history at Fort Battleford. The program looks more like the commemorative program developed during the Innes years. There is the recognition of Native and fur-trade history before the NWMP arrived and the story includes more than one point of view.

CONCLUSION

The mythic Canadian West where the Mounties heroically arrive bringing law and order as well as "civilization" to the land has proved hard to dislodge. Mountie images on everything from tea towels to refrigerator magnets for sale in tourist shops across this country serve as a sharp reminder of just how powerful and entrenched a national symbol the mounted policeman remains. Myth makers are still writing history to remind us of lessons that they believe need to be learned from the past, myth in these cases serving the cause of morality. The myths created from the past are deeply encoded with messages about who we are as Canadians and how we should act. The "March West" of 1874 has long stood, and continues to stand, for a new moral and cultural order that the NWMP brought to what was portrayed as an empty land, this in spite of considerable evidence from contemporary prairie dwellers and even missionaries who were astonished at just how cumbersome and incompetent the march onto the prairies in fact was.

Myths and myth makers often serve the ideologies of those who hold power and those who want that power to appear to be naturally and legitimately theirs. Their myths are built around "real people" and "real incidents" but these people and incidents are carefully "constructed" to include the facts that support the mythology and to selectively ignore those facts that might obstruct the clarity of the image.

Both myth makers and historians rely on the "facts" of the past. But historians by their craft are required to be vigilant about the "facts" and must deal with all of the "facts." Historians cannot simply tell a story to preserve a pure image, they must deal with all the information, all the facts, and must often be content to explain the great complexity of history, if necessary. Most importantly, the historian must present the context of historical events along with the multifaceted causality of history. The NWMP, for example, did not simply arrive in the West but were part of larger colonial and imperial enterprises that characterized much of the nineteenth century.

For the myth maker, time and context are unimportant. The Mountie in the tourist gift shop and the historical NWMP are one and the same, the image signified by either of them is what remains important. The Mountie signifies the law and order that Anglo-Canadians envisioned for the West, a law and order they thought the West needed. They were sent out to "maintain the right" for those who held power in central Canada and were about to hold power in the Canadian West. The myth maker, as Roland Barthes points out in the headnote to chapter 7, wants his image to remain above mere history.

At Fort Battleford, myth and history collided because the Mountie of the myth makers excluded the stories of many people, especially the history of the NWMP as they were seen by Métis and Aboriginal people of the prairies. As the complexity of the history at Fort Battleford is revealed through the history that the Cree and Métis tell, the image of the Mounties as harbingers of law and order or as agents of civilization is challenged. There already were laws in the West and there already were significant and varied cultures with a long presence on the prairies. Aboriginal groups had their own systems of government and of making and enforcing laws.

As the voices of First Nations' peoples are heard, the national narratives that had excluded them have had to adjust to accommodate their version of the past. Meanings and (establishing) the significance of events has changed as the result of the new perspectives. The history of the West has become more complex as more people are heard and as their point of view comes to be tolerated. The history of the West was no longer about the "great" settlement of the West but it was also about what happened to those who were already there. As Patricia Limerick points out in the headnote that begins this book, the inheritance of these original settlers does not only include great men, great events and great development, but it also includes a world on the brink of environmental disaster with pollutants, pesticides, a depleted ozone layer and nuclear waste. All of this does not easily evoke clear images of "progress" nor does the way of life of prairie tribes seem as unreasonable as it was once portrayed.

The myth of the Mounties needs to be balanced off against the historical evidence that shows them to be no more and no less than men of their times who carried the cultural baggage of the Victorian era they were part of. They are not and should not remain above history. They shared many — now discredited — ideas about race, gender and culture. As times change, so do attitudes, and the image of the Mountie should not remain timeless or above time; such myth making only leads to the intolerance inherent in the view that time does not change culture and society, and that new attitudes or ideas need not be entertained. Replacing myth with history is not intended to discredit the Mounties but rather return them to the less valorized context of being human (along with the rest of us), instead of on the pedestal where they have been for too long.

Members of the North West Council

David Laird	Lieutenant Governor	1877-81
Edgar Dewdney	Lieutenant Governor	1883-87
Amédée E. Forget	Clerk of Council	1877-87
Mathew Ryan S.M.	Ex-officio	1877-81
Lieut. Col. Hugh Richardson	Ex-officio	1877-87
Lieut. Col. James F. MacLeod	Commisioner NWMP,	1877-79
	appointed S.M. ex-officio	1881-87
Lawrence Clarke	Rep. from Lorne	1881-82
Lieut. Col. Acheson Gosford Irvine	Commissioner NWMP,	1883-87
	appointed	
Hayter Reed	Appointed	1883-87
Francis Oliver	Rep. from Edmonton	1883-84
D.H. Macdowall	Rep. from Lorne	1883-84
J.C.C. Hamilton	Rep. from Broadview	1883-84
T.W. Jackson	Rep. from Qu'Appelle	1883-85
W. White	Rep. from Regina	1883-84
J.H. Ross	Rep. from Moose Jaw	1883-87
Chas. B. Rouleau S.M.	Ex-officio	1884-87
T.G. Turriff	Rep. from Moose Mountain	1884-87
J.D. Geddes	Rep. from Calgary	1884-85
W.D. Perley	2nd member for Qu'Appelle	1885-86
S.A. Bedford	Rep. from Moosomin	1885-87
D.F. Jelly	Rep. from Regina	1885-87
J. Secord	Rep. from Regina	1885-87
R. Henry (Viscount Boyle)	Rep. from Macleod	1885-86
H.C. Wilson	Rep. from Edmonton	1885-87
S. Cunningham	Rep. from St. Albert	1885-87
C. Marshallsay	Rep. from Broadview	1885-86
	Rep. from Whitewood	1887
O.E. Hughes	Rep. from Lorne	1885-86
	Rep. from Prince Albert	1887
T.D. Lauder	Rep. from Calgary	1886-87
H.S. Cayley	Rep. from Calgary	1886-87
R. Crawford	Rep. from Qu'Appelle	1886-87
W. Sutherland	Rep. from Qu'Appelle	1887
F.W.G. Haultain	Rep. from Macleod	1887

Officers Commanding Battleford, 1878-1919

1876-80	Inspector J. Walker
1880-84	Superintendent W.M. Herchmer
1884-85	Superintendent L.N.F. Crozier
1885	Inspector W.S. Morris - temporarily, in absence of Crozier at Fort Carlton
1885	Inspector Dickens - temporarily, having evacuated Fort Pitt and moved to Battleford and being senior to Morris
1885	Superintendent S.B. Steele
1886	Superintendent S.B. Steele
1886	Superintendent A.R. Macdonell
1886-88	Superintendent J. Cotton
1888-89	Inspector J. Howe
1889-91	Inspector W.D. Antrobus
1891-95	Inspector J. Howe
1895-99	Superintendent J. Cotton
1899-1900	Inspector D.M. Howard - temporary Superintendent G.E. Sanders
1900-01	Inspector F.J.A. Demers
1901-04	Superintendent A.H. Griesback
1904-05	Inspector T. McGinnis
1905-06	Superintendent A.C. Macdonell, D.S.O.
1906-13	Superintendent J.A. McGibbon
1914-16	Superintendent C.H. West
1916-18	Inspector C.H.H. Sweetapple - for West
1918-19	Superintendent C.H. West
1919	Headquarters for district moved to Prince Albert

NOTES

Chapter One

1. Michael Ignatieff, "State, Civil Society and Total Institutions: A Critique of Recent Social Histories of Punishment," in Stanley Cohen and Andrew Scull (eds.), *Social Control and the Modern State* (London: Basil Blackwell, 1985), 75.
2. Ibid., 76.
3. Ibid., 93.
4. Ibid.
5. James Axtell, *The European and the Indian: Essays in the Ethnohistory of Colonial North America* (London: Oxford University Press, 1981). The concept has recently come under some criticism for focussing too much on how Natives changed, how they were unable to adapt to the new society ushered in by Europeans. But as Axtell has pointed out, this is not the fault of the methodology of acculturation but rather of those using the method. Thus the focus of the work by Axtell and others has looked at just how much whites learned from Native people, enabling the white men to absorb information that allowed them to survive in an unknown environment. A further trend that has emerged through the use of the acculturation model is the pronounced characteristic of racist beliefs in North America, especially in comparison with attitudes towards Natives in Europe. Perhaps mere physical distance explains this discrepancy in what otherwise were essentially the same cultural groups, some of which broke off from mother countries in Europe. The need to dominate or assimilate Native societies also emerges as a factor of white frontier culture.
6. Gerald Friesen, *The Canadian Prairies: A History* (Toronto: University of Toronto Press, 1984), 20.
7. Ibid., 186.
8. A. Rotstein, "Trade and Politics: An Institutional Approach," *Western Canadian Journal of Anthropology* 3, no. 1 (1973).
9. E.E. Rich, *The Fur Trade and the Northwest to 1857* (Toronto: McClelland and Stewart, 1967).
10. Arthur Ray, *Indians in the Fur Trade* (Toronto: University of Toronto Press, 1974).
11. John Milloy, *The Plains Cree: Trade, Diplomacy and War, 1790 to 1870* (Winnipeg: University of Manitoba Press, 1988), 6.
12. Ibid., 75-79.
13. Paul F. Sharp, *Whoop-Up Country: The Canadian-American West, 1865-1885* (Minneapolis: University of Minnesota Press, 1955), chapter 4.
14. Milloy, *The Plains Cree*, 119.
15. Ibid., 121.
16. Irene Spry, "The Transition From a Nomadic to a Settled Economy in Western Canada, 1856-96," *Transactions of the Royal Society of Canada*, vol. 6, series 4 (1968): 187-201.
17. Edward Hall, *The Dance of Life: The Other Dimension of Time* (Garden City: Doubleday, 1984).
18. Frederick Turner, *Beyond Geography: The Western Spirit Against the Wilderness* (New York: Viking Press, 1980), Part 1.
19. See, for example, Roy Harvey Pearce, *Savagism and Civilization: A Study of the Indian and the American Mind* (Baltimore: John Hopkins Press, 1965) and Philip Mason, *Patterns of Dominance* (London: Oxford University Press, 1971).
20. Sarah Carter, "The Missionaries' Indian: The Publications of John McDougall, John Maclean and Egerton Ryerson Young," *Prairie Forum* 9, no. 1 (Spring 1984): 27-44.
21. Spry, "The Tragedy of the Loss of the Commons in Western Canada," in Ian A.L. Getty and Antoine S. Lussier (eds.), *As Long as the Sun Shines and the Water Flows* (Vancouver: University of British Columbia Press, 1983), 204.
22. Ibid., 205.

23. Ibid., 211.

24. Ibid., 212.

25. Ibid., 220.

26. Ibid., 224.

27. Mason, *Patterns of Dominance.*

28. George Stanley, *The Birth of Western Canada: A History of the Riel Rebellions* (Toronto: University of Toronto Press, 1961).

29. Much of the material on the treaties has been taken from J.L. Taylor, "The Development of an Indian Policy for the Canadian Northwest, 1869-79" (Ph.D. dissertation, Queen's University, 1975).

30. Sarah Carter, *Lost Harvests: Prairie Indian Reserve Agriculture and Government Policy* (Montreal/Kingston: McGill-Queen's University Press, 1990).

Chapter Two

1. David Jules Prown, "Mind in Matter: An Introduction to Material Culture Theory and Method," *Winterthur Portfolio* 17, no . 1 (Spring 1982): 2.

2. Alan Gowans, *Building Canada* (Toronto: Oxford University Press, 1966), 8 .

3. Interview with Joe Guthrie in Walter Hildebrandt, "Fort Battleford: A Structural History." Manuscript Report Series No. 252 (Ottawa: Parks Canada, 1978), pp. 234-35.

4. Alan Gowans, *A History of the Gothic Revival* (Leicester, NY: Charles Eastlake, American Life Foundation, 1975), x. The Gothic Revival was part of a distinctive epoch within architectural history which for want of a better name can be called "Victorian." The older idea of some "battle of styles ... is rapidly giving way to recognition that all of the different styles of the Victorian era — Greek Revival, Roman Revival, Gothic Revival, and so forth have a common denominator [which is] the principle of borrowing forms from past styles because of their association with ideas of republicanism and civic virtue, Greek for associations with permanence and wisdom, Moorish for exoticism, and so on — the choice in any given case being determined by what sort of symbolic imagery social circumstances seem to call for ... the primary function of Gothic Revival architecture was to create symbolic imagery."

5. Ibid., 118-19: "Gothic was the style chosen for [the Parliament buildings]. That was no surprise; the architects hardly had an alternative. It was practically mandatory for them to express the country's close ties with Britain by taking as their model Westminster New Palace, home of the Mother of Parliaments in London."

6. Christopher Thomas, "Architectural Images for the Dominion: Scott, Fuller and the Stratford Post Office," *Journal of Canadian Art History* 3 (Fall 1976).

7. See, for example, Fort Battleford National Historic Park Library, Walker Letterbooks, 17 May 1877 to 21 February 1879, particularly the letter written by Inspector Walker to the Secretary of State, 17 December 1877. Correspondence between the federal government and officials at Fort Battleford shows that the architects in the Department of Public Works had a definite hand in dictating the shape these buildings on the frontier were to take.

8. This picturesque quality was not only to be achieved by the building but also by trees and landscaping. See A.J. Downing, *The Architecture of Country Houses* (New York: Da Capo Press, 1968), 28-29: "The Picturesque, is seen in ideas of beauty manifested with something of rudeness, violence, or difficulty. The effect of the whole is spirited and pleasing, but parts are not balanced, proportions are not perfect, and details are made. We feel at the first glance at a picturesque object, the idea of power is exerted, rather than the idea of beauty which it involves."

9. Hudson Holly, *Country Seats and Modern Dwellings* (Watkins Glen, New York: Library of Victorian Culture, 1977), 11.

10. Ibid., 19.

11. Downing, *The Architecture of Country Houses*, 21.

12. Ibid., 21ff.

13. George Hersey, "Replication Replicated on Notes on American Bastardy," *Perspecta, the Yale Architectural Journal*, nos. 9 and 10 (1965): 220.

14. Charles Lockwood, *Bricks and Brownstone, The New York Row House, 1783-1929: An Architectural and Social History* (Toronto: McGraw-Hill, 1972).

15. Ibid., 225.

16. Douglas Richardson, "Canadian Architecture in the Victorian Era: The Spirit of the Place," *Canadian Collector* 10, no. 5 (September/October 1975).

17. National Archives of Canada (hereafter cited as NA), RG 18, 1 August 1898, ibid., vol. 1165, file 28, 8 June 1890.

18. Ibid., vol. 1165, file 28, 8 June 1890.

19. Quote in L.H. Thomas, "The Saskatchewan Legislative Building and its Predecessors," *Royal Architectural Institute of Canada* 32 (1955): 250.

20. NA, RG 11, vol. 576, Walker to Commissioner, 17 December 1877.

21. Fred W. Peterson, "Vernacular Building and Victorian Architecture: Midwestern American Farm Homes," *Journal of Interdisciplinary History* 12, no. 3 (Winter 1982): 409.

22. Ken Hughes, "Boundless Horizon: Straight Line or Curved?," *NeWest Review* 9, no. 9 (May 1984): 9.

23. Ibid., 11.

24. Greg Thomas and Ian Clarke, "The Garrison Mentality and the Canadian West," *Prairie Forum* 4, No. 1 (Spring 1974): 83.

25. Ibid., 84.

26. Ibid., 85.

27. Gaile McGregor, *The Wacousta Syndrome: Explorations in the Canadian Landscape* (Toronto: University of Toronto Press, 1985).

Chapter Three

1. J.P. Turner, *The North-West Mounted Police 1873-1893*, 2 vols. (Ottawa: King's Printer, 1950); Edmund H. Oliver, "Saskatchewan and Alberta: General History, 1870-1912," in Adam Shortt and Arthur G. Doughty (eds.), *Canada and Its Provinces: A History of the Canadian People and Their Institutions By One Hundred Associates*, vol. 19 (Toronto: Glasgow, Brooks and Company, 1914), 147-280; John Hawkes, *The Story of Saskatchewan and its People* (Regina: S.J. Clarke, 1924).

2. R.C. Macleod, *The NWMP and Law Enforcement 1873-1905* (Toronto: University of Toronto Press, 1976).

3. Sarah Carter, "Categories and Terrains of Exclusion: Constructing the 'Indian Woman' in the Early Settlement Era in Western Canada," *Great Plains Quarterly* 13, no. 3 (Summer 1993): 147-61.

4. Edgar Z. Friedenberg, *Deference to Authority: The Case of Canada* (White Plains, NY: M.E. Sharpe, 1980).

5. A.L. Haydon, *Riders of the Plains: A Record of the Royal North-West Mounted Police of Canada, 1873-1910* (Edmonton: Hurtig, 1971), xxiii.

6. Ibid., 156-57.

7. Oliver, "Saskatchewan and Alberta."

8. Ibid., 148.

9. Ibid., 149.

10. Ibid., 163.

11. Haydon, *Riders of the Plains*, xviii-ix.

12. Ibid., 19.

13. Anthony Wilden, *The Imaginary Canadian* (Vancouver: Arsenal Press, 1980), 13.

14. Macleod, *NWMP and Law Enforcement*, 5.

15. Ibid.

16. Turner, *North-West Mounted Police*, vol. 1, 91.

17. Carter, *Lost Harvests*.

18. Macleod, *NWMP and Law Enforcement*, 29.

19. Turner, *North-West Mounted Police*, vol. 1, 267.

20. Ibid., 269.

21. A. Morris, *The Treaties of Canada with the Indians of Manitoba and the North-West Territories* (Toronto: Coles Canadiana Collection, 1971), 201-2.

22. Turner, *North-West Mounted Police*, vol. 1, 271.

23. Morris, *Treaties of Canada*, 209.

24. Ibid., 210.

25. Turner, *North-West Mounted Police*, vol. 1, 274-75.

26. Morris, *Treaties of Canada*, 238.

27. Hugh Dempsey, *Big Bear: The End of Freedom* (Vancouver: Douglas and McIntrye, 1984), 76.

28. Turner, *North-West Mounted Police*, vol. 1, 673.

29. Ibid., 651-52.

30. Ibid., 645.

31. John Tobias, "Canada's Subjugation of the Plains Cree, 1879-1885," *Canadian Historical Review* 64, no. 4 (December 1983): 519-48.

32. Turner, *North-West Mounted Police*, vol. 1, 475.

33. Ibid., 478.

34. Canada, *Sessonal Papers*, 1878, 8-9.

35. Turner, *North-West Mounted Police*, vol. 1, 475.

36. W.A. Waiser, "The North-West Mounted Police in 1874-1889: A Statistical Study," Research Bulletin No. 117 (Ottawa: Parks Canada, 1979).

37. A.J. Looy, "The Indian Agent and His Role in the Administration of the North-West Superintendency, 1876-1893" (Ph.D. dissertation, Queen's University, 1977).

38. Ibid.

39. Quoted in ibid., 104.

40. Carter, *Lost Harvests*.

41. Isabel Andrews, "Indian Protest Against Starvation: The Yellow Calf Incident of 1884," *Saskatchewan History* 28, no. 2 (Spring 1975): 41.

42. John Jennings, "The NWMP and Canadian Indian Policy, 1873-1896" (Ph.D. dissertation, University of Toronto, 1979).

43. Robert Jefferson, *Fifty Years on the Saskatchewan* (Battleford: Canadian North-West Historical Society, 1929), 108.

44. Ibid., 108.

45. Ibid., 109.

46. Ibid.

47. Ibid., 113.

48. Norma Sluman and Jean Goodwill, *John Tootoosis: A Biography of a Cree Leader* (Winnipeg: Pemmican Publications, 1984), 34.

49. Ibid., 35.

50. Ibid., 35-36.

Chapter Four

1. Douglas Sprague and John Finlay, *The Structure of Canadian History* (Scarborough: Prentice-Hall, 1984), 185

2. Carl Berger, *The Sense of Power: Studies in the Ideals of Canadian Imperialism 1867-1914* (Toronto: University of Toronto Press, 1970).

3. Walter E. Houghton, *The Victorian Frame of Mind, 1830-1870* (New Haven, CT: Yale University Press, 1963).

4. The *Nor'Wester* was the voice of the interests of the Canadian Party through the late 1850s and 1860s. In 1860 James Ross, the son of Red River historian Alexander Ross, bought out Buckingham's interest in the paper. In 1864 John Christian Schultz bought out Ross and in 1865 purchased Coldwell's interest in the paper.

5. *Saskatchewan Herald*, 25 August 1878.

6. Paul Rutherford, "The New Nationality, 1864-1897: A Study of the National Aims and Ideas of

English Canada in the Late Nineteenth Century" (Ph.D. dissertation, University of Toronto, 1970), 287.

7.   Saskatchewan Archives Board (Saskatoon) (hereafter cited as SAB), Effie Storer Papers, A186 II 5, "Prospectus of the Essex Record."

8.   Ibid.

9.   Ibid.

10. *Saskatchewan Herald*, 24 November 1883.

11. Ibid., 15 January 1887.

12. Rutherford, "The New Nationality." Almost as much as industrialization, the prospect of a new frontier excited the Conservatives. Often the Conservatives spoke of Canada's duty, sometimes as if imposed by God, to civilize the northern portion of the continent. By civilize, of course, he meant to exploit, to expand the Canadian economy westward. Obvious in Conservative rhetoric was the expectation that the frontier would play the role of economic catalyst in Canada's future similar to that played by the great plains of the recent American past.

13. *Saskatchewan Herald*, 25 August 1878.

14. Macleod, *The NWMP and Law Enforcement*, 74.

15. Ibid., 81.

16. Ibid., 79

17. *Saskatchewan Herald*, 16 December 1878.

18. Ibid., 13 January 1879.

19. Ibid., 31 January 1881.

20. Ibid.

21. Ibid., 8 March 1884.

22. Ibid., 23 August 1884.

23. Ibid., 18 January 1886.

24. Ibid., 10 May 1886.

25. Ibid., 5 Feburary 1892.

26. Ibid., 11 June 1911.

27. Ibid., 27 January 1879.

28. Ibid., 12 January 1880.

29. Ibid., 17 January 1880.

30. Ibid., 8 January 1887.

31. Ibid. 7 July 1888.

32. Ibid., 27 May 1883.

33. Ibid., 2 May 1883.

34. Ibid., 7 January 1897.

35. Ibid., 15 February 1886.

36. Ibid., 13 September 1880.

37. Alan McCullough, "Papers Relating to the North-West Mounted Police and Fort Walsh." Manuscript Report Series No. 213 (Ottawa: Parks Canada, 1977), 185-218.

38. *Saskatchewan Herald*, 9 February 1880.

39. Ibid., 29 February 1880.

40. Ibid., 9 May 1881.

41. Ibid., 10 November 1883.

42. Ibid., 28 October 1882.

43. Ibid., 9 June 1883.

44. Ibid., 27 February 1885.

45. Ibid., 2 November 1885.

46. Ibid., 18 October 1886.

47. Ibid.

48. Carter, "Categories and Terrains of Exclusion," 152.

49. Ibid., 155.

50. Ibid., 158.

Chapter Five

1. Douglas Sprague, *Canada and the Metis, 1869-1885* (Waterloo: Wilfrid Laurier University Press, 1988), ix .
2. Stanley, *The Birth of Western Canada.*
3. John Tobias, "Protection, Civilization and Assimilation: An Outline History of Canada's Indian Policy," *Western Canadian Journal of Anthropology* 6, no. 2 (1976).
4. Sprague, *Canada and the Metis,* 167-77.
5. Ibid., ix.
6. Blair Stonechild, "The Indian View of the 1885 Uprising," in F. Laurie Barron and James Waldram (eds.), *1885 and After: Native Society in Transition* (Regina: Canadian Plains Research Center, 1986).
7. SAB, NWMP Diary, A186 IV 22, 4 March 1885.
8. Ibid., 7 March 1885.
9. Ibid., 12 March 1885.
10. Ibid., 16 March 1885.
11. Arlean McPherson, *The Battlefords: A History* (Saskatoon: Modern Press, 1967), 79.
12. SAB, NWMP Diary, A186 IV 22, 26 March 1885; 27 March 1885; 29 March 1885.
13. Ibid., 29 March 1885.
14. SAB, Effie Storer Papers, A186 II 5, "Inside the Stockade," chapter 9.
15. SAB, NWMP Diary, A186 IV 22, 12 April 1885.
16. Ibid., 3 April 1885.
17. Ibid., 4 April 1885.
18. Sluman and Goodwill, *John Tootoosis.*
19. Ibid., 42.
20. Ibid., 56.
21. Ibid., 48.
22. Ibid., 61.
23. Ibid., 70.
24. Ibid., 74.
25. SAB, NWMP Diary, A186 IV 22, 6 April 1885.
26. Ibid., 11 April 1885.
27. Ibid., 14 April 1885.
28. Ibid., 18 April 1885.
29. Ibid., 22 April 1885.
30. Ibid., 23 April 1885.
31. Ibid.
32. Fort Battleford National Historic Park Library (hereafter cited as FBNHP Library, Cassels Diary), Lt. R.S. Cassels Diary, North-West Field Force, 23.
33. Ibid.
34. Ibid., 25.
35. Ibid.
36. Desmond Morton, *The Canadian General: Sir William Otter* (hereafter cited as *Otter*), (Toronto: Hakkert, 1974), 75-123.
37. Ibid., 110.
38. Ibid.
39. Ibid., 111.
40. FBNHP Library, Cassels Diary, 27.
41. Fort Battleford Library Collection, Lieutenant-Colonel Hamlyn Todd, "North-West Rebellion, 1885; Recollections, Reflections and Items: The Diary of Lieutenant-Colonel Hamlyn Todd commanding the company of Sharpshooters in that Expedition," 29 April 1885.
42. Morton, *Otter,* 111.

43. Desmond Morton and R.H. Roy (eds.), *Telegrams of the North-West Campaign 1885* (Toronto: Hovey, 1978), lxix.
44. Morton, *Otter*, 112.
45. Ibid., 113.
46. Ibid.
47. Ibid.
48. FBNHP Library, Cassels Diary, 33.
49. Morton, *Otter*, 119.
50. Ibid., 121.
51. FBNHP Library, *North-West Mounted Police Fort Battleford Post Journal, 1885* (hereafter cited as *Post Journal*), 20 June 1885.
52. W.B. Cameron, *Blood Red the Sun* (Calgary: Kenway Publishing, 1926), 197-99.
53. Ibid., 207.
54. Ibid., 209-12.
55. FBNHP Library, *Post Journal*, 27 June 1885.
56. McPherson, *The Battlefords*, 109.
57. SAB, *NWMP Diary*, A186 IV 22, 20 August 1885.
58. John Archer, *Saskatchewan: A History* (Saskatoon: Western Producer Prairie Books, 1980), 89.
59. Jefferson, *Fifty Years on the Saskatchewan*, 121.
60. Ibid., 123.
61. Ibid.
62. Ibid., 125.
63. Ibid.
64. SAB, Campbell Innes Papers.
65. Jefferson, *Fifty Years on the Saskatchewan*, 128.
66. Ibid., 125-26.
67. Dempsey, *Big Bear*.
68. Jefferson, *Fifty Years on the Saskatchewan*, 136.
69. Ibid., 136-37.
70. Ibid., 140.
71. Ibid., 143.
72. Ibid., 147.
73. Ibid., 152.
74. Tobias, "Canada's Subjugation of the Plains Cree," 545.
75. Ibid., 547-48.

Chapter Six

1. Turner, *The North-West Mounted Police*, vol. 2, 304.
2. Ibid., 377.
3. See Jennings, "The NWMP and Canadian Indian Policy."
4. Tobias, "Protection, Civilization and Assimilation."
5. NA, RG 10, vol. 3674, file 11, p. 422, N.F. Davin, "Report on Industrial Schools for Indians and Half-Breeds."
6. Ibid., 10-11.
7. Ibid., 14-15.
8. Ibid., 2.
9. J. Gresko, "White 'Rites' and Indian 'Rites': Indian Education and Native Responses in the West, 1870-1910," in A.W. Rasporich (ed.), *Western Canada: Past and Present* (Calgary: McClelland and Stewart, 1975), 174.
10. Carter, *Lost Harvests*, 143.
11. Ibid.
12. Ibid., 143.

13. Ibid., 145.
14. Ibid., 145.
15. Charles Koester, "Nicholas Flood Davin: A Biography" (Ph.D. dissertation, University of Alberta, 1971), 135.
16. *Saskatchewan Herald*, 21 September 1885.
17. Sarah Carter, "Agriculture and Agitation on the Oak River Reserve, 1875-1895," *Manitoba History* 6 (Fall 1983): 2-10.
18. Canada, Department of Indian Affairs, "The Facts Respecting Indian Administration in the North-West," 1886.
19. Canada, House of Commons, *Debates*, "Malcolm Colin Cameron (Huron West)," 15 April 1886.
20. Ibid., 719.
21. Ibid., 720.
22. Ibid.
23. Ibid., 722.
24. Ibid.
25. Ibid., 723.
26. Ibid.
27. Jennings, "The NWMP and Canadian Indian Policy," 7.
28. Ibid., 98.
29. Ibid., 102. See also Berger, *The Sense of Power*.
30. Jennings, "The NWMP and Canadian Indian Policy," 117.
31. Waiser, "The North-West Mounted Police in1874-1889," 32-33.
32. Jennings, "The NWMP and Canadian Indian Policy," 196.
33. Ibid., 198.
34. Ibid., 273.
35. Ibid., 220.
36. Ibid., 220-21.
37. Ibid., 250.
38. Ibid., 299.
39. Ibid., 325.
40. Kenneth J. Tyler, "Kapeyakwaskonam (One Arrow)," *Dictionary of Canadian Biography*, Vol. 11: 1881-1890 (Toronto: University of Toronto Press, 1982), 461-62.
41. Jennings, "The NWMP and Canadian Indian Policy," 346.
42. Ibid., 247.

Chapter Seven

1. NA, RG 84, box 1057, file FBA-2, "J. Stuart to Deputy Minister," 14 March 1951.
2. Ibid.
3. Ibid., "Memorial and Museum Plans," 1 July 1950.
4. Ibid.
5. NA, RG 84, box 1057, file FBA-28, vol. 1 (1949-54), pt. 2, 7 June 1949, file U. 325-10-1.
6. Ibid., box 1057, file FBA-2, "Campbell Innes to Dr. H.C. Keenleyside," 14 February 1949.
7. Ibid., "T.L.R. MacInnes to W.P. Crommarty," 27 October 1948.
8. Ibid., RG 84, box 1057, file FBA-28, vol. 1 (1949-54), pt. 2, 7 June 1949, file U. 325-10-1.
9. Ibid.
10. "Plaque at Fort Battleford Marks Restoration of Site," *The Optimist* (Battleford), 11 September 1952.
11. C. James Taylor, "National Historic Parks and Sites, 1880-1951: The Biography of a Federal Cultural Program" (Ph.D. dissertation, Carleton University, 1986), 146.
12. Ibid., 159.
13. Ibid., 236.
14. Ibid.

BIBLIOGRAPHY

Primary Sources

National Archives of Canada
      Record Group 10 — Indian Affairs Records
      Deputy Superintendent Letterbooks
      Field Office Correspondence
      Black Series Headquarters Files
      Headquarters Letterbooks

Government Publications (Canada)

Sessional Papers. Annual Reports of the Department of the Interior, 1874-80.
Sessional Papers. Annual Reports of the Department of Indian Affairs, 1880-1914.
Sessional Papers. Annual Reports of the Commissioner of the North West Mounted Police, 1875-1914.
Sessional Papers. Annual Reports of the Department of Agriculture, 1875-1914.
Debates of the House of Commons, 1878-1914.
Senate Journals, 1887, Vol. 21, Appendix 1.
Department of Indian Affairs. "The Facts Respecting Indian Administration in the North West." 1886.

Manuscript Collections

Fort Battleford National Historic Park Library
      Diary of Lt. R.S. Cassels, North-West Field Force
      Lieutenant-Colonel Hamlyn Todd, "North-West Rebellion,1885; Recollections, Reflections and Items: The Diary of Lieutenant-Colonel Hamly Todd commanding the company of Sharpshooters in that Expedition," 29 April 1885.
McCord Museum, McGill University
      Hayter Reed Papers
National Archives of Canada
      Edgar Dewdney Papers
      Sir W. Laurier Papers
      Sir J.A. Macdonald Papers
Saskatchewan Archives Board
      Campbell Innes Papers
      NWMP Diary, A186 IV 22
      Effie Storer Papers, A186 II 5
Newspapers
      Calgary *Albertan*
      Regina *Leader*
      Saskatchewan Herald

Theses

Andrews, I.A., "The Crooked Lakes Reserves: A Study of Indian Policy in Practice From the Qu'Appelle Treaty to 1900" (M.A. thesis, University of Saskatchewan, 1972).

Carter, Sarah, "Man's Mission of Subjugation: The Publications of John Maclean, John McDougall and Egerton R. Young, Nineteenth Century Methodist Missionaries in Western Canada" (M.A. thesis, University of Saskatchewan, 1981).

Drake, E.G., "The Territorial Press in the Region of Present Day Saskatchewan, 1878-1905" (M.A. thesis, University of Saskatchewan, 1951).

Dyck, N.E., "The Administration of Federal Indian Aid in the Northwest Territories, 1879-1885" (M.A. thesis, University of Saskatchewan, 1970).

Falk, G.A., "Missionary Education Work Among the Prairie Indians, 1870-1914" (M.A. thesis, University of Western Ontario, 1972).

Foster, J.E., "The Anglican Church in the Red River Settlement" (M.A. thesis, University of Alberta, 1966).

Getty, I., "The Church Missionary Society Among the Blackfoot Indians of Southern Alberta, 1880-1895" (M.A. thesis, University of Calgary, 1971).

Gracie, B.A., "The Agrarian Response to Industrialization in Prairie Canada, 1900-1935" (Ph.D. dissertation, McMaster University, 1976).

Hildebrandt, Walter, "P.G. Laurie: The Aspirations of a Western Enthusiast" (M.A. thesis, University of Saskatchewan, 1978).

Jennings, John, "The NWMP and Canadian Indian Policy, 1873-1896" (Ph.D. dissertation, University of Toronto, 1979).

Kaye, B., "The Historical Geography of Agriculture and Agricultural Settlement in the Canadian Northwest, 1774-1830" (Ph.D. dissertation, University of London, England, 1976).

Kennedy, J.J., "Qu'Appelle Industrial School: White 'Rites' For the Indians of the Old North-West" (M.A. thesis, Carleton University, 1970).

Larmour, J., "Edward Dewdney, Commissioner of Indian Affairs and Lieutenant Governor of the North West Territories, 1879-1888" (M.A. thesis, University of Saskatchewan, 1969).

Leighton, J.D., "The Development of Federal Indian Policy, 1840-1890" (Ph.D. dissertation, University of Western Ontario, 1975).

Looy, A.J., "The Indian Agent and His Role in the Administration of the North-West Superintendency, 1876-1893" (Ph.D. dissertation, Queen's University, 1977).

Milloy, John S., "The Plains Cree: A Preliminary Trade and Military Chronology, 1670-1870" (M.A. thesis, Carlton University, 1972).

Pannekoek, F., "Protestant Agricultural Missions in the Canadian West to 1870" (M.A. thesis, University of Alberta, 1970).

Richardson, N.A., "Men With a Mission: Canada's Indian Administration in the North-West, 1873-1900" (M.A. thesis, University of Calgary, 1980).

Surtees, R.J., "Indian Reserve Policy in Upper Canada, 1830-1845" (M.A. thesis, Carleton University, 1966).

Taylor, J.L., "The Development of an Indian Policy for the Canadian Northwest, 1869-79" (Ph.D. dissertation, Queen's University, 1975).

Tyler, K., "A Tax-Eating Proposition: The History of the Passpasschase Indian Reserve" (M.A. thesis, University of Alberta, n.d.).

Venne, S., "The Process of Assimilation: The Plains Cree of the Touchwood Agency, 1880-1896" (Honours thesis, University of Victoria, 1976).

Unpublished Sources

Tyler and Wright Research Consultants Ltd., "The Alienation of Indian Reserve Lands During the Administration of Sir Wilfrid Laurier, 1896-1911:"

1. Chekastapasin Reserve #98, a report prepared for the Federation of Saskatchewan Indians, 1978.

2. Pheasant's Rump #68 and Ocean Man #69, reports prepared for the Federation of Saskatchewan Indians, 1978.

3. Stoney Plain #135, a report prepared for the Indian Association of Alberta (n.d.).

4. The St. Peter's Reserve, a report prepared for the Manitoba Indian Brotherhood (n.d.).

Tyler, K., "A Brief History of the Thunderchild Band, 1876-1920." Federation of Saskatchewan Indians, Regina.

Books and Book Chapters

Ankli, R.E. and R.M. Little, "The Growth of Prairie Agriculture: Economic Considerations," in *Canadian Papers in Rural History*, edited by D.H. Akenson. Langdale Press, Gananoque, Ontario, 1978.

Archer, John, *Saskatchewan: A History*. Western Producer Prairie Books, Saskatoon, 1980.

Axtell, J., *The European and the Indian: Essays in the Ethnohistory of Colonial North America*. Oxford University Press, London, 1981.

Bartlett, R.H., *The Indian Act of Canada*. Native Law Centre, Saskatoon, 1980.

Bennett, J.W., *Northern Plainsmen: Adaptive Strategy and Agrarian Life*. AHM Publishing Co., Arlington Heights, IL, 1969.

Berger, Carl, *The Sense of Power: Studies in the Ideals of Canadian Imperialism 1867-1914*. University of Toronto Press, Toronto, 1970.

Berkhofer, R.J., Jr., *Salvation and the Savage: An Analysis of Protestant Missions and American Indian Responses, 1787-1862*. University of Kentucky Press, Lexington, 1965.

——. *The White Man's Indian*. Alfred A. Knopf, New York, 1978.

Bolt, C., *Victorian Attitudes to Race*. University of Toronto Press, Toronto, 1970.

Bradley, I., *The Call to Seriousness: The Evangelical Impact on the Victorians*. Jonathan Cape, London, 1976.

Brett, E.A., *Colonialism and Underdevelopment in East Africa: The Politics of Economic Change*. Heinemann, London, 1973.

Cairns, H.A.C., *Prelude to Imperialism: British Reactions to Central African Society, 1840-1890*. Routledge and Kegan Paul, London, 1965.

Cameron, W.B., *Blood Red the Sun*. Kenway Publishing, Calgary, 1926.

Carlson, L.A., *Indians, Bureaucrats and Land: The Dawes Act and the Decline of Indian Farming*. Greenwood Press, Westport, 1981.

Carter, Sarah, *Lost Harvests: Prairie Indian Reserve Farmers and Government Policy*. McGill-Queen's University Press, Montreal/Kingston, 1990.

Chamberlain, J.E., *The Harrowing of Eden: White Attitudes Towards Native Americans*. The Seabury Press, New York, 1975.

Clifton, J.A., *The Prairie People: Continuity and Change in Potowatomi Culture, 1665-1965*. Regents Press of Kansas, Lawrence, 1977.

Cumming, P.A. and N.H. Mickenberg, *Native Rights in Canada*. Indian-Eskimo Association of Canada, Toronto, 1972.

Dempsey, H., *Charcoal's World*. Western Producer Prairie Books, Saskatoon, 1978.

Fisher, R., *Contact and Conflict: Indian-European Relations in British Columbia, 1774-1890*. University of British Columbia Press, Vancouver, 1977.

Fowke, V.C., *Canadian Agricultural Policy: This Historical Pattern*. University of Toronto Press, Toronto, 1946.

——. *The National Policy and the Wheat Economy*. University of Toronto Press, Toronto, 1974.

Fried, M.H., "Economic Theory and First Contact," in *New Direction in Political Economy*, edited by M. Leons and F. Rothstein. Greenwood Press, Westport, 1979.

Getty, I.A.L. "The Failure of the Native Church Policy of the CMS in the North-West," in *Religion and Society in the Prairie West*, edited by Richard Allen. Canadian Plains Research Center, Regina, 1974.

Gresko, J. "White 'Rites' and Indian 'Rites': Indian Education and Native Responses in the West, 1870-1910," in *Western Canada Past and Present*, edited by A.W. Rasporich. McClelland and Stewart, Calgary, 1975.

Hall, Edward, *The Dance of Life: The Other Dimension of Time*. Doubleday, Garden City, 1984.

Hanks, L.M. and J.R. Hanks, *Tribe Under Trust: A Study of the Blackfoot Reserve in Alberta*. University of Toronto Press, Toronto, 1950.

Hargreaves, M.W.H., *Dry Farming in the Northern Great Plains*. Harvard University Press, Cambridge, 1957.

Harrod, H.L., *Mission Among the Blackfoot*. University of Oklahoma Press, Norman, 1971.

Hildebrandt, W. and Hubner, B., *The Cypress Hills: The Land and Its People*. Purich Publishers, Saskatoon, 1994.

Hodgetts, J.K., *Pioneer Public Services: An Administrative History of the United Canadas, 1841-1867*. University of Toronto Press, Toronto, 1965.

Houghton, Walter E., *The Victorian Frame of Mind, 1830-1870*. Yale University Press, New Haven, 1973.

Horsman, R., *Expansion and American Indian Policy*. Michigan State University Press, East Lansing, 1967.

Jaenen, C., "Missionary Approaches to Native Peoples," in *Approaches to Native History of Canada*, edited by D.A. Muise. National Museum of Man, Ottawa, 1975 (Mercury Series No. 25).

Jefferson, Robert, *Fifty Years on the Saskatchewan*. Canadian North-West Historical Society, Battleford, 1929.

Jennings, F., *The Invasion of America: Indians, Colonialism and the Cant of Conquest*. University of North Carolina, Chapel Hill, 1975.

Kiernan, V.G., *The Lords of Human Kind: European Attitudes to the Outside World in the Imperial Age*. Penquin Books, Middlesex, 1972.

Knight, R., *Indians at Work: An Informal History of Native Indian Labour in British Columbia, 1888-1930*. New Star Books, Vancouver, 1978.

Leslie, J. and R. Maguire, eds., *The Historical Development of the Indian Act*. Indian and Northern Affairs Canada, Research Branch, Ottawa, 1978.

Light, Doug, *Footprints in the Dust*. Turner-Warwick, North Battleford, 1987.

Mandelbaum, D.G., *The Plains Cree: An Ethnographic, Historical and Comparative Study*. Canadian Plains Research Center, Regina, 1979.

Mardock, R.W., *The Reformers and the American Indian*. University of Missouri Press, Columbia, 1971.

Mason, Philip, *Patterns of Dominance*. Oxford University Press, London, 1971.

McGregor, Gaile, *The Wacousta Syndrome: Explorations in the Canadian Landscape*. University of Toronto Press, Toronto, 1985.

McPherson, Arlean, *The Battlefords: A History*. Modern Press, Saskatoon, 1967.

Meyer, R.W., *The Village Indians of the Upper Missouri: The Mandans, Hidastas and Arikaras*. University of Nebraska Press, Lincoln, 1977.

Morris, A., *The Treaties of Canada With the Indians*. Coles Canadiana Collection, Toronto, 1971.

Morton, Desmond, *The Canadian General: Sir William Otter*. Hakkert, Toronto, 1974.

Morton, Desmond and R.H. Roy, eds., *Telegrams of the North-West Campaign 1885*. Hovey, Toronto, 1978.

Morton, W.L., "Agriculture in the Red River Community," in *Contexts of Canada's Past*, edited by A.B. McKillop. Macmillan, Toronto, 1980.

Nix, J.E.N., *Mission Among the Buffalo: The Labours of the Reverends George M. and John C. McDougall in the Canadian Northwest,1860-1876*. The Ryerson Press, Toronto, 1960.

Patterson, E.P., *The Canadian Indian: A History Since 1500*. Macmillan, Toronto, 1972.

Pearce, Roy Harvey, *The Savages in American: A Study of the Indian and the Idea of Civilization*. John Hopkins Press, Baltimore, 1953.

——, *Savagism and Civilization: A Study of the Indian and the American Mind*. John Hopkins Press, Baltimore, 1965.

Price, R., ed., *The Spirit of the Alberta Indian Treaties*. Butterworths, Toronto, 1979.

Priest, L.B., *Uncle Sam's Stepchildren: The Reformation of United States Indian Policy, 1865-1887*. Octagon Books, New York, 1969.

Ray, Arthur, *Indians in the Fur Trade*. University of Toronto Press, Toronto, 1974.

Rich, E.E., *The Fur Trade and The Northwest to 1857*. McClelland and Stewart, Toronto, 1967.

Sahlins, M., *Stone Age Economics*. Aldine, New York, 1972.

Scott, D.C., "Indian Affairs, 1867-1912," in *Political Evolution of Canada and Its Provinces*, edited by Adam Shortt and A.G. Doughty. T and A Constable, Toronto, 1914.

Sharp, Paul F., *Whoop-Up Country*. University of Minnesota Press, Minneapolis, 1955.

Sheehan, B.W., *Savagism and Civility: Indians and Englishmen in Colonial Virginia*. Cambridge University Press, Cambridge, 1980.

——, *Seeds of Extinction: Jeffersonian Philanthropy and the American Indian*. University of North Carolina Press, Chapel Hill,1973.

Sluman, Norma and Jean Goodwill, *John Tootoosis: A Biography of a Cree Leader*. Pemmican Publications, Winnipeg, 1984.

Stanley, G.F.G., *The Birth of Western Canada*. University of Toronto Press, Toronto, 1961.

Street, B.V., *The Savage in Literature: Representations of "Primitive" Society in English Fiction, 1858-1920*. Routledge and Kegan Paul, London, 1975.

Thompson, J., *The Harvests of War: The Prairie West, 1914-1918*. McClelland and Stewart, Toronto, 1978.

Trennert, R.A., Jr., *Alternative to Extinction: Federal Indian Policy and the Beginnings of the Reservation System*. Temple University Press, Philadelphia, 1975.

Turner, Frederick, *Beyond Geography: The Western Spirit Against the Wilderness*. Viking Press, New York, 1980.

Usher, J., "Duncan of Metlakatla: The Victorian Origins of a Model Indian Community," in *The Shield of Achilles: Aspects of Canada in the Victorian Age*, edited by W.L. Morton. McClelland and Stewart, Toronto, 1968.

Van Every, D., *Disinherited: The Lost Birthright of the American Indian*. William Morrow and Co., New York,1966.

Walden, Keith, *Visions of Order: The Canadian Mounties in Symbol and Myth*. Butterworths, Toronto, 1982.

Wallace, A.F.C., *The Death and Rebirth of the Seneca*. Knopf, New York, 1970.

Wallace, W.S., ed. *The Macmillan Dictionary of Canadian Biography*, 3rd ed. Macmillan, Toronto, 1963.

Wessell, T.R., ed., *Agriculture in the Great Plains*. Agricultural History Society, Washington, 1977.

Will, G. and G. Hyde, *Corn Among the Indians of the Upper Missouri*. University of Nebraska Press, Lincoln, 1917.

Wood, L.A., *A History of Farmer's Movements in Canada: The Origins and Development of Agrarian Protest, 1872-1924*. University of Toronto Press, Toronto, 1975.

Zaslow, M., *The Opening of the Canadian North, 1870-1914*. McClelland and Stewart, Toronto, 1971.

Articles

Andrews, Isabel, "Indian Protest Against Starvation." *Saskatchewan History* 28, no. 2 (Spring 1975): 41-51.

Baker, R., "Indian Corn and its Culture." *Agricultural History* 1 (1974).

Bennett, B., "Study of Passes For Indians to Leave Their Reserves." Paper submitted to the Department of Indian and Northern Affairs, Ottawa, 1974.

Berkhofer, R.F., Jr., "Model Zions For the American Indian." *American Quarterly* 15 (1963).

——, "The Political Context of a New Indian History." *Pacific Historical Review* 40, no. 3 (August 1971): 357-82.

Brass, Eleanor, "The File Hills Ex-Pupil Colony." *Saskatchewan History* 6, no. 2 (Spring 1953): 66-69.

Brown, R.G., "Missions and Cultural Diffusion." *American Journal of Sociology* 50 (1944/45): 214-8.

Carter, Sarah, "Agriculture and Agitation on the Oak River Reserve, 1875-1895." *Manitoba History* 6 (Fall 1983): 2-10.

——, "Categories and Terrains of Exclusion: Constructing the 'Indian Woman' in the Early Settlement Era in Western Canada." *Great Plains Quarterly* 13, no. 3 (Summer 1993): 147-61.

——, "The Missionaries' Indian: The Publications of John McDougall, John Maclean and Egerton Ryerson Young." *Prairie Forum* 9, no. 1 (1984): 27-44.

Dick, L., "Estimates of Farm Making Costs in Saskatchewan,1882-1914." *Prairie Forum* 6, no. 2 (1981): 183-201.

Fisher, A.D., "Cultural Conflict on the Prairies: Indian and White." *Alberta Historical Review* 16 (Summer 1968): 22-29.

Frank, A.G., "The Development of Underdevelopment." *Monthly Review* (September 1966).

Hildebrandt, Walter, "P.G. Laurie: The Aspirations of a Western Enthusiast." *Prairie Forum* 8, no. 2 (1983): 157-78.

Jorgensen, J.G., "A Century of Political Economic Effects on American Indian Society, 1880-1980." *Journal of Ethnic Studies* 6, no. 3 (Fall 1978): 1-82.

Looy, A.J., "Saskatchewan's First Indian Agent: M.G. Dickiesen." *Saskatchewan History* 33, no. 3 (Autumn 1979): 104-15.

Martin, C., "The Metaphysics of Writing Indian-White History." *Ethnohistory* 26, no. 2 (1979).

Moodie, D.W. and B. Kaye, "The Northern Limit of Indian Agriculture in North America." *Geographical Review* 59 (1969): 513-29.

Pearce, R.H., "From the History of Ideas to Ethnohistory." *Journal of Ethnic Studies* 2, no. 1 (Spring 1974): 86-92.

Raby, S., "Indian Land Surrenders in Southern Saskatchewan." *The Canadian Geographer* 17, no. 1 (Spring 1973): 36-52.

Raby, S., "Indian Treaty No. 5 and The Pas Agency, Saskatchewan, N.W.T." *Saskatchewan History* 25, no. 3 (Autumn 1972): 92-114.

Rotstein, A., "Trade and Politics: An Institutional Approach." *Western Canadian Journal of Anthropology* 3, no. 1 (1973): 1-23.

Spry, Irene, "The Transition From a Nomadic to a Settled Economy in Western Canada, 1856-96." *Transactions of the Royal Society of Canada*, vol. 6, series 4 (1968): 187-201.

Tobias, John, "Canada's Subjugation of the Plains Cree, 1879-1885." *Canadian Historical Review* 64, no. 4 (December 1983): 519-48.

Tyler, Kenneth J., "Kapeyakwaskonam (One Arrow)." *Dictionary of Canadian Biography*, Vol. 11 (1982), pp. 461-62.

Waiser, W.A., "The North-West Mounted Police in 1874-1889: A Statistical Study." Parks Canada *Research Bulletin*, No. 117 (November 1979). Ottawa.

Walker, J.W., "The Indian in Canadian Historical Writing." *Canadian Historical Association Historical Papers* (1971): 21-51.

Wessel, Thomas, "Agriculture, Indians and American History." *Agricultural History* 58, no. 1 (1976): 9-20.

Williams, G., "The Hudson's Bay Company and the Fur Trade: 1670-1870." *The Beaver*, Outfit 314:2 (Autumn 1983): 4-86.

INDEX